Ken
Engleman
813 Eton Dr.
333-3426

MW01378958

METAL FLASHING WOOD SHINGLE ROOF

WOOD SHINGLE ROOF

CEILING SHEET METAL ROOF

T. GUTTER

D.S. D.S. D.S. D.S.

CONCEALED D.S.

WOOD RAIL

SECOND FLOOR

WOOD BRACKETS

WOOD

WOOD COLS. PIPE COL. BATTEN DOOR

FIRST FLOOR WOOD BRICK

6" 3" CONC. SLAB

6"

CONC. SLAB

BASEMENT FLOOR

HISTORIC HOMES OF
PONCA CITY
and Kay County

John Brooks Walton and Kathy Adams

JBW PUBLICATIONS ~ TULSA

ACKNOWLEDGMENTS

First of all, we thank the group of people who have given financial support to make this book possible.
We are also grateful to the family members of the original owners of these historic houses and to the people who live
in and care for them today. Special thanks are also due to Pat Lloyd Deisenroth, Paul McGraw, Connie Pruitt, Darlene
Platt, Shelley Howe Rutherford, Sarah Theobald-Hall for her work with our text, and Michelle Weeks for her photography.
Four very helpful historians were Karen Dye, Marilee Helton, Trish Gossard, and Jacque Graham. — KA and JBW

SOURCES FOR MATERIAL

ARCHIVES

Ponca City News, Ponca City Library, Marland's Grand Home, Marland Mansion, Pioneer Woman Museum, Glass
Negative, Laura Streich historic files, *Newkirk Herald,* Newkirk Heritage Center, *Blackwell Journal,* Blackwell Museum,
Blackwell Public Library, *Tonkawa News,* Tonkawa Historical Society, and McCarter Museum

PUBLICATIONS

Residential Architecture of John Duncan Forsyth
Pieces of the Past by Marilee Helton
Ponca City Mayors by Kathy Adams
Autobiography of a Pioneer Woman by Virginia Cannon Cronin
The Last Run by the Ponca City Chapter of the D. A. R.
Rooted in the Past-Growing for the Future by North Central Oklahoma Historical Association, Incorporated
Madness in the Heart by Edward Donahoe
Dictionary of Architecture by Henry H. Saylor
Gateway Historic District by Marlys Bush Thurber & Associates
Made Out-a Mud by Luke Robinson
Life and Death of An Oilman by John Joseph Matthews

ISBN 0-9759799-0-6
Copyright ©2004 by Kathy Adams and John Brooks Walton
All rights reserved, including right of reproduction in whole or in part in any form
Printed in China

Design, editorial assistance, and production management by Carol Haralson

Page one: Marland Mansion: Covered porch connecting artist's studio to the original guest quarters.
Page two: The Dr. George Nieman house.
Page five: Detail from the Johnson-Pitts house.
Page eight: Staircase tower of the Riehl house.
Page ten: Dr. W.A.T. Robertson house.
Page 224: Entrance gate to the Dr. George Nieman house.

This book is dedicated to Louise Abercrombie, for many years a staff writer for *The Ponca City News*. Her numerous writings on the historic homes of Ponca City, including a series of stories of the homes built in the 1920s by E. W. Marland's "lieutenants," have been a valuable aid in the writing of this book.

CONTENTS

Preface 9

Introduction: Ponca's Beginnings 11

CENTRAL AND DOWNTOWN

Marland's Grand Avenue Home 16

Miss Lottie's House 21

The McFadden-Edgington House 22

The Mary French Barrett House 25

The Collins Houses 27

The Christmas Party House 30

MIDTOWN

DeRoberts-Calkins Mansion 32

The State Flag House 36

Ponca's First Flour Mill:

   D.J. Donahoe House 37

Joe Donahue-Goldenstern House 39

South Seventh Street Sisters 40

Anthony-Mall House 42

Gammie House 43

Dr. George Nieman's House 44

Gill-Lessert Family Home 47

E. M. Trout House 49

Dr. R. B. Gibson Home 50

Handley-Mertz Houses 52

Lessert-Howe House 54

"I Like Ike" House 58

The McElroy House 60

The Pickrel-Casey House 63

GATEWAY HISTORIC DISTRICT

The W. A. T. Robertson House 66

O. F. Keck House 68

Sixth Street Rooming House 70

"God Bless America" House 72

The R. P. Baughman House 74

The Barnes Family Homes 75

COUNTRY CLUB-HILLCREST

Dillard Clark Estate 80

Another "Lieutenant's" House 82

The Lackey-Alcorn House 86

Ponca's "House of Seven Gables" 88

The "Seven Stables" 91

Marland Polo Barn 93

ACRE HOMES

The Edward J. Sheldon House 98

The Forsyth-Neal House 100

The Loft House 101

Clyde Muchmore House 103

The Tom Irby Houses 105

The White Picket Fence House 108

Casey -Skidmore House 110

Drs. Browne and Neal House 112

Last Tribal Chief's House 114

John Whitehurst Family Home 116

Pat's Potato Chips Houses 119

"Master of the Hounds" House 121

Lincoln-Gibson House 123

Harper Baughman House 124

House on the Street of
Many Children 127

The Johnson-Pitts House 129

C. W. Arrendell House 131

THE MARLAND ESTATE

Marland Mansion 134

Marland Stable 142

Marland Gate House 143

Invitation to a Party
at the Marland Mansion 144

John Duncan Forsyth 145

ARCHITECTS
AND THEIR HOUSES

Bob Buchner's Ponca Houses 148

William Caton's Ponca Houses 154

RURAL PONCA

The 101 Ranch "White House" 158

The Big V 161

LOST PONCA

The George H. Brett Mansion 164

Ponca's First (and only)
Brick Yard 166

NEWKIRK

Newkirk's First Hospital 168

The Anton Horinek House 169

The Chappell Houses 170

The Native Limestone House 172

The Lancet Dome House 173

The P. W. Smith House 174

A Colonial Revival 175

The Israel Tipton House 176

The Sam K. Sullivan House 177

The Home of the Judge
and Miss Mittie 178

Amanda's House 179

The J. P. K. Mathias House 180

BLACKWELL

The McKee-Becker House 182

The G. E. Dowis House 184

The Denton House 186

Mrs. Daisy Riehl's House 188

The Sylvester Jack Walton Home 191

Miss Louise's Family Homes 193

The West-Dyer Story 195

The Turvey Farm 197

Lowery Mansion 198

The Frenchman's House 199

Blackwell's Triplets 201

The Goodson Ranch 204

TONKAWA

The House That Petroleum Built 206

Tonkawa's Mail-Order House 207

The Wiley William
Gregory House 208

The First Banker's House 209

The Seven Cedars House 210

Jones-Burr House 212

The Plumb Houses 214

The Major's House 215

The Doenges Story 216

The McCafferty Story 218

White Wonder Flour 220

The C. C. Bell House 222

PREFACE

WHILE ATTENDING a high school class reunion shortly after completing my first book on Tulsa's historic homes, I was asked by a fellow classmate, Joyce Patterson Dunham, "Why don't you write a book on the historic homes of Ponca City?" I confessed it might be an interesting subject but then changed the conversation.

Over the next several years, Joyce continued to ask the same question at each of our reunions. I would respond with "I'm too busy with my architectural practice" or "I question the financial feasibility of such a book."

Christmas of 2002, as I was completing my third book on Tulsa's historic homes, I received a holiday card from Joyce and her husband Howard. Her enclosed note again asked the familiar question: "Why not?" I put the card away for a few days but upon reading it again I said to myself, "Why don't I write a book on the historic homes of Ponca City?"

So Joyce, now you can quit asking me.

JOHN BROOKS WALTON
Tulsa, Oklahoma

THIS BOOK is more than a collection of stories about houses and their architectural styles. It is also a book of memories about the citizens of Ponca City and Kay County who have contributed to the way we live today. Pride and honor are qualities that have prevailed in Kay County since the Cherokee Strip Land Run of 1893. The historic homes of Kay County provide a window of understanding on communities that have endured and prospered for over one hundred years.

Co-authoring *The Historical Homes of Ponca City and Kay County* has helped me realize some important things about myself. With the completion of this book, I have now taken an advance course in "how to write a book," and the research is what I have enjoyed the most—it has been a fascinating treasure hunt.

KATHY ADAMS
Ponca City, Oklahoma

INTRODUCTION: PONCA'S BEGINNINGS

In the spring of 1893, B. S. Barnes had sold his furniture manufacturing company in Adrian, Michigan, and was in Arkansas City, Kansas, to participate in the opening of the Cherokee Strip. For many days prior to the opening of the Strip, Barnes traveled by team and buggy inspecting the counties designated "K, C, O, and P" (later Kay, Grant, Garfield, and Noble). He observed many allotted townsites already established by the United States Government. On his trip into eastern K County, Barnes discovered a wagon road from Arkansas City leading southward and crossing the Arkansas River at a point one mile southeast of today's Arkansas River bridge. The crossing had been used for many years by buggies and wagons because of its gentle slope into the river's shallow water. This ancient road continued south and east to numerous settlements including Tahlequah and Muskogee. Located about a mile to the north and west of the crossing was a natural spring where travelers stopped to refresh themselves and water their horses.

The abundance of water and the fact that the spring was located near the wagon road convinced Barnes that this was the logical site for his contemplated townsite.

The spring would be within the city limits of his township and just above it was level, open ground ideal for building sites. Railroad tracks were nearby. So this became the site for B. S. Barnes's new settlement which would someday be called Ponca City. In July of 1893, he announced his plans and organized the Ponca Townsite Company in Arkansas City to sell certificates for building lots.

On September 16, 1893, Barnes made the run into the Cherokee Strip, traveling in his two-seater buggy driven by a pair of black horses trained to run a fast race. His luggage consisted of a tent, bedding, clothes, and food supplies. Upon reaching his new townsite, Barnes discovered several people already there; soon afterwards hundreds of people dotted the landscape. His first act was to help bring order out of the chaos and to act as peacemaker for the settlement of many of the contested claims in the area. During the first few days after the Run, many slept under the open skies while others enjoyed the privacy of a tent. The only available water supply was the nearby spring. The new citizens could either travel there for water or have it hauled to them for fifteen cents a barrel.

It took four days to complete the survey of the town, and on September 21, 1893, a wood platform was erected for the drawing of the lots, which were then recorded in a large bound book. Since over 2,300 certificates had been sold, it took two days to complete the drawing, But with its completion, the noise of hammers and saws filled the air as the building of Ponca City began.

The night after the completion of the drawing a mass meeting was held to select provisional city officers. Among those chosen were B. S. Barnes as mayor and W.E. McGuire as clerk.

Within sixty days the opening of the Chreokee Strip land run of 1893, Ponca City had a new two-room school house, and the town's first church, the Methodist Church, was completed within four months. But only one mile to the north of B. S. Barnes's proposed new city was the platted town of Cross. It had been established as a township by the United States government and was predicted to become the largest city in the county with its post office, telegraph, and "box car" train station.

By 1894, Ponca City had repeatedly asked the Santa Fe Railroad to grant the town a railroad station. Their constant reply was that Ponca and Cross were too close together for both towns to have a station, and Cross already has one.

One very dark night a crowd of young Ponca men, including B. S. Barnes's son, Louis, hitched up a team of black horses and drove them to Cross. There they hitched the team to the town's "box car" station and hauled it to Ponca. They left the stolen station on a railroad spur. The next morning most of the Ponca townspeople were at their new depot to flag down the oncoming train. When the approaching train stopped, a small girl and young Louis Barnes boarded the train and gave out cards saying, "Trains stop in Ponca just as they do in Chicago." Louis handed out cigars to the male passengers and his young lady companion distributed bouquets of wildflowers to the ladies. And that is how Ponca obtained its first train depot.

Barnes's new city also had some difficulty in obtaining its own post office, but after lengthy negotiations, it did receive one. The post office was called New Ponca because the Santa Fe Railroad had established a station named Ponca only four miles south of the new city at the Ponca Indian Reservation.

In retrospect, the town of Cross was larger and had city facilities from the very start. But Ponca had something else—its boosters with their strong determination to establish a city. What Ponca lacked in material benefits it made up for in its citizens' ambition and civic ardor. With these strong qualities, the early-day Ponca City leaders would create the great and beautiful city that we have today. —JBW

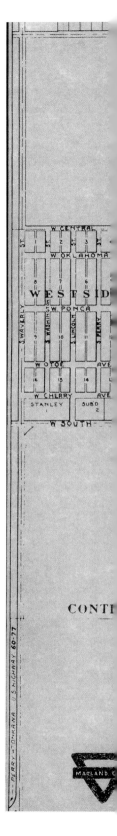

COMMEMORATIVE MAP OF PONCA CITY IN THE 1930S.

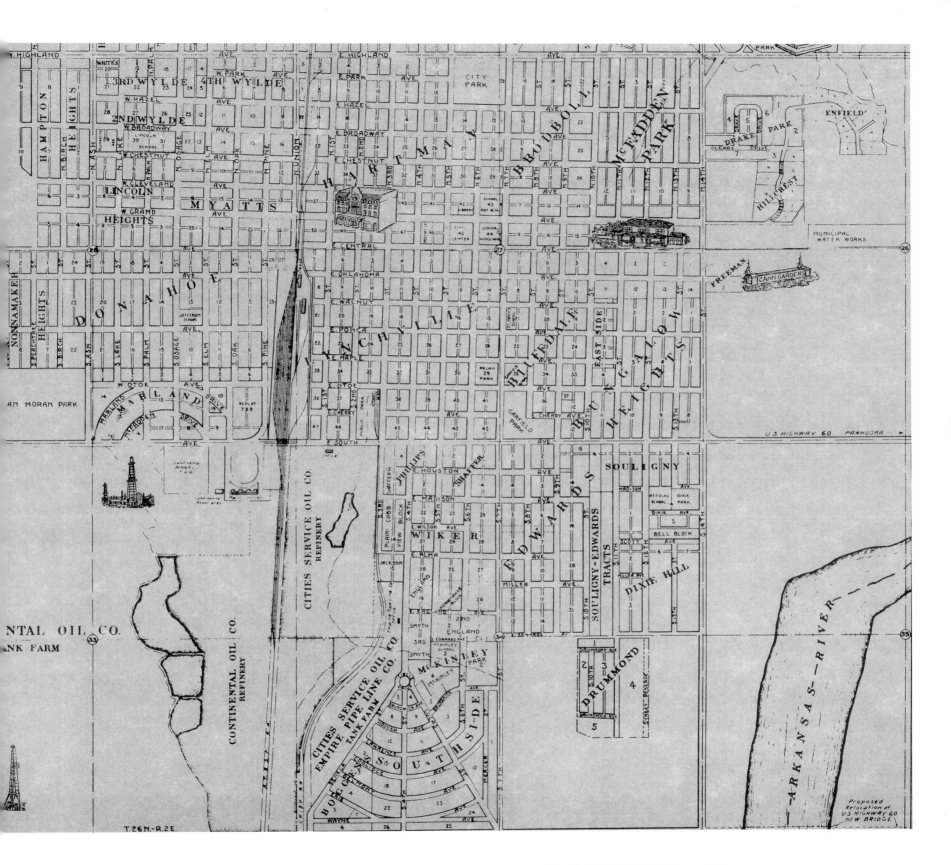

Certain Service

THE motorist of today gains through the regular use of MARLAND HIGH GRADE MOTOR OILS a certain service. This certain service has not only made possible the Marland slogan, "ALWAYS THE SAME—ALWAYS GOOD," but has proven the truth of Marland Quality and dependability of performance.

THE certain service of the Marland Service Stations has made the servicing of motor cars a pleasure instead of the distasteful chore as was the case a few years ago. Speedy, willing attendance, free water and air, quality products together with courteous, personal attention and an honest desire to serve on the part of the station salesman make Marland certain service desired by every motorist.

At the Sign of the Red Triangle

Marland Oils

Always the Same — Always Good

CENTRAL AND DOWNTOWN

With the discovery of oil in northern Oklahoma and the new wealth that came with it, Ponca City was transformed from an agricultural community into a thriving modern city with many beautiful new homes. Hundreds of new homes were built in the late teens and early 1920s in the central part of the city, and many still stand today, some eighty years later, testaments to the belief of Poncans in the life and future of their community.

As Ponca City grew, its residential areas would spread along both sides of Grand Avenue, extending west to the John Hampton Farm and east to Fourteenth Street. E.W. Marland would build his first home at 1000 East Grand Avenue, with several of his "Lieutenants" and family members building their homes close by on East Central Avenue. —KA-JBW

1000 E. GRAND AVENUE

Marland's Grand Avenue Home

Much has been written about E.W. Marland's Grand Avenue home and of its regal lifestyle during the Marland early years. Those halcyon days occurred before I was born so my first remembrances of the mansion are from the Dan Moran years. Moran was sent to Ponca City to become president of Continental Oil Company after its takeover of Marland Oil Company. During the Moran years, one saw very little activity around the house, and at night only a few dim lights could be seen glowing from inside.

Completed in 1916, the house was designed by Solomon Layton, the architect who also designed the Oklahoma governor's mansion in Oklahoma City. Contractor for the project was O. F. Keck. When completed, the Grand Avenue home stood at the west end of a property that extended four blocks to the east terminating at

1920S AERIAL VIEW OF THE FORMAL GARDENS OF E. W. MARLAND'S FIRST HOME; BELOW: THE STAIRCASE DURING THE PARIS YEARS.

Fourteenth Street. The home's formal gardens were designed by Marland's personal Japanese gardener, Henry Hatashita. The mansion and the gardens overlooked the Marland Golf Course, which lay between North Tenth and North Fourteenth Streets and from Grand Avenue to East Highland.

In 1940, Jay and Jessie Paris became the owners of the Marland Grand Avenue home. I vividly recall the Parises' years in the house for my best high school friend, Halsey Davis, was their nephew. Through the years, Halsey and I spent many memorable hours in the Paris home. Jay and Jessie had one daughter, Patricia, and when she had friends spending a weekend night in her bedroom suite during her teen years, Halsey and I would often be in attendance, sleeping in the "Lincoln Bedroom."

During the Paris years, the entrance foyer with its grand split staircase was the

HISTORIC HOMES OF PONCA CITY AND KAY COUNTY ~ 17

DURING THE PARIS YEARS, THE BASEMENT SWIMMING POOL, THE DINING ROOM, A POSTCARD VIEW OF THE FRONT OF THE HOUSE. FACING PAGE: THE LIBRARY FIREPLACE.

background for many Ponca City brides posing for wedding portraits. In the center of the foyer was a marble-topped table beneath the elegant crystal chandelier. Often there would be a large bouquet of fresh flowers sitting on the table. At the base of the staircase was a small table desk and atop it was one of the four downstairs phones and a small desk lamp that was always left on. The most interesting item in the foyer was a marvelous Swiss music box resting on its matching tall legs. This wind-up musical instrument played numerous tunes but the winding and playing of it was off limits to teenagers. Like the small table desk, this music box remains in the home today and is still off limits, not only to teenagers, but to today's visitors.

To the right of the foyer is the beautiful oak-paneled library. In the early Paris years, the original Marland furniture was in the room. This parlor set consisted of a massive

18 ~ HISTORIC HOMES OF PONCA CITY AND KAY COUNTY

mohair-covered couch and matching chairs in what I often refer to as the 1920s "Mickey and Minnie Mouse" style. An ornate oak executive style desk stood in the north corner of the room, and in the winter there was always a cheerful fire burning in the fireplace.

The Paris home was filled with many fine paintings but the grandest of these was the very large painting that covered a large part of the west wall in the library. Although I had always enjoyed beautiful artwork, I was not a student of the arts. To me this painting was just a wonderful picture that showed Ponce de Leon and his soldiers with their bright red uniforms standing in a forest. Later I was to learn that the forest was the Florida Everglades and the artist was Thomas Moran. Years later, Pat Paris told me the history of the painting. Her father purchased it in 1939 for $12,000, and it hung in their library until her mother sold it in 1965 for $65,000. Eventually the painting would hang in Oklahoma City's Cowboy Hall of Fame (now the National Cowboy and Western Heritage Museum) until it was sold to the State of Florida for over $3 million.

To the left of the foyer is the formal living room, where several of the Parises' furnishings are still in place, including a pair of curved wingback chairs. On the east wall of the living room was a spinet piano and a French hutch that flanked the door to the

sunroom. Atop the piano were a pair of hurricane lamps in green milk glass. Behind the living room is the formal dining room with its black walnut wood wainscot and hand-painted wall murals, all from the Marland years. The beautiful Chippendale dining room furniture was purchased by Jay Paris for this room on one of his buying trips to the Furniture Market in Chicago. The Victorian rosewood sideboard is an antique purchased by the Parises in New Orleans. All the dining room furniture that was part of the Paris years remains in the house today.

Off the living and dining rooms is the large sunroom on the east side of the house. This wing balances a similar wing at the west end that served as a glassed-in garage.

The sunroom has a bold black and white marble floor, and all of the rattan furniture is from the Paris years. Today the furniture has been painted but originally it was natural rattan with brightly colored floral cushions.

Beyond the dining room is the original butler's pantry and kitchen which was slightly modified to fit the Parises' needs. Off the kitchen is a long hall leading to the garages. There is a back staircase and an opening into the foyer from this hall plus two rooms located on the back of the house. The first room, used as a breakfast and sitting room, was furnished in Early American maple pieces. Mrs. Paris spent a great deal of time in this cozy space.

The home's grand staircase leads to a large upstairs sitting room. During the Paris years this space was furnished in reproduction Victorian style furniture, including an antique pump organ. Jessie Paris enjoyed pumping and playing vintage tunes on the organ for us.

The Paris master bedroom was located on the northeast corner of the second floor. It had rose-colored walls and maroon bedspreads and drapery. A pair of tall four-poster beds dominated the room. Behind the master bedroom was the master bath and dressing room which connected to a sleeping porch on the southeast corner of the house. This sleeping porch was daughter Pat's bedroom, and the adjoining bedroom was her sitting room. Opposite the master bedroom on the west end of the house was the main guest bedroom. This very large space was furnished in a painted bedroom suite that might well have been original with the house. Also at the west end was another sleeping porch and the "Lincoln bedroom," named for its very, very tall Victorian bed not unlike the one in the White House in Washington, D.C. The grand staircase rises to the third floor with its bedrooms on the south and attic storage spaces on the north. The third floor bedrooms were used as George Marland's bedroom suite and during the Paris years they became storage rooms.

The basement of the Marland Grand Avenue home consists of a series of rooms, including an indoor swimming pool situated below the east veranda of the house. The staircase leads you into a larger foyer space that connects to the billiard room with its oak bar across one end of the room. One Christmas, we had our high school social club dance in the basement of the home. During the festivities, Jay Paris called me over to the bar and said, "John, I have just put a new bag of peanuts on the bar and I want you to sample them." The peanuts were in a large silver bowl that, unknown to me, was sitting on a small metal button embedded into the bar top. As I put my hand into the bowl, Mr. Paris pressed a button behind the bar that sent electrical currents to the metal button and thus to the silver bowl. As I touched the silver bowl, my handful of peanuts flew into the air, scattering to the four corners of the room.

The dance guests were stepping on peanuts throughout the remainder of the evening.

The basement swimming pool had its own dressing rooms with private dressing booths. One summer Halsey and I both had daytime jobs, so after work we spent a delightful and relaxing time in the Paris pool. These nightly swims were spent when no others would be using the pool. One evening Halsey and I decided to be daring and go "skinny dipping." First we turned out all of the lights and then removed our bathing suits. (I guess we did not want to see each other in the nude.) I remember the moment well for Halsey was standing on the diving board and I was afloat on a raft in the pool when the lights came on. Mrs. Paris had out-of-town guests and was showing them the indoor swimming pool.

The attached three-car garage was a thing of beauty in its own right. The Paris automobiles included a large black Cadillac limousine and a Pontiac convertible that Jay had purchased at the 1940 Car Show in Detroit, Michigan. The convertible was a metallic maroon with matching leather interior. Near the floor on the passenger side was a metal tube that held an umbrella with fabric the same color as the car. One summer evening, Halsey borrowed his uncle's convertible and we went driving down South Pine Avenue with the top down. (We thought we were really cool.) We soon passed a very cute young girl walking along the sidewalk and as we passed we smiled and she smiled back. We decided to try our luck at "picking her up." She was agreeable, but after traveling only a few blocks we discov-

ered that our new friend was only twelve years old. We took her to her destination without delay.

After Jay Paris's death in the mid 1950s, his widow, Jessie, continued to live in the Grand Avenue home until 1965, when she sold it to the City of Ponca to be used as a Cultural Center. At that time, she told her daughter, Patricia, to come and pick out anything she wanted from the home. There was nothing Pat desired. (Remember that this was the 1960s, and everyone, including me, wanted contemporary furniture and houses.) Many years later, Pat related the incident to me and said how fortunate she was that her mother had the foresight to know that someday her daughter's tastes would change. Jessie Paris had saved many of the family heirlooms, awaiting the time when her daughter would once again treasure them. And she did —JBW

919 E. GRAND AVENUE
Miss Lottie's House

Charlotte (Lottie) Marland was the sister of oilman E. W. Marland. Her brother owned the property located on the northwest corner of Grand Avenue and North Tenth Street. Marland's original intent was to build a twelve-unit apartment complex on the property to house employees of the Marland Refinery and Kay County Gas Companies. Instead E. W. Marland built a home for his maiden sister, Lottie. Completed in 1916, the house was designed by George Forsythe of the firm Layton and Forsythe Architects who also designed Marland's Grand Avenue home.

We were taught in architectural school that a building should be designed to complement the lot on which it sat. The Lottie Marland house is an excellent example of that design theory. The L-shaped plan with the entrance at the intersection of its legs points directly to the intersection of the streets and has a wonderful view of Marland's Grand Avenue house. The semicircular front terrace, centered with its fountain and fish pond, helps to further orient the house to the lot. The house is designed in the Italianate Revival style with a stucco exterior and Italian clay barrel tile roof. The entrance foyer is dominated by a graceful staircase. The first floor contains large formal living and dining rooms and a card room surrounded by casement windows and storage cabinets for folding card tables and chairs. In the butler's pantry is a dumbwaiter serving the first and second floors and the basement. The second floor of the house had two large bedroom suites with the master bedroom measuring twenty by twenty-five feet in size.

Lottie Marland lived in Ponca City for only twelve years but maintained a very active and visible life as a community leader while there. She was president of the hospital guild and established the Charlotte Marland Fund at the hospital. Lottie was also known for her interest in music and was an ardent supporter of the advancement of the fine arts. She was an active communicant of Grace Episcopal Church to which she bequeathed the lovely furnishings from her home. She owned the first electric car in Ponca City and enjoyed doing her shopping using this unique mode of transportation. The one-seated vehicle was guided not by a steering wheel but by a swinging tiller similar to a boat's steering mechanism.

Miss Charlotte (Lottie) Marland died in July of 1927, after a long illness. She was fifty-eight years old. Hundreds of people attended the funeral which was held in her home. The burial service was read by the Reverend Frederic W. Sandford, rector of Grace Episcopal Church. The mayor requested that all downtown businesses be closed at the time of the funeral. In reporting Lottie's funeral the *Ponca City News* noted that "solemnity settled over the city at 5:00 P.M. in a tribute to Miss Charlotte Marland." —JBW

HISTORIC HOMES OF PONCA CITY AND KAY COUNTY ~ 21

210 S. TENTH STREET

The McFadden-Edgington House

William Hartman (Bill) McFadden was born in Moundville, West Virginia, in 1869. At the age of fifteen, he went to work for the McIntosh-Hemphill Steel Mills in Pittsburgh, Pennsylvania. In applying for his $3.50-per-week job, he announced to his interviewer that someday he would become president of the company. McFadden kept his promise, and twenty-seven years later he became president of McIntosh-Hemphill.

McFadden left Pittsburgh in 1911. He believed he had failing heath and so relocated to Hot Springs, Arkansas, with its numerous mineral bathhouses for those wishing to take "the cure."

A BRONZE STATUE OF MCFADDEN DEPICTED AS *THE PLAINSMAN*, COMMISSIONED BY E. W. MARLAND.

Soon after arriving in Hot Springs, McFadden met John McCaskey, an early-day associate of E. W. Marland and the Miller brothers in Ponca City, Oklahoma. From McCaskey, McFadden learned of the 101 Ranch and its "wide open spaces." Shortly after his visit with McCaskey he "came west" and pitched a tent on the prairie, not far from the 101 Ranch, where E. W. Marland and George Miller were drilling for oil. They had drilled eight wells in a row, and all were dry. (McCaskey, who had financed Marland's move to Ponca City to search for oil, sent Lew Wentz to find out what E. W. was doing with "all of my money.")

After the eighth dry well, the wildcatters approached McFadden for additional financing. As the story went, Bill McFadden had a large sum of cash inside a pillowcase. E. W. Marland said to George Miller, "How are we going to get that 's.o.b.' to put up some money?" McFadden, who overheard the question, replied, "Just make the 's.o.b.' a good proposition."

With McFadden's financing, the next well was a gusher. It was named "Willie Cries for War." From this strike came the foundation for the Marland, Miller, and McFadden Oklahoma oil fortunes. When the Marland Oil Company was founded, Bill McFadden was named executive vice-president. He served in that capacity until 1928, when E. W. was forced out of the company. McFadden once reflected, "E. W. and his oil company made $25 million and it took him until 1928 to spend it all." Bill McFadden's thrifty and cautious nature kept him from participating in the chances taken by Marland and the Miller brothers. Thus McFadden emerged from the Great Depression still a very wealthy man.

After being a bachelor for many years, Bill McFadden married Mrs. Helen Charlotte Williams-Levi of Pittsburgh, Pennsylvania, in 1920. Their wedding attendants were E. W. and Mary Virginia Marland.

McFadden held the office of Ponca City's mayor for six years, serving from 1913 until 1919. During his terms in office, the construction of the Civic Center auditorium began in 1917. The still incomplete building was used on October 2 of that year to send off 141 Kay County soldiers leaving for duty in World War I. Bill loved a parade and was the Grand Marshall of the Cherokee Strip parades held during his administration. In 1931, the McFaddens moved to Ft. Worth, Texas, but continued to own a home in Ponca City for a number of years. After relocating to Texas, Bill kept his Ponca City interests alive by returning whenever possible to ride at the head of the annual Cherokee Strip parades.

William Hartman McFadden died in 1956 at the age of eighty-seven. Clyde Muchmore, the publisher of the *Ponca City News* and a close friend of McFadden's, wrote that he was "one of the most dynamic forces ever to come to Ponca and to Oklahoma. He had a part in all of our civic and business development. We who knew Bill well can certainly give him full credit for the spirited growth of our community."

The Edgington Years

L. D. Edgington purchased the First National Bank in 1933 and was its president until his retirement in 1954. At one time, he owned the First National Bank of Tenneco and the Shidler National Bank. L. D. Edgington is remembered as an honest man who handled many business transactions with a simple handshake. The Edgingtons purchased the home in 1940, and in later years their daughter, Betty Edgington Andrews, would refer to the family home as "McFadden's Imagination." It seems that when the house was being built, Mr. McFadden would often tell the workmen to add another room or change a recently built part of the house. Perhaps this is the reason that upon entering the front door, the second floor staircase is almost too close for comfort. When the Edgingtons had Betty's wedding reception in the home, a note was attached to the front door asking the guests to enter through the sunroom doors. The reason was the architectural detailing of the front door and its nearby location to the staircase and the dining room door.

The attractive exterior of the McFadden–Edgington Dutch Colonial style home has a semi-circular front portico supported by Ionic columns and an interesting array of dormer windows. One enters directly into the living room with its fireplace on the south wall of the room. Flanking the fireplace are pairs of arched

THE ORIGINAL CARRIAGE HOUSE SHOWING THE BREEZEWAY THAT CONNECTS IT TO THE MAIN HOUSE.

French doors leading into the sunroom that originally had a black and white marble tiled porch. A single arched door to the right of the staircase opens into the large formal dining room, (Yes, it is a tight squeeze at the staircase and the dining room and front entrance doors.) Behind the dining room was the butler's pantry, breakfast room, and kitchen. Today, these spaces are opened into one large area and a fireplace has been added. Off the kitchen is a narrow porch and an attached "washroom." The porch continues as a breezeway leading to the carriage house. A pull-up door in the floor of this area led to the wine cellar below ground level. The second floor of the home contained a sitting room, three bedrooms, and two-plus baths. The original showers in the baths were lined with tin.

Today the McFadden-Edgington home is owned by Fred and Sue Boettcher. When excavating for the Boettcher family pool in the backyard, the workmen discovered huge slabs of buried concrete, likely the remains of the original dog runs. This discovery confirmed the rumor that the property was originally the site for E. W. Marland's dog kennels. Further support for the dog kennel theory was discovered when the original wood floors in the dining room were removed. Beneath the floor was a concrete floor with a large floor drain. Above the dining room is a second floor bedroom and when the plaster was removed from its walls, wood boarding was discovered. These two items occurred in only this portion of the house so it is assumed that this was the original dog kennel with a storeroom above. —JBW

921 E. CENTRAL AVENUE
The Mary French Barrett House

Whenever I attend one of my numerous class reunions, a group of us enjoy driving around Ponca City and looking at many of the houses we grew up with. Always on one of these Ponca house tours, someone will say, "Let's drive by Mary French Barrett's house."

The Mary French Barrett house was built in 1913 by William Knox Moore. Moore had arrived in Ponca at the beginning of the twentieth century and started his career as City Attorney and Justice of the Peace. In 1916, he joined the Marland Oil Company legal department to become head of that division.

The Moore-Barrett house is located at 921 East Central, (remember that Marland's Grand Avenue home was not completed until the Christmas of 1916) and for several years it stood at the eastern boundary of the city. Today's house is much larger than the original for in the early 1920s, the two-car garage wing was added with the large room above it becoming W. K.'s library. During this same period the sunroom was added on the east side of the house. This addition included a first floor sunroom and a second floor screened sleeping porch which was later

HISTORIC HOMES OF PONCA CITY AND KAY COUNTY ~ 25

enclosed to become part of the master bedroom suite.

In 1929, W. K. Moore left Marland Oil Company to enter private law practice. Continental Oil had taken over Marland Oil Company and during this transition many of Marland's executives were forced to find other careers.

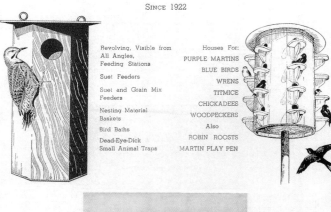

THE BARRETT YEARS

In 1941, Jack and Lea Barrett purchased the W. K. Moore house for $6,000. Jack Barrett was raised in Wynnewood, Indian Territory, and attended business college in Guthrie, Oklahoma, where he earned his room and board by caring for a herd of cows. Jack would teach bookkeeping and penmanship at the business college until 1917, when he took the position of bookkeeper with Charlie Duncan Ford Motor Company in Ponca. In July of that same year, Jack enlisted in the United States Army and saw duty in France and Germany during World War I. Barrett returned to Ponca City in 1919, and in 1925 he joined the Marland Oil Company. He remained there after its merger with Continental Oil Company, retiring in 1955, as supervisor of station auditors.

Lea French Barrett's parents arrived in Cross, Oklahoma Territory, in 1893. Her father, J. A. French, brought with him his two fine brood mares and a single sire. From these three fine horses, the French stable built an excellent reputation for the breeding of trotter and pacer horses. On June 20, 1920, Jack Barrett and Lea French were married. They had one daughter, Mary French Barrett (my classmate and friend.) After his retirement from Continental, Jack turned his attention to the photography of birds and to his old hobby of building bird houses and birdfeeders. He and Lea became well known as "birders." They exhibited their bird houses and feeders at county fairs and gave lectures and slide presentations about their feathered friends for garden clubs, civic organizations, churches, and Girl and Boy Scout groups.

The next time you are taking a Sunday afternoon drive around beautiful Ponca City, do not forget to say, "Why don't we drive by Mary French Barrett's House?" —JBW

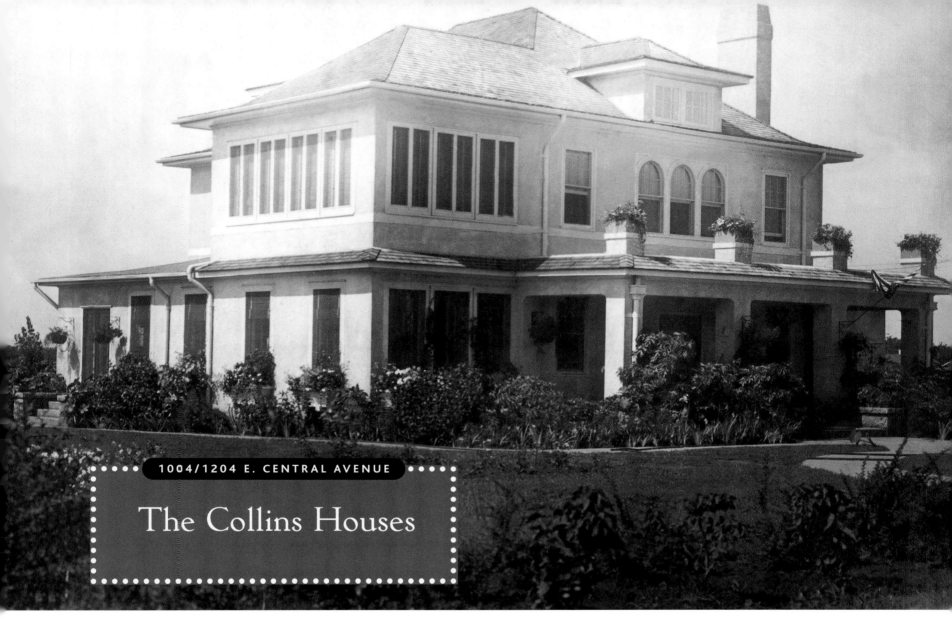

1004/1204 E. CENTRAL AVENUE

The Collins Houses

EARLY-DAY PHOTO OF THE SAM COLLINS, SR. HOME.

Samuel Cavin Collins, Sr. was born in Philadelphia, Pennsylvania, in 1850. In 1871, he married Lydie Elizabeth Miller and from that union five children were born: Mary Virginia, Margaret, Nellie, Bessie, and Samuel C. Collins, Jr.

In 1895, Margaret Collins married George Roberts. Their family included four children, George, Lydie, Ernest, and Virginia.

In 1903, Mary Virginia Collins married Ernest Whitworth Marland. Mary Virginia and her husband would eventually adopt two of Margaret and George Roberts's children and raise them as their own. The two adopted children were Lydie and George. After Mary Virginia's death, her husband, E. W. Marland, would have the adoption of Lydie annulled, and they would marry on July 14, 1928, in Flourtown, Pennsylvania.

SAM C. COLLINS, SR. HOUSE

The two-story structure with a large third floor attic has a stucco facade. A series of three arched windows above the front porch roof and the sweeping roof overhangs are all part of the architectural integrity of the house. Designed by Solomon Layton, the attached two car garage has large windows similar to Marland's Grand Avenue garages.

SAM C. COLLINS, JR. HOUSE

In 1916, Samuel Cavin Collins, Jr. married Florence Weisenberger in Philadelphia, Pennsylvania. They had two daughters, Lydie Virginia and Florence Ann.

There is some evidence that the Sam C. Collins, Jr. home was originally built for Colonel Franklin Kenney, a nephew of E. W. Marland. But soon after its completion in 1922, the ownership of the house was transferred to Collins, making it questionable if Kenney ever occupied the house. Sam Collins, Jr. was director and vice-president of marketing for Marland Oil Company. He and E. W. Marland were good friends in Pennsylvania before Marland arrived in Ponca City.

The house was designed by Layton, Smith and Forsythe of Oklahoma City, the same architectural firm that had designed Marland's home at 1000 East Grand Avenue. The Mediterranean style three-story stucco structure has a red clay tile roof that blends with the red tile front porch. Massive stucco brackets with a circular motif seem to support the decorative planter box above the front entrance. The east terrace has French doors leading into the formal living room and on the grounds are an incinerator, a storm cellar, a cistern and a reservoir for kerosene used to operate the original radiator heating system. Today the central heating system is fired by natural gas.

A passage in the book *The Life and Death of an Oilman* describes a visit by E.W. Marland to the Sam Collins, Jr. home: "The comfortable living room where they sat was beautiful and restful. But, after looking around, E. W. said, 'Sam, you ought to have a good oil painting there above the fireplace.' 'I know,' answered Sam, 'but I don't want oil paintings and I can't afford expensive rugs. What's the use of having expensive things you don't want?' Marland replied, 'You want beautiful things for that is what makes life worthwhile.'"

The floors throughout the house are of quarter-sawn white oak in the Mission-Craftsman style. There are bookcases with leaded glass doors also in white oak. The large living room is bright and sunny with its many windows which are part of the seventy-seven window units in the house. The living room mantelpiece is of wood with applied plaster classical reliefs which, when painted to match the mantelpiece, give the appearance of being hand carved.

The kitchen is fitted with a call bell system designed to summon servants to both front and back doors and also to the various rooms in the house. The number that appeared in an oak box indicated where a household staff member was needed. The second floor consisted of two bedroom suites and a sleeping porch. The third floor was used for servants' quarters and has two bedrooms, a bath, and a huge storage room the entire width of the house. A full basement houses the laundry room with its large metal sinks, used for the household washing.

Sam Collins, Jr. resigned his position with Marland Oil Company in 1928, when it was taken over by Continental. He died in 1957 and his wife, Florence Collins, continued to live in the family home until her death in 1977. —JBW

FACING PAGE: THE SAM COLLINS, SR. HOUSE TODAY.

RIGHT: THE SAM COLLINS, JR. HOUSE AT 1204 E. CENTRAL AVENUE.

903 E. CENTRAL AVENUE

The Christmas Party House

The federal Colonial Revival style house located at 903 East Central welcomes you with an imposing double doorway flanked by Corinthian pilasters. The house was built in 1928 for the Markham family. Ten years after its completion, the home was purchased by J. J. (Jim) Young and his wife, Marcella.

As a young man, Jim Young started his career in the oil business as a roustabout. He would work his way up the ladder to become a lease foreman and later a drilling contractor. Jim's success in the oil business was attributed to hard work and insight into its future growth. Jim was the stepson of Dan Mooney, and together they owned one-third interest in the development of the Jens Marie Hotel. In later years, Young would serve as its manager. In 1946, Jim developed the land west of the hospital, naming the streets in the development after his four children: Mary, John, Jane, and Joe.

The layout of the Markham-Young house was designed for entertaining. The oversized rooms on the ground floor include the formal entrance hall, the living and dining rooms, the sunroom and a huge kitchen. The elaborate chandeliers and the wide plaster ceiling moldings highlight the ten foot ceilings. The detached garage had servants' quarters above. When the family's son, John, was in high school, this area was converted into a private poker and recreational space for him and his friends.

The large basement club room held two pool tables and two ping pong tables, and the adjoining "poker room" was a popular weekly gathering place for leaders in the community such as D. J. Donahoe, Lew Prunty, and Lew Wentz. Even Senator Robert S. Kerr once attended one of these poker parties. One of the busboys from the Jens Marie often served as bartender.

In my visit with Jim and Marcella's son, John, I learned much about life in his family home during the 1940s and 1950s. The Youngs were staunch Democrats, so every four years they hosted a Presidential "Watch Party." During the 1948 election when Truman was finally declared winner in the early hours of the morning, over 200 guests who had attended the Youngs' Watch Party stayed until the last vote was counted. In 1952, presidential candidate Adlai Stevenson visited the Young home during his campaign in Oklahoma. Another early-day remembrance was that since the Youngs' home was only two blocks from the Marland Golf Course, friends would often gather at the house, walk over to play golf, and then return to the house for alcoholic refreshments.

Jim and Marcella Young were famous for their Christmas parties for children. In the first years, these parties started with just a few families, but soon more people were invited until over 300 were attending the festivities. Santa Claus was always on the scene talking to each of the children and asking about their Christmas wishes. Each child was given a gift. Sandwiches and cookies were served and everyone sang Christmas carols.

What a wonderful childhood Christmas memory to have. —KA

MIDTOWN

In the Midtown area, business owners and oilmen who prospered from the newly burgeoning regional oil industry of the teens and 1920s built some of Ponca City's most notable homes. They surrounded them with spacious landscaping and beautiful gardens and shade trees.

In May, 1922, the *Ponca City News* reported that many of the homeowners had participated in the annual "City Beautiful" campaign and that "lawns are clean, unsightly places have been eliminated and parking areas along the 150 blocks of paved streets have been improved. Many citizens have planted alfalfa and garden crops on the vacant lots to prevent weeds from infesting those places." — KA

505 W. GRAND AVENUE
DeRoberts-Calkins Mansion

Charles DeRoberts was born in Burlington, Iowa, in 1843. He married Carrie Mendenhall and came to Oklahoma in 1893 with the opening of the Cherokee Outlet. He settled in the Township of Cross, which was located at North Union Street between West Albany and Hartford Avenues. There DeRoberts established the Commercial Bank of Cross. Later he was offered a corner lot at First Street and Grand Avenue as an inducement to relocate his bank to Ponca City. He did relocate his bank to Ponca City but held out for an additional lot and so was given both the north corner lots at that intersection.

DeRoberts moved the frame and steel structure from Cross to his newly acquired east corner lot and would build a three-story brick building on the west lot where his son-in-law, Charles Calkins, opened the Calkins Mercantile Store. When DeRoberts decided to replace his original bank with a brick structure, he put the building on skids and moved it to the 500 block on West Grand Avenue. There the relocated building continued as a bank until the new building was completed. Eventually DeRoberts had the structure relocated to its present location after rotating it ninety degrees. From this humble structure was created the DeRoberts-Calkins mansion. It is said that several elm trees were located on the property where the house was to stand. In order to prevent damage to those trees, they were carefully dug up and balled and moved to a temporary spot until the house was put in its final location. Today we would call it "instant landscape." The relocation and remodel of the house was started in 1906 and completed in 1907.

In 1912, the house was severely damaged by a tornado, and when rebuilt it was enlarged and enhanced as it appears today—a beautiful Greek Revival mansion. The architect for this marvelous creation was C. N. Terry of Wichita, Kansas, and the architect's original drawings are still in existence. The stately Ionic columns support the first and second floor verandas and are of stamped metal which could be ordered from an architectural metal catalog. The exterior of the mansion might be described as a melody of fine scale and proportion accentuated with exquisite detailing.

The focal point of the front foyer is the massive staircase leading to the upper floors and the original brass lantern which is still in place in the foyer. To the right of the foyer was the living room with its delicate carved wood mantlepiece. Beyond the living room was the sunroom surrounded with windows on three sides. To the left of the foyer was the formal dining room. Its original chandelier is of alabaster marble, handcrafted in Italy in 1908. Other rooms on the ground floor were a butler's pantry, kitchen, and breakfast room.

Charles DeRoberts was Ponca City's third mayor, serving from 1898 until 1901. During his term in office, long-distance phone service was made available, and the city's first water works system was installed in 1900. DeRoberts owned the first gasoline-powered automobile in Oklahoma. It was manufactured by the Automobile Company of America and was called the "dos-e-dos," for it was an open air vehicle built for the passengers to sit back-to-back. Mr. DeRoberts died on May 1, 1915, at the age of seventy-one, and his funeral was held in the family home. His eulogy referred to him as a builder, not a knocker and concluded by saying: "If there is any word that will express his activities it is 'helpfulness.' He loved to counsel and he loved to advise, intelligently, unobtrusively, and sympathetically. He loved to help the failing business manager, farmer, artisan or laborer. He had a higher object in life than making money."

THE CALKINS YEARS

Charles F. Calkins was married to the DeRobertses' daughter. He came to Indian Territory at the urging of his father-in-law and established the C. F. Calkins Mercantile Store in the township of Cross. Like DeRoberts, Calkins relocated his store to Ponca City at 120 East Grand Avenue. The Calkins Mercantile would open its doors each morning between 5:00 and 6:00 A.M. in the summer so customers could shop in the cool of the day. Many arrived in wagons from towns as far away as Pawnee, Hominy, and Tonkawa. Some would come the previous day, camp out for the night, and then do their early morning shopping before returning home that same day.

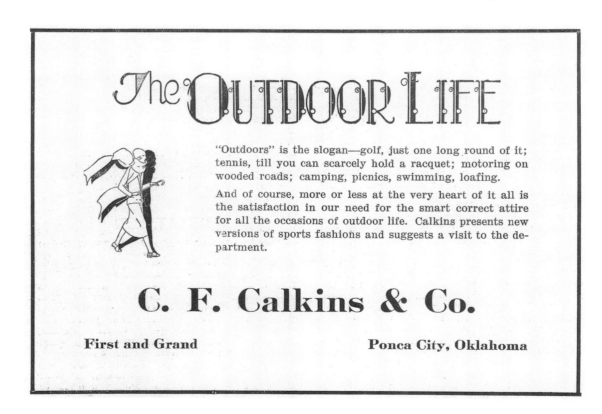

34 ~ HISTORIC HOMES OF PONCA CITY AND KAY COUNTY

Calkins had a good relationship and trade with the local Native Americans. A system of collecting from them was established by several of the local merchants. The Indian Agency would set a day to pay the various tribesmen once every six months. It became the practice of their creditors to line up and as the tribesmen were paid, they would hand over their check to the first creditor. He would give back the change from what was owed him and so down the line until all current bills were paid.

In 1926, Calkins sold his store and retired from the business world. Mr. and Mrs. Calkins enjoyed traveling and made several trips around the world. They especially liked India and many of their vast collections were from that country. Their collection of paintings included such artists as Moran and Corot. A fine rose-colored silk hanging that once adorned a Chinese palace was included in their collection. Today only one piece from the collection remains—a pen and ink sketch of the home by well-known artist Birger Sandzen remains in the mansion.

THE MATZENE YEARS

Richard Gordon Matzene was born in London on September 19, 1880. He grew up and attended schools in Denmark and Italy, but after the death of his parents he made his home with an aunt and uncle in England. His interest in art led him to the study of photography. He become a professional photographer and was recognized as one of the foremost photographers in the country.

Matzene was a well-known traveler. He made eight trips around the world and for several years maintained a studio in Simla, Himachal Prodesh, India. While there, he received an invitation from the King of Nepal to visit Kathmandu, Nepal, to make photographs of various members of the royal family. At that time, Nepal was a closed country. Europeans could enter the country only after receiving official invitations from the government. Matzene is said to have been the twenty-seventh outsider to visit Nepal.

During the last years of his life, Matzene made his home with Mr. and Mrs. Charles Calkins in the Calkins mansion at 505 West Grand Avenue. Richard Gordon Matzene bequeathed the Matzene collection of Oriental and Modern Art to the Ponca City Library where it can be seen today. He died on August 27, 1950, at the age of seventy.
—KA

I would like to add "my two cents" about the Matzene collection in the Ponca City Library. Whenever I come to Ponca and have the time, I enjoy visiting the library to see the small but wonderful Matzene collection. My favorite is the not-too-large Chinese Mandarin dressed in bright red. He hangs in the southeast reading room—don't miss him on your next tour.

As a child, my introduction to Impressionist art occurred when the large Birger Sandzen landscape was hung in the northwest reading room at the Ponca City Library. My first view of the painting was from a great distance and I was "taken" with this rather unusual style of painting. Then, upon closer view, the painting became nothing but big globs of paint—what a surprise.
—JBW

601 MCFADDEN DRIVE
The State Flag House

Louise Funk and George Rogers Fluke were both raised in Shawnee, Oklahoma. George would attend Northwestern University in Chicago, and Louise would study at Columbia University, the Art Student League in New York City, and the Art Institute in Chicago. Louise and George were married in 1924, and in 1928, they moved to Ponca City. The Fluke family home is at 601 McFadden Drive, located in the Marland Model City District.

In the 1920s, the original state flag was deemed unacceptable by the military leaders at Ft. Sill, Oklahoma. They, with other concerned citizens and organizations, including the Daughters of the American Revolution, sponsored a statewide contest for a new state flag design. A friend of Louise, who knew of her talents and training, urged her to enter the flag contest. Louise spent many hours at the Oklahoma Historical Museum in Oklahoma City poring over pictures and relics of Indian lore in doing the research for her submittals. (She entered two designs.) Louise Fluke's design for our state flag was unanimously selected by a panel of judges and then adopted by the state's Tenth Legislature in 1925.

The Flukes had one son, George Rogers, Jr., who remembers his mother not only for her talent as an artist but also for her beautiful penmanship. Today, the Flukes' son has the original three-by-five-foot silk flag his mother hand decorated. It was the first new state flag to fly over the Capitol in Oklahoma City. George, Jr. remembers from growing up in Ponca City that his father "was an avid fisherman and we would go on many fishing trips to places including Canada and Red River, New Mexico. It was fun camping out."

Susanne Abbott Bullock's mother was a close friend and neighbor of Louise Fluke. Today, Susanne has her mother's copy of the Oklahoma state flag that Louise had hand-colored: "The flag has a sky blue field with a circular rawhide shield of an American Indian warrior. The shield is decorated with six painted crosses, the symbol of stars, and the lower half of the shield is fringed with seven pendant eagle feathers. Superimposed upon the face of the shield is a calumet or peace pipe crossed at right angles with an olive branch. The blue of the field signifies devotion. The shield signifies defensive or protective warfare—but always surmounted by and subservient to the olive branch and peace pipe which betokens the love of peace and the part of a united people."

The state name was added to the flag in 1941.

Marquetta Brown wrote a book telling the history of our state flag and in 1984, a story of Louise Fluke and her state flag appeared in the newsletter of the First Presbyterian Church in Oklahoma City. The article ended with the words, "An hour with Mrs. Fluke makes Oklahoma history come alive." —JBW

36 ~ HISTORIC HOMES OF PONCA CITY AND KAY COUNTY

502 S. SEVENTH STREET
Ponca's First Flour Mill: D. J. Donahoe House

A small flour mill was started in Ponca City in 1893 by Robert Maxwell and Lee McCord. This mill was one of the main anchors of early-day Ponca City. The original facility consisted of a small wooden shanty with minimum equipment and only five employees. Upon its completion a celebration was held for the townspeople. A long rope was tied to the whistle atop the mill, and the citizens lined up to take turns blowing the whistle. The first sack of flour was ground on April 4, 1894, and that night, the merchants of Ponca held a banquet in honor of the mill owners. The first sack of flour was put up for auction and was purchased by Mayor B.S. Barnes for $150.

The years after the Land Run of 1893 were difficult ones, with drought burning up the crops of the settlers, and the mill fell upon hard times. In 1895, three brothers, Dan, Ed, and John Donahoe, purchased the mill at a sheriff's sale. The Donahoes added new buildings, new grain elevators, and new equipment to the mill, making it one of the finest of its kind in the area. Three years later, Dan bought out his brothers' shares and became the mill's owner. At one time, the top of the grain elevators were lined with lights that could be seen as a landmark and a "lamp in the window" to Poncans returning home. The tall mill elevators also bore the legend "Ponca City — the Best Place in the World."

Over the years, Dan Donahoe would become very prosperous through ranching, grain milling, and real estate development. He was also instrumental in bringing the Rock Island Railroad to Ponca and was one of the founders of the Ponca City Chamber of Commerce, originally known as the Board of Trade.

Dan Donahoe had received his law degree from the University of Wisconsin in 1891. He was twenty-eight years old when he made the Cherokee Strip Land Run in 1893. He staked a claim, but gave it to another man with a family who was unable to find an unclaimed parcel. Upon arriving in Ponca City, his first lodging was in a tent hotel. The large tent was divided into stalls with straw heaped on the ground for bedding and rented for twenty-five cents a night. The tent hotel also had stalls with cots but their costs were considerably higher, so Dan elected to sleep on the straw bedding.

HISTORIC HOMES OF PONCA CITY AND KAY COUNTY ~ 37

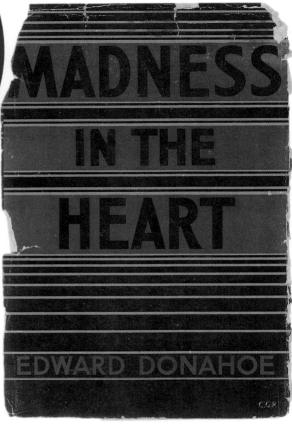

EDWARD DONAHOE, AUTHOR OF *MADNESS IN THE HEART*, ORIGINAL DUST JACKET OF HIS BOOK, AND A LIST OF THE BOOK'S FICTIONAL CHARACTERS.

In 1898, Daniel J. Donahoe married Margaret McGraw, and in 1910 they built their family home at 302 South Seventh Street. Built in the Craftsman Style, the house was designed by Solomon Layton, the architect for Marland's Grand Avenue house. The exterior of the Donahoe house features wide overhangs and a hard-fired red brick facade. The end gables are stucco with a half-timber design. In 1917, a sleeping porch was added to the rear of the house, and in 1921 Layton designed a bedroom and solarium addition on the south end of the house.

D. J. and Margaret had two sons, D. J. Jr. (Dee), who took over the family business, and Edward, who became a writer. In 1937, Edward Donahoe published a book entitled *Madness in the Heart.* The book used fictitious names and places, but it was the disguised tale of Ponca City, and in particular of the Donahoes, the McGraws, and E. W. and Mary Virginia Marland. E. W. Marland became Marcus Sigourney and the Soldani sisters were called the Marenge girls. Ponca City was called Pleasant Prairie, and the names of the Arcade and Jens-Marie Hotels were changed to Savoy and Sooner. Many social scandals of Ponca City were highlighted. Edward's father, D. J., purchased and burned every copy of the book he could find, so any remaining copies have become much-sought-after items. On the title page of the book, Ecclesiates, chapter 9, verse 3, is quoted: *"—The heart of the sons of men is full of evil, and madness is in their heart while they live—"*

The library of the Donahoe house is where D. J. had his desk and books, and in his final years, he spent a great deal of time in this room. Margaret McGraw Donahoe died in 1936, and D. J. continued to live in the family home until his death in 1946, at the age of eighty-one. The Donahoe home remained in the family but stood virtually empty for the next thirty-five years.

Reading D. J. Donahoe's memoirs in *The Last Run,* published by the Ponca City Chapter of the Daughters of the American Revolution, makes me question his support for our nation's early-day Women's Suffrage Movement. At the conclusion of his essay, Donahoe wrote, "Today [1939], although there are eleven million men out of work, there are also eleven million women engaged in the business world. My belief is, that if those eleven million women would turn their jobs over to the eleven million unemployed men, our economic problems would be solved." —JBW

902 S. SEVENTH STREET
Joe Donahue-Goldenstern Home

In 1923, Ursula Dellaplain purchased the lot on the southwest corner of South Seventh Street and South Avenue. In 1924, the Dellaplains built their "airplane bungalow" there at a cost of $1,400. In that same year, the house was sold to J. W. (Joe) Donahue. In 1930, Joe and Vera Goldenstern purchased the home from the Donahoes and, for the next forty-four years, the house at 902 South Seventh Street would be the Goldenstern family home. Joe Goldenstern, a well respected leader in the community, was in the used oil field equipment business.

The exterior of the house is dark red brick with a porch extending across the front. A partial second story wing sits in the middle of the first floor roof line. Beyond the front porch is the long living room, which also spans the width of the structure. Behind the living room are the formal dining room, breakfast room, and kitchen, plus two downstairs bedrooms and a bath. The second floor of the Donahue-Goldenstern house has two additional bedrooms and a bath.

The "airplane-bungalow" style was popular during the 1920s. The main mass of the house was one story with only a partial second floor, making for a smaller structure than a full two-story house. This second floor could provide excellent ventilation on three sides and was often a single room used as a sleeping porch.

The name "airplane bungalow" reflects the shape of the houses. The second floor wing was usually located at the rear of the house and the front porch often extended out on each side of the main body of the first floor. These extensions were sometimes a porte cochere at one end and a continuation of the porch at the opposite end. With this configuration, the second floor resembled the tail of an airplane and the front porch extensions formed the wings of the plane. The Donahue-Goldenstern house is a modified version of this design.

Ponca City has several versions of "airplane bungalows" throughout the city. I grew up in an "airplane bungalow" house in Wichita, Kansas, so I always take special notice when I drive by those houses similar to my family home. —KA

1103/1107 S. SEVENTH STREET
South Seventh Street Sisters

Charles F. Martin and his wife, Marie, were both from Little Rock, Arkansas. They arrived in Ponca City in 1919, when Charles became an official with the Francoma Oil Company. In 1922, the company was purchased by Marland Oil, and Martin became vice-president of Marland's land department. Later Martin resigned this position to become an independent oil operator. Charles and Marie Martin built their home at 1103 South Seventh Street, but in 1929, Charles Martin died at the age of forty-five, leaving Marie a widow with three children, two sons, Charles and Bill, and a daughter, Gloria.

The Martin family home is not unlike its next door neighbor, the Bogan-Beard house. Both houses are in the Craftsman-Bungalow style of architecture with dark red brick facades capped with terra cotta barrel red tile roofs. The Martin-Harris home has two large formal living rooms, plus a sunroom, dining room, breakfast room, butler's pantry, and kitchen. The full basement has a club room and wine cellar and the second floor houses four bedrooms and four baths.

In 1934, Marie Martin married Colonel T. D. Harris, who had served in World War I. Colonel Harris owned Green Gables Farm, which many of us remember. This pristine farm was located on North Waverly Road, just north of West Hartford Avenue, and its white farmhouse was capped with a green gabled roof. During the Darr School of Aeronautics years, its British Commander, Fesler Susser, lived at Green Gables.

Marie Martin Harris's next door neighbor was A. L. Bogan, who gave the City of Ponca the land and money to build Bogan Swimming Pool in south Ponca. With the advent of the Depression years, Bogan did not have the cash to complete the swimming pool. Without any fanfare, Marie silently gave the money to complete the Bogan Pool.

Marie was active in the social life of the Marland era in Ponca City and was one of the hostesses during the original grand opening of the Marland Mansion in 1928. In 1933, she attended the first inauguration of President Franklin D. Roosevelt and participated in the social activities surrounding the inauguration. Marie was accompanied to Washington, D. C. by her longtime friend and fellow Poncan, Blanche Lucas. The story is told by Marie's daughter, Gloria Martin Williams, of how Blanche and Marie arrived at one of the inaugural dinners early so they could rearrange the place cards for Blanche

THE HOUSE AT 1103 SOUTH SEVENTH STREET.

THE HOUSE AT 1107 SOUTH SEVENTH STREET.

to be seated next to Jim Farley, the Postmaster General of the United States. The reason for this change in seating arrangements was that Blanche Lucas wanted to be appointed Postmistress of Ponca to replace her deceased husband, Frank Lucas. It worked. —JBW

Next door to the Martin-Harris home is the Bogan-Beard home. Both houses have similar facades with their brick exterior and red tile roofs. The Bogan-Beard house was built in 1922, for a Mr. Rickerd who was a local road contractor. In 1923, the home was sold to A. L. Bogan for $28,000. Bogan's business interests included the Murray, Majestic, and Mission movie theaters and would later include the Poncan and Ritz movie houses. Because of this interest in the entertainment world, it was said that many movie and vaudeville stars were guests in the Bogan home, including Will Rogers and Mae West.

Bogan gave the land and built the Bogan Swimming Pool (now known as Ambuc Pool), which he gave (with the help of Marie Martin Harris) to the City of Ponca. Unfortunately, Bogan experienced financial difficulties with the advent of the Great Depression, and in the late 1930s the home was sold to W. D. (Bill) Beard, owner of the Ponca City Ice Company, and later president of Ponca City Savings and Loan. Bill and his wife, Inez, and their two children, David and Ruthie, would occupy the home until 1970. The Beards were good friends of Governor Johnston Murray and his wife Willie. Mrs. Murray would come to Ponca and give piano lessons to both David and Ruthie along with several other Ponca City children.

The classically designed front entrance opens into a wide center hall. On one wall of the hall is a hand-painted mural depicting the Osage hills and trees with the artist's own home included in the artwork. To the right of the central foyer is the living room, and to the left is the formal dining room which connects the the butler pantry and kitchen. The focal point of the living room is the decorative tile mantelpiece with its center medallion design. The living room is large enough to house two grand pianos, and the pair of French doors flanking the fireplace opens onto a long, long porch. What is now the library was originally the smoking room. Located off the living room, this rooms was used by the master of the house and his male guests. An exhaust fan in the space kept the cigar and cigarette smoke from entering the rest of the house.

A full basement includes a knotty-pine club room with space for a billiard table and even a table for the game of ping pong. Gun and trophy cases were on each side of the club room fireplace. The second floor of the Bogan-Beard house includes the master bedroom containing built-in cabinets with leaded glass doors and the floor in the inlaid woods in a parquetry design. There are four bedrooms and two baths on the second floor level.

One of my favorite areas in the home is the large and spacious attic. A pull-down ladder in this space leads up to a skylight that, when opened, offers a "pigeon's eye" panoramic view of Ponca City. — KA

HISTORIC HOMES OF PONCA CITY AND KAY COUNTY ~ 41

1220 S. EIGHTH STREET
Anthony-Mall House

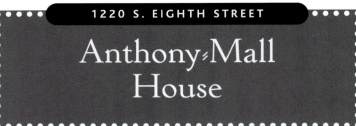

In 1924, George J. Cannon, a prominent local architect, designed this Dutch Colonial style house for Ida Soldani Anthony. The following year, Cannon would design a home for her uncle, Godance Soldani. The Godance Soldani mansion is located at 819 East Central Avenue and today is the home of the Ponca City Art Center. George Cannon was also the architect for the original Rock Cliff Country Club which today is the home of the Veterans of Foreign Wars organization.

Located at 1220 South Eighth Street, the Anthony home is remembered by many Poncans as the residence of Dr. Werner Mall, an eye-ear-nose-and-throat physician who lived in the home until 1969. In 1947, the Malls completed a major addition to the house, designed by another local architect, M. D. (Doc) Timberlake. The 3,700-square-foot house has a facade of field limestone and wood siding. The house has four bedrooms at the second floor, each with its own private bath. Also at the second floor are numerous storage closets with some housing wood rods to hang quilts and linens.

Six fireplaces are found in the house, three wood-burning and three with gas logs. The decorative tile surround at one of the fireplaces features hand-painted tiles imported from Spain. Another unique feature of the home is the three "porthole" style windows that can be opened for ventilation.

The original stone columns at each end of the south porch and the similar stone posts flanking the driveway help to relate the house to its spacious yard. The stone posts seem to indicate that originally there was a wood or iron fence surrounding the property with a matching gate at the drive.

In 1988, the home was converted into Ponca City's first bed and breakfast and was called the Mall-Bright House. I remember visiting the home during that time period and recall how the living room, or gathering room as it was then called, had such a very "homey" and cheerful feel with its furniture arranged around the hearth of the very large stone fireplace. Janet Bright owned a large collection of heirloom quilts and displayed several of them on the walls at the staircase leading to the second floor. Janet's specialty was her "homemade" breakfasts. For these wonderful meals, she used fruit from the fruit trees in the yard and fresh vegetables from her garden. Another of her specialties were her homemade bread and rolls. When Janet's husband was transferred to Houston, Texas, the property once again became a private single family home.

Dr. Werner Mall was an avid gardener. It is said that he had over seventy-five varieties of roses growing in his garden plus many species of lilies and irises. Today evidence of the good doctor's gardening skills can still be seen on the grounds of this historic South Ponca City home. —KA

408 S. TENTH STREET
The Gammie House

James Gammie was born in Scotland, and, at an early age, was apprenticed to a stonecutter in Aberdeen, Scotland, to learn the trade of a stonemason. Upon immigrating to the United States, James first arrived in Boston, Massachusetts. He would slowly work his way across the country until he reached Arkansas City, Kansas. James and his wife, Lois, had six sons. The two younger boys, Thomas and Robert, were James's children and the other four, Angus, Kyler and the twins, Wilbur and Wilfred, were Lois's children from a previous marriage.

James Gammie became infected with the fever of the Cherokee Strip Run of 1893. He made the Run on foot, traveling in a southerly direction. After walking for several hours, he staked his 160-acre claim between Blackwell and Ponca City. After he staked his location notices, Gammie built a fire and prepared for the coming of night. Next morning, he discovered a rival homesteader who had filed and camped on the same quarter section of land. After several days of negotiating, James offered the other claimant fifty dollars down and another fifty dollars at some indefinite future date. His offer was accepted.

The second summer after staking their claim, the Gammie family's finances were at an all time low. It was decided to divide their meager cash supply, so James took twenty-five cents and went in search of work and left the remaining one dollar for Lois and the boys to survive on. When he reached Niotaze, Texas, James worked for

the greater part of the summer and was paid in money, seed, wheat, a pig, a plow, a bushel of grapes, and some vegetables.

Upon his return to Oklahoma, Gammie was soon hired to construct Ponca City's first stone building for the George Brett Implement Company, located at 100 East Grand Avenue. Later he became the manager of the Ponca City Quarry owned by E. W. Marland. This quarry provided the stone for the Marland mansion, the Ponca City Federal Building and Post Office and many other stone structures in Ponca City.

In 1927, Gammie's son, Thomas Gammie, built his unusual silver gray limestone house at 408 South Tenth Street. The cut stone is laid in the random ashlar pattern and the house includes such interesting features as the stone railing enclosing the front porch and the large lintel stones used on each end of the arched opening at the front porch. At the gabled ends of the Gammie house are parapet walls instead of roof overhangs, and the garage and quarters at the rear of the lot are of similar design. A low stone wall on the south side of the property continues around the back of the lot where it serves as a retaining wall. The Thomas Gammie house was built on land owned by his father, James, and since the father and son were partners in the stone contracting business, it is surmised that the house was built to showcase the high quality of their craftsmanship. —KA

George Nieman arrived in Ponca City at the age of eleven, just two months after the Cherokee Strip Land Run in 1893. During his boyhood days, young George was a local paper boy. Later he would attend medical school. Upon his graduation, the young Dr. Nieman was asked to return to Ponca for a few months while a local physician was on vacation. George accepted the offer but soon discovered that no one wanted their former newsboy as their doctor. One day he received a call from the Big V Ranch reporting the stabbing of the ranch foreman. When Dr. Nieman arrived, the victim was near death, so with the help of a cowboy and the cook, Nieman performed the surgery on the ranch house dining room table. Dr. George stayed with his patient for seven nights knowing that if the man died he would have no future in Ponca City as a medical doctor. His patient survived, and Dr. George Nieman practiced medicine in Ponca City for many, many years.

George Nieman married Louise Soldani in 1908. Unfortunately Louise and their first child both died in childbirth. Dr. Nieman's second wife was Grace Taliaferro Nieman.

The Nieman's first house was built in 1913 at 417 South Eighth Street. An extensive remodel was completed on the original structure in the late 1920s. Designed by the architect George Cannon, the remodeled home was in the southwestern style often called Pueblo Revival. The house is enclosed with a stucco fence and with its wrought-iron accents and the mission bell hanging in the belfry, it is a fine example of what one might see in Santa Fe and Taos, New

Mexico. To add more Southwest flavor to the home, an authentic Spanish well is located in the front lawn, with ornamental iron accents. The well was filled with ice to chill the champagne for the 1938 garden wedding of the Niemans' daughter, Louise. There are four bedrooms in the home, each with its own fireplace.

The original house remodel was in a U shape at the rear, but later this space was enclosed for a library. The Niemans loved Santa Fe and spent many vacations in its environs. The plaster relief above the music room mantel depicts a New Mexico Pueblo scene. I remember riding my bicycle down South Seventh Street and turning left at St. Mary's School just to study this very unusual southwestern style home.

The Niemans had two children, Louise and Hal. Hal was killed in a polo game accident at the University of Oklahoma when he was twenty-two. (Polo was a pre-war varsity sport at Oklahoma University; after the tragic accident the school's polo field was renamed in Hal's honor.) The children's pets included a baby buffalo given to them by the 101 Ranch. When he became too large to be a pet he was transferred to the Nieman farm east of Ponca. Unfortunately he died in a freak accident while making the journey, so his head was stuffed and for many years adorned a special spot above the library mantel.

Dr. George Nieman was a true "horse and buggy doctor." He would often make midnight buggy rides into the Osage, which meant fording the Arkansas River or crossing it when it was frozen over. He often reflected later on his early-day medical practice, at a time when "Ponca had a population of 1,800 people, which included eighteen doctors, and eighteen saloons." —JBW

418 N. SECOND STREET

Gill-Lessert Family Home

M. G. Gill arrived in Ponca City in 1901 to work for the J. M. Hayden Furniture and Undertaking establishment. Four years later, Gill married Eudora Bonham, a spunky young lady who had staked a claim in western Kay County during the Cherokee Outlet Land Run.

In 1919, the Gills purchased the Hayden operation along with the Smith Funeral Home and relocated their business to 104 East Grand Avenue, the future site of the Poncan Theatre. In 1925, the Gills closed their furniture business and devoted their time entirely to being funeral directors. In that same year, the new Gill Funeral Home building was completed. Located on the southwest corner of North Second Street and East Cleveland, the beautiful two-story structure was said to have cost $35,000. The drawings for the Gill Building show the architect to be H. R. Vorhies. However, newspaper articles of the period included Mr. and Mrs. Gill as also being the architects.

M. G. Gill was a very tolerant man and understood the fleeting nature of life. He was a friend to the Native Americans in a time when they knew few white friends who understood their feelings and emotions. He conducted the first Indian funeral in Ponca City, and his mortuary would continue to serve the nearby Indian tribes for many years.

The M. G. and Eudora Gill home is located at 418 North Second Street and was built about the same time that the Gill Mortuary building was constructed. In 1932, the Gills' only child, Dora Ellen, married Joe W. Lessert in the Gill living room, and today the Gill-Lessert home has housed four generations of family who still own the farm that Eudora Bonham Gill homesteaded. Joe and Dora had three children, two sons and one daughter. Their son, M. G. Lessert, his wife, Virginia, and their two children live in the family home.

The entrance foyer in the Gill-Lessert house features a fine Arts and Crafts staircase leading to the second floor. All of the woodwork in the house has its original natural finish. The formal living room, forty feet in length, is to the right of the foyer. Off the living room is the equally large dining room that can seat twenty people. The sunroom in the home is actually an extension of the formal dining room and is separated by oak columns. M. G. Lessert recalls the weekly Sunday dinners which the entire family were expected to attend. On the left of the entrance foyer is the cozy den with its brick fireplace.

Several of the original chandeliers and wall sconces in this finely preserved home have crystal prisms hanging from their arms, but the most interesting is the sunroom

fixture with its shades or light bulb covers. Made of Czechoslovakian colored glass, they are in the form of small beaded flowers wired together, giving a colorful and unusual effect.

The stairway hall leads to the the five bedrooms on the second floor and a back stair takes you to the breakfast room and kitchen area.

During World War II, the Gill-Lessert family had a "Chicken Park" in their back yard. It was M. G., Lessert's job to gather the eggs each morning, and his grandmother Eudora had the task of chasing down a chicken for the family's evening meal.

In 1993, the Gill-Lessert Funeral Home merged with the Trout Funeral Home, ending over seventy years of service to the community. The Gill Building is still intact and so is the original hearse once driven by a pair of fine horses. Another early-day vehicle that still exists is the 1923 Sayers-Scoville Cadillac ambulance. —KA

314 N. FOURTH STREET
E. M. Trout House

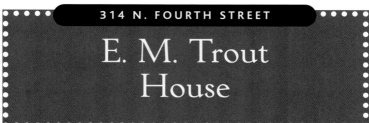

Ernest M. Trout, his wife, Nelle, and their eldest son, Ernest, Jr., came to Ponca City in 1918. Trout's first position was with the Marland Oil Company, but two years later he joined the McCaskey-Wentz Oil Company, where he worked in the insurance department for the next eleven years.

Trout's first home was in the 900 block on South Sixth Street. The Trout twins, Jim and John (Jack), were born in 1921. Shortly after, Lew Wentz arrived at the Trouts' doorstep in his Cole eight-cylinder car. He said, "You have doubled the size of your family, so you need a larger car." With that, he handed the keys of the Cole to Ernest and drove off in the family's ancient Model T Ford.

In 1923, the Trouts built their new home at 314 North Fourth Street. The house was financed by Lew Wentz. The four-square wood frame structure is two floors in height with a front porch extending across the front of the house. The large living room has its fireplace on the south wall and the staircase on the north wall. According to the Trouts' son, Ernie, "The living room was large enough to play touch football in—which we did, until we were caught." Behind the living room is the large formal dining room that connects to a breakfast nook and the kitchen. The first floor also has a bedroom. Upstairs there are three bedrooms and a lovely sitting room with French doors. In 1928, Phyllis Marie was born in one of the second floor bedrooms.

The Trout living room was also the site of weekly family musicals, Ernie, Jr. would recall. "Mom would play the grand piano, I played the cello, and the twins each played the violin." Ernie continued, "All of the houses on the block had horse hitching rings embedded into the curbs. The house next door had a limestone hitching post carved to resemble a tree stump. During World War II, when the ice truck came by to make deliveries, the driver would tie his horse to the post. We loved to jump on the back of the wagon and eat pieces of ice."

The Trout Funeral Home opened its doors on November 9, 1936 in a modest frame bungalow located on the southwest corner of Grand Avenue and South Oak. Ernie, Jr. recalls, "Here we were in the funeral home business and none of the family had ever seen a dead body." In 1942, the Trout Funeral home purchased the DeRoberts-Calkins mansion and relocated the funeral home to the mansion at 505 West Grand Avenue.

The slogan "Jack and Jim—The Minnow Men" was launched when the Trout twins started their careers in the minnow business. Their father helped them build a concrete pond in the back yard, which they stocked with minnows seined from the Arkansas River. After advertising their new business venture, they slept on cots outdoors during the summer months to accommodate the predawn fishermen of Ponca City. The customers drove down the alley and stopped to buy bait. Within three summers, Jack and Jim Trout earned over $1,000 from the sale of minnow bait.

And that was during the years of the Great Depression. —KA

418 N. FOURTH STREET
Dr. R.B. Gibson Home

Robert Barry Gibson was born in Campabella, South Carolina, in 1896. His father was a farmer who also operated a saw mill and a cotton gin and would become a member of the South Carolina legislature. After Robert's first year in college, his family's farm home was destroyed by a fire in which several of his siblings were killed. After the tragic fire, Robert and his brother, Walter, returned to the farm and spent the next year rebuilding their family home. Upon its completion, Robert Gibson, along with several friends, decided to "go west" to seek his fortune. After arriving in Oklahoma City, the other members of the group elected to return to South Carolina, but Robert remained in Oklahoma and soon enrolled in the school of medicine at the University of Oklahoma.

After his graduation, young Dr. Gibson practiced medicine in Oklahoma City until he enlisted in the United States Army Medical Corps and served as a doctor on the battlefields in France. In 1919, Gibson returned to Oklahoma City and seriously considered locating his medical practice in Kingfisher, Oklahoma. But he had heard of the oil boom in Ponca City and so decided to check Ponca out as a possible city to practice medicine. He rented a room in the Arcade Hotel where he soon became friends with the hotel's desk clerk, Roy Black. This friendship and his exploration of the town convinced Gibson to establish himself as a doctor of medicine in Ponca City.

Helen Wingo was raised on a farm near Inman, South Carolina. She and Robert Gibson met when both were attending a nearby boarding school. In 1921, Helen and Robert were married. In later years Helen would reflect that she was born, raised, and married in the family home that her grandfather had built with tools he had fashioned by hand.

The newlyweds' first lodging in Ponca City was in the front bedroom of a frame Victorian house located at 211 North Fourth street. (Members of my family lived there for over fifty years. In 1987 I gave the property to the First Christian Church.) The Gibsons remember accessorizing their

NATIVE AMERICANS PERFORMING ON GRAND AVENUE AT WHAT WAS PROBABLY AN EARLY DAY CHEROKEE STRIP CELEBRATION. NOTE MCKINNEY AND GIBSON SIGN AT THE SECOND FLOOR WINDOW LEVEL.

living quarters with orange crates collected from the Tom O'Neal Grocery Store. In the late 1920s, Robert and Helen Gibson built their first Ponca City home. Located at 615 East Chestnut, it sat on the back half of a corner lot. The frame bungalow with its comfortable front porch had two bedrooms, living and dining rooms, a breakfast room, and kitchen.

In 1935, the Gibsons purchased a large frame two-story house at 418 North Fourth Street. The old house was sold at a sheriff's sale and was in need of much repair. With the help of a local architect, the house was soon converted into a fine family home. A large wraparound front porch that extended onto an open terrace was added. The terrace connected to a French door opening off the library. This door could be used by Dr. Gibson's patients after office hours.

Upon entering the Gibson home you are in the large living room. To your left is the staircase leading to the second floor. Its delicate balusters and stained railing are open to the living room. Above the Adams style living room mantelpiece hung a Robert Wood California coastline landscape painting. In one corner of the room sat the grand piano, and hanging nearby were photo portraits of sons Bob and Charles, taken by Morton Harvey. In the living and dining rooms were matching handwoven Sarouk rugs. Once, when as teenagers, Charlie and I were spending an evening alone in his home, and we decided to roast marshmallows in the living room fireplace. One of us dropped a sticky marshmallow on the rug and in an attempt to remove it we used a knife to cut some of the rug's pile. (I hope Mrs. Gibson never learned of this drastic measure.)

The Gibson library is paneled in knotty pine with open book shelves on one wall surrounding the outside French door. The furnishings in the room were country English oak. There was a guest bedroom and bath on the first floor, and three bedrooms, including the master bedroom, and bedrooms for each of the sons on the second floor level. Charles recalls how the family would close all of the bedroom doors at night and open the windows during the winter to provide healthy ventilation while sleeping. He remembers the rooms as being cold, cold and he and his brother Bob would hang their clothing on the open stair rail in the upstairs hall so they would be warm upon dressing the next morning. When I asked Charles to recall his memories of growing up in the family home, they seemed to be of a catastrophic nature. The first was when he pushed his brother through a large plate glass window. Another was when he was burning off the dry grass on the front lawn, he set the family's prize pine tree on fire. It burned to the ground.

Both of Dr. R. B. Gibson's sons followed in their father's footsteps. Dr. Bob would practice medicine in Ponca City while Dr. Charles would open his practice in Chickasha, Oklahoma. The Gibsons' granddaughter, Toni Gibson, lived in the family home for many years. —JBW

Handley-Mertz Houses

The Handley brothers, Charles and Fred, opened the Handley Brothers Meat Market shortly after statehood. The original location was 121 East Grand Avenue. In the late 1920s, the business was moved to 307 East Grand. The Handley brothers' father, Francis M. Handley, once served as mayor of Wichita, Kansas.

Charles Handley and his wife, Clara, had three daughters, Hattie, Beth, and Charlene. In 1908, Charles came to Ponca City where he worked as a cattle buyer for Swift and Company, shipping stock from Ponca to Chicago, Kansas City, and Ft. Worth, Texas. Seeing the abundant supply of quality beef available on the hoof, Charles and his brother opened their family meat market. In the late 1920s, Charles bought out his brother and changed the name to Handley Meat Market. The market continued in operation until the early 1940s.

500 N. FOURTH STREET

52 ~ HISTORIC HOMES OF PONCA CITY AND KAY COUNTY

1201 E. CENTRAL

LEFT, THE MERTZ HOUSE AT 1201 EAST CENTRAL; FACING PAGE: THE HANDLEY HOUSE AT 500 NORTH FOURTH STREET.

The Charles Handley home is located at 500 North Fourth Street. Sitting on the northwest corner of the intersection, it has a "prairie box" exterior and floor plan that are similar to those of many of the larger houses of its era. Its long front porch opens into the living room which spans across the front of the house. Behind the living room is the formal dining room with a side porch opening onto East Chestnut Avenue. The second floor has three bedrooms.

On Wednesday, January 15, 1919, Hattie Handley, the eldest daughter of Charles and Clara Handley, married Howard A. (Jack) Mertz, a mechanic for the Marland Oil Company. The couple would become the parents of three sons (Charles, who was killed in combat during World War II, Forrest, and Don) and three daughters (Elaine, Martha, and a daughter who died in infancy).

Starting as a mechanic at the age of sixteen for Marland Oil, Jack Mertz came by his mechanical skills naturally, for his father, Roy Mertz, operated a machine shop in Ponca for many years. Jack Mertz would become superintendent of transportation and then construction superintendent for Continental Oil Company. Later he became mechanical superintendent of the Conoco Refinery.

In 1947, Jack and Hattie Mertz built their "dream house" at 1201 East Central Avenue. Its exterior of native limestone cut in the random Ashlar pattern is capped with a hip roof not unlike those of many of the "ranch style" designs of post World War II. A unique feature of the Mertz home is its construction. Built like a commercial building, it has steel floor joists and three-inch-thick concrete floor slab that cover the full basement area. In the basement are a forty-foot-long club room, a bedroom and bath, plus a large utility room. Oftentimes during the tornado season, there would be forty to fifty of the Mertzes' neighbors and friends seeking shelter in the family basement.

Jack Mertz was a close associate of Conoco's president, Dan Moran, and the two could often be seen sitting on a curb in the refinery area drawing up a plan or idea on a yellow legal pad.

In 1948, Don and Forrest Mertz purchased their grandfather's machine shop on South Second Street in Ponca. Upon handing over the business to his grandsons, Roy Mertz reminded them of his business policy, established years ago: "Whatever you make, make it right." On November 1, 1967, articles of incorporation changed the firm's name to Mertz Incorporated. Through the years, this company has successfully negotiated numerous business contracts with leaders of business and government throughout the world.

Through the years, the company continued to operate under the same philosophy as did Roy Mertz in his little machine shop in 1927. "Whatever you make, make it right." —JBW

HANDLEY'S MEAT MARKET
307 E. Grand   Phone 470
Real Quality — Quick Service

SPECIALS FOR SATURDAY
7-lb. Pail Lard or Compound $1.00
7-lb. choice Veal Shoulder steak $1.00
Veal Chops, lb. 20c
Veal Loin and T-Bone, lb. 25c
Boiling Beef, lb. 12½c
Pot Roast of Beef or Veal, lb.
  12½c and 15c
Choice Pork Roasts, lb. 14c
Nice Lean Pork Steak, lb. 17½c
Fresh, Pure Pork Sausage, lb. ...20c
Fresh Pork Liver, lb. 10c
Fresh Pork Hearts, lb. 15c
Fresh Spare Ribs, lb. 16c
Back Bones, 3-lbs. for 25c
Fresh Side Pork, lb. 25c
1st Grade Sliced Bacon, lb. 35c
Wilson's Certified 1-lb. box bacon 35c
Heavy Airship Bacon, whole
  or half, per lb. 20c
Dry Salt Pork, lb. 17½c
Choice K C Corn Fed Baby Beef
  Roast, any cut, per lb. 25c

EXTRA SPECIAL!
FOR SATURDAY ONLY!
We have 500 pounds those good old fashioned picnic hams, lb. 17c
(While they Last)

Fresh Fish, Shrimp and Fresh Oysters
We have some very choice K C Corn Fed Baby Beef Loins. Try a nice thick Loin to broil.

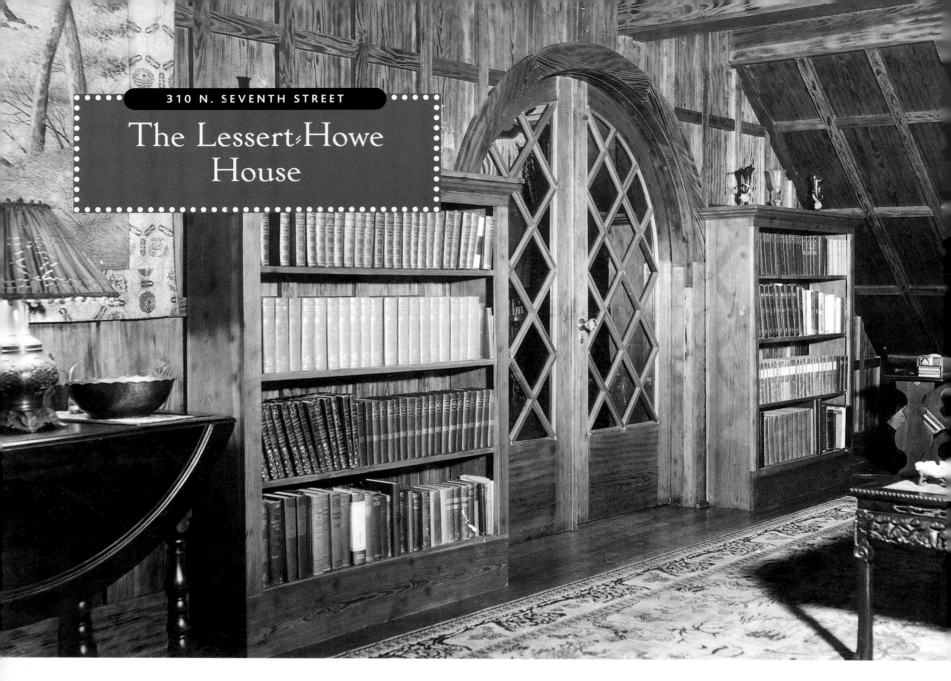

310 N. SEVENTH STREET
The Lessert-Howe House

In 1799, a Frenchman named Michel Roy was adopted into the Kansa Indian tribe and allowed to marry one of the tribe's young women. Later, more Frenchmen would be adopted by the Kansa tribe. Four of these French traders, named Pappan, Lessert, Prue, and Revelett, would marry the four daughters of Michel Roy. Eventually the Lessert, Prue, and Revelett families would integrate into the Osage tribe, while the Pappans remained with the Kansa tribe.

Clement (called Clemore by the Indians) Lessert married Michel Roy's daughter, Julia Roy. Clement was a French trader who knew seven languages and operated the first trading store in Kansas City (Westport). He was hired as a government scout when the

Santa Fe Trail was being surveyed from Westport to Santa Fe, New Mexico. For these services, he received eighty acres of land where the Union Train Station in Kansas City now stands. From this grant of land, Clement gave fourteen acres to the Catholic Diosese for a church and a cemetery which are still standing. Clement and Julia had nine children, seven girls and two boys. The sons were Frank and Louis Benjamin. Frank married Susan Pappan and Louis married Margaret Kavanaugh, an Irish immigrant.

Margaret Kavanaugh Lessert would divorce her husband, Louis, and build her Ponca City home in 1917. Located at 310 North Seventh Street, it was a one-story Mediterranean-style bungalow. A porch penetrated by graceful arched openings wrapped around the south and east sides of the house. Its exterior had a tan stucco and gravel finish with dark brown trim. On November 11, 1918, Margaret Lessert planted an American elm tree in the middle of her back yard to commemorate the signing of the Armistice Agreement ending World War I. For many years this tree would form a large umbrella canopy over the entire rear yard.

In 1927, Margaret Lessert gave the home to her son, William (Will) Kavanaugh Lessert, who did a major remodel on the home. This included the addition of a second floor in the middle of the house. The east porch was enclosed into a sunrooom-library. The arches in these spaces were enclosed with wood and glass casement windows in a diamond shaped pattern. The overall result was terrific. The completed project included the sunroom-library, living room, formal dining room, guest bedroom, kitchen, and breakfast room at the first floor, and three bedrooms at the second floor level. A staircase in the library led to a balcony and then upward to the second floor. The foyer-library was paneled in hard oak shipped from Florida and the cedar paneling in the living and dining rooms was from the state of Washington. A large double car garage flanked with a servant's quarters and a laundry room on each side was also added. Above this space was a large club room which housed Will's three grand pianos, for he was an accomplished musician.

Will Lessert was also an artist and decorated several areas in the house with his artwork. This included the breakfast room mural depicting Spanish ships afloat on a

FACING PAGE: BOOKCASES AND FRENCH DOORS IN THE LIBRARY-SUNROOM; RIGHT: THE LIBRARY-SUNROOM.

HISTORIC HOMES OF PONCA CITY AND KAY COUNTY ~ 55

LEFT: THE DINING ROOM, SET WITH A TEA SERVICE THAT BELONGED TO E. W. MARLAND. BELOW: A BALCONY LOOKING DOWN INTO THE LIBRARY-SUNROOM.

green blue ocean with floating clouds in the sky, cartoon characters in the upstairs nursery, and a lady dressed in blue in the downstairs bath. The door to the club room above the garage also had a mural painted by Will, an Indian prayer with the River of Life running through it. Included in the design was a symbolic large green snake. The original living room chandelier was an electrified wagon wheel taken from a wagon that had made the 1893 Cherokee Strip Run.

When the Lessert house was first built, the corner lot to the south was vacant and for sale. The Lesserts' original intent was to someday purchase this lot, making it their front lawn, so the front of the house would face south. But they put off the purchase of the property until someone else bought the lot and built a house on it. So today the Lessert house faces east overlooking North Seventh Street.

56 ~ HISTORIC HOMES OF PONCA CITY AND KAY COUNTY

EXTERIOR OF THE LESSERT-HOWE HOUSE.

THE HOWE YEARS

Dr. Julius Holland Howe was born in Spencerville, Ohio, in 1886. He attended medical school in Louisville, Kentucky, and specialized in the field of urology. After a five-year engagement, he and his fiance, Rose Taylor Knasel, were married on May 11, 1917. The Howes moved to Ponca City in 1930, when Dr. Howe became associated with the Neiman-Northcutt Clinic. In 1937, Holland and Rose purchased the Lessert house, which would be their family home for the next forty-seven years.

Through the years, the Howes furnished their home with fine family and European antiques, including several pieces they were able to purchase from the Marland Estate. Among the Marland items were a large silver tea service with a matching silver water pitcher, the daybed that E. W. slept on, and his billiard table made in 1903 in Buffalo, New York. Another item from the Marland collection was a cast stone Japanese "snow lantern" designed by Marland's Japanese gardener. This piece has been returned to the Marland estate by the Howes' only daughter, Dr. Shelley Howe Rutherford. Dr. Rutherford was a professor at Oklahoma State University until her retirement. Her only daughter, Shelley Rutherford Zuhdi, carries on the family tradition as a teacher of Latin and history at the high school level in Shawnee, Oklahoma.

In growing up next door to the Lessert-Howe house, I became very familiar with this lovely home. Since my lifetime desire was to become an architect, I often wondered why the second floor window trim on our neighbor's house was different from the first floor window trim. I discovered the answer over sixty years later while researching this article. The reason was that the Lessert-Howe house had its beginnings as a single story structure and when the second floor was added ten years later, they changed the design of the second floor window trim.
—JBW

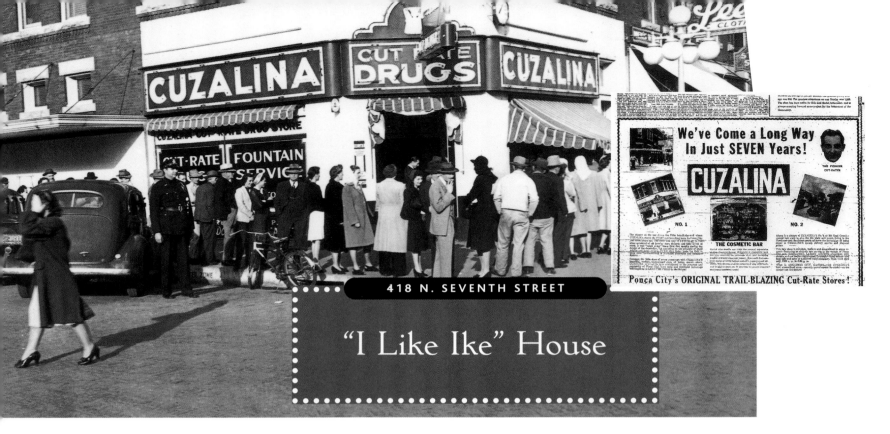

"I Like Ike" House
418 N. SEVENTH STREET

At the age of sixteen, T. J. Cuzalina opened his own drug store in Hartshorne, Oklahoma. In 1921, he relocated to Ponca City and established the Cuzalina Drug Store at the corner of East Grand Avenue and North Second Street. T. J. soon became one of Ponca's best supporters, and in the 1940s he began writing a newspaper column titled "Just Poppin Off." The column was not only featured in the *Ponca City News* but also in the *New York Times* and the *Denver Post*. I remember the time when T. J. thought that we should stop calling our town Ponca City, and begin calling it Ponca. His reason was that everyone now knew that Ponca was a fine city so it was not necessary to add the word "city" to its name. This promotion lasted several weeks in his column but finally "died on the vine."

This popular column evolved into a campaign for General Dwight D. Eisenhower to become President of the United States, many years before he was nominated by the Republican Party in 1952. T. J. sent out over 121,000 letters to druggists nationwide urging their support for Eisenhower. He also had thousands of campaign buttons made, reading first "Draft Ike" and then "I Like Ike," which became the National Republican Party's slogan. When Dwight D. Eisenhower was elected President, Cuzalina sent him a wire. It read: "Hot Ziggity Dog and Congratulations— T. J."

In the early 1940s, T. J. Cuzalina sponsored a Fourth of July public fireworks display. The first one was held behind his home on a vacant lot. Soon the crowds attending these annual fireworks displays forced the performance to move to Blaine Stadium.

The Cuzalina home is located at 418 North Seventh Street. The modified Mediterranean style of architecture features both flat and pitched roofs while the arched front door helps to accentuate the style of the house. The detached garage at the rear was later attached to the house by a connecting wing.

T. J. and his wife, Geneva Lavina Whiting Cuzalina, were both natives of Harthshorne, Oklahoma. The couple had two daughters, Karoline Cuzalina Hron and Marian Cuzalina Gibson. Toni Gibson, daughter of Bob and Marian Gibson, recalls a story her mother told about how the two sisters would sit in the family porch swing chanting to the rhythm of the swaying swing:
GE-NE-VA
LA-VI-NA
CUZ-A-LIN-A

One of my sisters, Jackie Walton Rigg, and Marian Cuzalina were good friends. Living only a block apart, they would often attend Sunday school and church together. Afterwards they would go to the drug store where Marian would create exotic refreshments behind the soda fountain. After having indulged, they would go to the cosmetic counter and try on the latest shades of fingernail polish and lipstick. (I am sure the store manager dreaded their Sunday morning visits.)

My childhood memories of the Cuzalina Drug Store were of the large sign T. J. had painted on the west side of his building—a large hatchet with the slogan "Let's Bury Hatchet Kerr." I still do not understand its meaning, but it was probably conceived when Kerr was running for either senator or governor. I also recall the weekend a large bus parallel parked on North Second Street by the drug store. When its large window coverings were removed and a folding platform arose on three sides of the vehicle, the public could walk around the platform and view a miniature animated circus. This unique creation was sponsored by the LIFE-SAVER company. I visited the exhibit many times and purchased an ice cream cone at the Cuzalina Drug on each visit.

While in junior high school, I attended a high school homecoming football game. When the football queen was crowned, she and her attendants were driven around the football field in Karoline and Marian Cuzalina's four-door Packard convertible. This cream-colored automobile with its red leather interior was the envy of everyone in the stadium.

In the 1998 book *Ponca City Mayors*, T. J. Cuzalina is recognized as twice a mayoral candidate, but never a winner of public office. However, he deserves recognition for his contributions to Ponca City and for his efforts in promoting Dwight D. Eisenhower as President of the United States. T. J. also conceived the idea of the Cherokee Strip Golf Classic as a benefit for the Kay County Council for Retarded Children. Many top stars of the entertainment world and business and professional leaders from all over the country came to Ponca City at his invitation to help make the tournament the success it was—and still is.

In 1952, T. J. Cuzalina finally met Dwight D. Eisenhower. The meeting took place at a golf tournament in Denver, Colorado. T. J.'s comment was, "You just have to look at General Eisenhower to see he is a good man and a natural leader. For he is as plain as an old shoe."

Today, T. J. Cuzalina's grandson, Bobby Gibson, has adopted his grandfather's tradition of writing interesting and provocative items in a regular column in the *Ponca City News*. —JBW

Every so often, someone says something to you or reminisces about something that means a lot to you. That particular thing happened to me just yesterday. I was talking to Ole Steve Struble, and he began to tell me a story about when he was a little boy. His parents had taken him into my Granddad T. J. Cuzalina's Drug Store, and my Granddad gave him a toy jet just for being a good well-behaved boy in his store. Sometimes I truly think things happen for a reason. I had been preoccupied all day, and that story really lifted me up, and made me feel good. Thanks Steve, you don't know how much that made my day.
And now that we are "Marching" into Spring,
Give me a call and make my telephone ring.
One and two bedrooms, we have one for you,
Because living at the Paladin is the thing to do!

Call Bobby Gibson

Paladin APARTMENTS
301 W. HARTFORD, PONCA CITY
762-7164

AN ITEM IN THE *PONCA CITY NEWS* BY T.J. CUZALINA'S GRANDSON, BOBBY GIBSON.

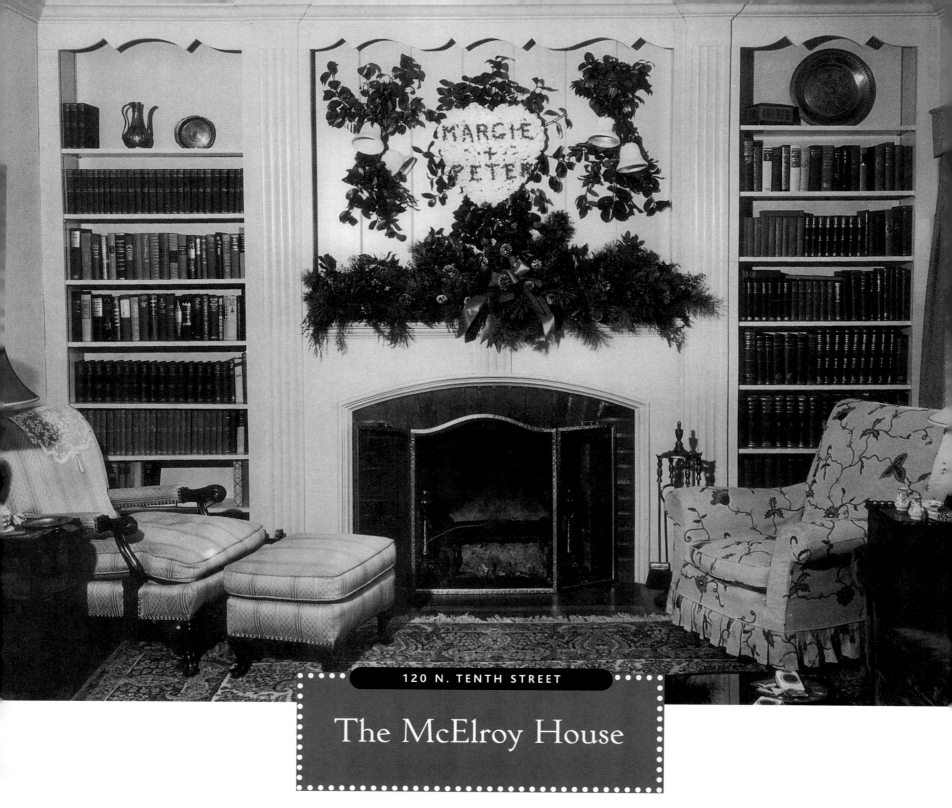

120 N. TENTH STREET

The McElroy House

In 1919, Dr. Tom McElroy had made the decision to go to California to establish his medical practice with a fellow graduate. He stopped off in Tulsa, Oklahoma, to visit an uncle, Dr. Frank Reisling, and Tom liked Tulsa so well that he decided to remain there instead of traveling on to California. In 1921, E. W. Marland was staying at the Mayo Hotel in Tulsa and became ill. Tom was the hotel doctor on call and attended to Marland's illness. A friendship soon developed, and in 1921 Dr. Tom McElroy moved to Ponca City to open his medical practice. When E. W. Marland opened a medical center at the Marland Oil Company, Dr. McElroy was appointed its director, a position he held until Marland Oil became Continental.

A native of Mingo Junction, Ohio, Dr. McElroy served in the Army Medical Corps during World War I. On December 24, 1923, Thomas McElroy married Marjorie Cryselda Taylor in Kansas City, Missouri. A spring wedding had been planned but Tom had found a house in Ponca that could be purchased at a very good price. Marjorie was given the choice of either a Caribbean cruise or the Ponca City home as a wedding present—the cruise became history.

FACING PAGE: ANNOUNCING DAUGHTER MARJORIE MCELROY MOOTE'S ENGAGEMENT, DECEMBER, 1947. TOP: THE ORIGINAL "AIRPLANE BUNGALOW" FACADE, APRIL 13, 1939. BOTTOM: THE HOUSE IN 1941 AFTER REMODELING BY ARCHITECT WILLIAM M. CATON.

HISTORIC HOMES OF PONCA CITY AND KAY COUNTY ~ 61

Located at 120 North Tenth Street, the "airplane bungalow" was owned by F. P. Rickard. He must have been having some difficulties, for McElroy purchased the house including all of the furnishings, even the bathroom "bath mat." The first floor of the McElroy home contained the living room with its archway opening into the dining room, the kitchen with an enclosed back porch, and two bedrooms and a bath. The second floor had one large bedroom with an adjoining nursery.

After an attempted robbery, Dr. McElroy kept his loaded World War I .45-caliber service revolver under the bed mattress. Shortly after the burglary attempt, Tom was awakened in the middle of the night by a disturbance downstairs. As he approached the sounds in the darkened house, he fired two shots at the would-be intruder. He soon discovered he had put one hole in his camel hair top coat hanging on the family hall tree and the other in the nearby closet door. The late night disturbance had been caused by wind rattling the closet door and flapping the coat on the hall tree.

In 1940, the McElroys decided to remodel their family home. William N. Caton of Winfield, Kansas, was the architect for the project, which was completed in 1941. The porte cochere at the south of the house and the front porch were enclosed, while the original bungalow design gave way to a southwestern or ranch style.

For many years the original front porch of the McElroy home was their outdoor living room. On Saturdays and Sundays during spring, summer, and fall, they spent much time on the porch watching the golfers on the Marland Golf Course across the street from their home. In the winter when there was snow, Tom McElroy would hook up the sleds behind his Ford and take his daughter and her friends for a sleigh ride across the fairways on the nearby course.

The McElroys' daughter, Marjorie McElroy Moote, recalls that "We were on the front porch in August of 1935, when we heard the news of the plane crash in Alaska killing Will Rogers. He was a favorite of my father's for Dad had met and seen him when the Miller Brother's 101 Ranch was in operation."

Marjorie Cryselda McElroy died peacefully and with a quiet dignity on March 4, 2002, at the age of 103. —JBW

MRS. MCELROY AND FIVE-YEAR-OLD MARJORIE IN THE SIDE YARD, 1931.

200 N. TENTH STREET
Pickrel-Casey House

The house at 200 North Tenth Street was built in 1918 for John Alcorn and designed by Elmer Boillot, a well-known Kansas City architect. With its deep overhanging eaves and stucco exterior, the design of the house is in the Prairie Style, a style that was first created by architect Frank Lloyd Wright at the turn of the century.

In 1928, a three-way "house switch" occurred. John Alcorn purchased the home of William Lackey at 8 Hillcrest and sold his home to Fred Pickrel, who was moving to Ponca from Oklahoma City to manage the Poncan Theatre. In the third part of this "house move triangle," Lackey planned to relocate to Oklahoma City and so purchased Fred Pickrel's Oklahoma City home.

The Pickrel household included Fred and his wife, Ferne, their daughter, Barbara, and Ferne's mother, Fannie Blanton Street. The house has a sunroom off the formal living room that opens onto a front terrace and a covered front porch. Pairs of French pocket doors separate the sunroom and the dining room from the living room. Adjoining the kitchen area was the maid's room and a back staircase leading to the second floor of the house. Today this space has been incorporated as part of the kitchen. The second floor of the house had three bedrooms and a

overnight guests in the Pickrel home. Fred brought musicals, plays, and famous entertainers to the Poncan. The list included The John Phillip Sousa Band, Sigmund Romberg, and Sally Rand, who appeared on the stage with only her fans and a large transparent bubble balloon. There were many house parties given by the Pickrels for these famous personalities with Grandmother Street doing her part by making "bathtub gin" for each occasion.

The original view from the front porch of the home was the Marland Golf Course. Built in the 1920s by E. W. Marland, the course extended from Grand Avenue north to East Highland Avenue and from North Tenth Street to North Fourteenth Street. When Bayard Stewart would come to visit her grandparents in Ponca, she always felt as if it were Easter. Bayard would spend hours gathering stray golf balls hidden among the shrubs and grasses in her grandparents' front lawn. In fact, she recalls, finding golf balls was more fun than searching for Easter eggs.

THE STEWART-CASEY YEARS

In 1948, Clyde Stewart, his wife, Barbara Pickrel Stewart, and daughter, Bayard, returned to Ponca when he was transferred by Conoco. They first lived in the garage apartment on the Dillard Clark estate located at 10 Hillcrest. After that structure caught fire, they relocated to Barbara's family home on North Tenth Street for a period of time. Bayard remembers her grandparents' home was always kept dark during the hot summer afternoons. She recalls the formal dining room as the coolest room in the house and that when she and her friends came in from swimming they always "plopped down" in this room.

In 1960, Bayard Stewart married Charles Casey and, like Bayard's parents, the new couple too lived in the Dillard Clarks' garage apartment for their first two years of married life. In 1971, Ferne Pickrel died and left the family home to her granddaughter, Bayard. Bayard and her husband, Charles, became the third generation to live in the home. Bayard recalls the many happy hours she spent in the house as a child. Her grandparents' close friends included the Dillard Clarks, the Louis Barneses, the Cad Arrendells, and members of the Donahoe family. Bayard knew them all as "Aunt and Uncle," in the family tradition.

Today Grandmother Ferne's original living room furniture still resides in one of Ponca City's most historic houses. —KA

small sitting room. One was the master bedroom, another was Grandmother Street's bedroom, the third served as the guest bedroom, and the sitting room became Barbara's bedroom. There is an original servants' quarters in the backyard (Ferne Pickrel told her husband she was not moving to Ponca unless she had a full-time, live-in housekeeper). The attached garage on the north side of the house has doors on both the east and west to allow one to drive into the garage from North Tenth Street and exit onto East Cleveland Avenue.

The Pickrel years covered the "heyday" of live theater entertainment at the Poncan Theatre, and many performers were

GATEWAY HISTORIC DISTRICT

In 2001, North Sixth Street was designated a historic district from East Cleveland Avenue to the limestone gateway leading into Pioneer Park. The large family homes along North Sixth Street echo the good times during which they were built, and its tree-lined brick paving helps to remind one that these homes, with their gracious front porches, have been here for nearly a century. And through the years they have patiently watched and hosted much of Ponca City's early history.

Residences of historic North Sixth Street have included mayors, builders and bankers and even a lumberyard owner. The inventor of a revolutionary ice chest and an oil baron or two have all owned property on North Sixth Street.

Now let us travel down historic North Sixth Street where we will visit the home of Ponca City's first mayor's son, the home of the builder of Marland's Grand Avenue house and the home of Ponca's first doctor to own a microscope. —JBW

202 N. SIXTH STREET
The W.A.T. Robertson House

Dr. W. A. T. Robertson moved to Ponca City in 1898, five years after the Land Run of 1893. A native of Quebec, Canada, Dr. Robertson received his medical training in Montreal. Before relocating to Ponca he settled in Junction City, Kansas, where he practiced his profession of medicine for two years. After arriving in Ponca, he would eventually marry Miss Lillian Bemis, and from this union the couple had two daughters.

In 1908, Dr. Robertson became a United States citizen, which came as a surprise to his many friends who had always assumed the doctor was already an American citizen. His fellow physician, Dr. George Niemann, once said, "Dr. Robertson was the first modern doctor to arrive in Ponca with a microscope."

In 1906, the Robertsons purchased land on which to build a home at 202 North Sixth Street and the following year they started construction. After the completion of the house, the tax assessment on the property was $2,700. At that time the average home in Ponca was assessed at $750 or less.

The Robertson home was one of the few "high-style" homes that was built in early-day Ponca. The exterior foundation walls and porch railings are of rough-hewn limestone quarried from a nearby quarry. Its gambrel roof is Dutch Colonial in style and permits more floor space at the second floor level. The detailing on the exterior of the house is very eclectic with fluted Ionic columns at the front porch and the arch-topped entry with its smaller Ionic columns on each side. There are bull's eye and leaded glass windows, Palladian windows and even a carved shell above an upper-story window. The fan light and sidelights at the front door are original with their leaded glass panels. Upon entering the house, you are in a small vestibule designed to keep the cold outside air from entering the other rooms in the house.

Once inside the main hall foyer, the full impact of the home's classical style is visible. The sweeping staircase rises to the second floor, and oak Ionic columns separate the entry hall from the front parlor. Fortunately the original stained woodwork has never been painted. The front parlor has beautiful sets of leaded glass windows at the upper sashes. The front and back parlors are separated by heavy oak pocket doors. The back parlor features a massive oak mantle and boxed oak beams at the ceiling. Opposite the fireplace wall is a deep bay window with a trio of leaded glass panels similar to those in the front parlor

The highlight of the formal dining room is the built-in china cabinet with leaded glass doors matching the pattern of the leaded glass windows. There are three bedrooms on the second floor with one of the bedrooms opening onto a small porch above the entry.

Dr. Robertson was always very active in the community and following his retirement from the practice of medicine he enjoyed walking in the downtown business district, visiting and joking with his many friends and former patients. He served on the early day Ponca City Board of Trade, which later became the Chamber of Commerce, and was an active horseman. He owned several mares with his brother, Major John Robertson, who also relocated to Ponca from Canada.

Dr. Robertson enjoyed recalling his first days as a young bachelor in Ponca. He and George L. Miller of the 101 Ranch were good friends and attended many social affairs together. Robertson claimed that Miller always kept his derby hat hanging in Robertson's office so when he came to town Miller could hang up his cowboy hat and replace it with his derby. Then Miller and the good doctor would go socializing. —KA

210 N. SIXTH STREET

O. F. Keck House

Oscar F. Keck left his wife in Colorado and came to Oklahoma for the Land Run in 1893. He boarded a train in Arkansas City, Kansas, and jumped off at the present site of Ponca City while the train was traveling twenty-five miles per hour. He soon staked out his claim and since there was no else around, Keck held the title of "Ponca's first citizen." When the Ponca Townsite Company held the drawing for city lots, Oscar Keck drew the lot at 210 North Sixth Street. There he built a small two-room structure, the first house built in Ponca. Later it would become the first house to have gas and electricity, and still later one of the first to have a telephone. Much later Keck built his large two-story house around the first one with the original two-room core becoming the living room.

Oscar Keck opened a carpenter shop in a tent and was soon hired by the Townsite Company to build a school building. The first years in Ponca City were very wild and dangerous for cowboys would get drunk and start shooting up the town. They would ride by Keck's shop, forcing the workmen to hide under work tables to protect themselves from flying bullets. Keck became Ponca's largest building contractor, building Marland's Grand Avenue home, the auditorium section of the Civic Center and the original *Ponca City News* building located at the northwest corner of North Third Street and East Cleveland. Keck also built the Soldani mansion at East Central and South Ninth Street, which today houses the Ponca City Art Center.

The Keck home is a square, box-like two-story structure with a sunroom and second floor sleeping porch wing on the south side of the house. The first floor consists of the formal living room across the front of the house, the formal dining room and kitchen area including a butler's pantry, breakfast room and kitchen. The second floor houses three bedrooms and the upstairs sleeping porch. Across the front of the house is a long front porch with a very slight sloping roof. Oscar and his wife, Dorothy Belle, were charter members of the First Christian Church, and they had one daughter, who became Mrs. Marvin Hatcher.

Oscar Keck was well known in Ponca for his outside Christmas decorations. In the days when most homes only exhibited a single electric red candle light bulb hanging in a chenille wreath purchased at the local F. W. Woolworth Store, the Keck's house and yard were ablaze with Christmas lights. Atop the fireplace chimney was a spotlit Santa Claus climbing down the chimney with his bag of toys. A very tall pine tree located at the north side yard was covered with blue lights plus other blue lights were scattered on various shrubbery.

In 1935, the Kecks' outdoor Christmas decorations received a new addition. Atop the front porch roof were five names spelled out in blue neon lighting. They were: CECILE, ANNETTE, EMILIE, MARIE, and YVONNE. These were the names of the famous Dionne quintuplets who were born in Ontario, Canada, on May 28, 1934.
—JBW

O. F. KECK
RESIDENCE
210 NORTH 6TH

HISTORIC HOMES OF PONCA CITY AND KAY COUNTY ~ 69

The original house was built in 1898 as a two-room frame structure for Frank and Cora Lessert. The second owners of the property were Ben and Maggie Lessert, who sold the home to H. P. Gott and his wife, Margaret, in 1906 for $2,000. Mr. Gott was an early-day businessman who ran a very successful hardware and tin shop in downtown Ponca City. In 1917, the Gotts relocated to Winfield, Kansas, where Mr. Gott founded the Gott Manufacturing Company, which made portable insulated water coolers. It was later purchased by Rubbermaid Corporation and is still in operation in Winfield.

In 1924, Mrs. Anna Post purchased the Gott house, borrowed $7,500, and did a complete remodel, including the addition of a second floor. With the help of her stepdaughter, Ethel, Anna Post opened the newly remodeled home as the Sixth Street Rooming House.

The remodeled house was designed by George J. Cannon in a modified English style, with lap siding and stucco-and-half-timber-gables. It sits on a corner lot. The detached double-car garage with an apartment above was added in 1925. The arched front door with its small roof cover enters into a "not-so-large" foyer with a staircase leading to the upper floor. On the right are French doors leading into the living room. The mantelpiece in the living room has tan and gray ceramic tile in the style known as Arts and Crafts. Behind the living room is the dining room with another pair of French doors separating the two spaces. A bay window on the north wall of the dining room has a high window unit with a diamond-shaped glass pattern. Its placement was intended to allow a buffet or sideboard to be put beneath it.

Off the dining room was Mrs. Post's suite of rooms, including a bedroom, bath, and sitting room. With its own outside entrance, this self-contained unit even had its own doorbell. Upstairs in the North Sixth Street Boarding House are three large bedrooms and a master bedroom suite consisting of a bedroom and sitting room. The mantelpiece in the master suite is similar to that of the living room fireplace. All the bedrooms have large closets, and the single second floor bathroom is ample enough to include a large linen closet as well.

Mrs. Post's roomers were all single women. Many worked at Continental Oil or were teachers in the Ponca City Public School system. In 1946, Marie O'Neil purchased the property and continued to operate it as a rooming house. Several of her roomers remember Mrs. O'Neil as very kind, but a very strict landlady. Male visitors were only allowed in the living room, which she called the parlor. A visitor at a recent historic house tour related to today's owners that she met her future husband while living there. He was the brother of another roomer, who introduced him when he was visiting. After their initial introduction, her husband-to-be kept coming back again and again, ostensibly to visit his sister. —KA

304 N. SIXTH STREET
"God Bless America" House

In 1924, Frances Smith Catron wrote in her thesis, "I have reached my majority with a right to vote, and I vote Ponca City the best town on the map." She was born in Linnaeous, Missouri, in 1877. In 1903 she married an attorney, Edward M Catron, in Kansas City. The couple moved the same year to Ponca City, where Edward became supervisor of music for the Ponca City schools. Frances was an accomplished pianist who immediately began bringing music and culture to the city.

Frances Smith Catron began her music career with the Ponca City schools in 1910. She taught music, and later, after Edward's death, became supervisor of music for the elementary and junior high schools. Upon her retirement in 1947 (my 1947 graduating class presented her with a silver tea service), she soon came into demand as a speaker describing her many trips to Africa, Europe, Egypt, Scandinavia, and the South Sea Islands as well as travels in the U.S.

My Roosevelt Grade School music class looked forward to Mrs. Catron's visits, during which she would often sing for us. Her voice reminded me of the sound of a beautiful clear bell. In later years Frances shared her home with her sister and brother-in-law, Mr. and Mrs. Carl Metcalf. I was their paper boy while in junior high school, and I always enjoyed seeing Mrs. Catron sitting on the front porch awaiting my arrival (I was usually late).

In 1969, the Ponca City Music Club, the Twentieth Century Music Club, and the Ponca City chapter of the Daughters of the American Revolution sponsored a tribute to Mrs. Catron in the Marland Grand Avenue home. On that occasion a spokesman, on behalf of others who had known her, celebrated Frances Smith Catron as "one whose entire life was dedicated to service above self, to giving more than receiving, and a life of great productivity and achievement."

As director of music for Ponca's schools,

Mrs. Catron was the founder of the annual spring music festival, whose first concert was performed at Garfield School. Later these concerts were held in Blaine Stadium. The schools' music classes would rehearse separately, then gather at the stadium to perform as a group. At the 1940 festival, the closing song was a recently written patriotic number by Irving Berlin. Today the chorus of "God Bless America" has almost become our national anthem. But in 1940, we sang the verse before singing the chorus:

While the storm clouds gather
Far across the sea,
Let us pledge our allegiance
To a land that's free.
Let us all be grateful
To a land so fair
As we raise our voices
in a solemn prayer.

God Bless America . . .

Mrs. Catron was truly the first lady of music in Ponca City. —JBW

MRS. FRANCES SMITH CATRON.

HISTORIC HOMES OF PONCA CITY AND KAY COUNTY ~ 73

310 N. SIXTH STREET
The R.P. Baughman House

When R. P. Baughman ran for the office of mayor of Ponca City in 1905, the *Ponca City Democrat* wrote: "Mr. Baughman is young, ambitious, energetic and public spirited. He is interested in the future growth and development of our city. He is competent in every way to fill the position to which he has been nominated. He is progressive, broad-minded and businesslike and will be a mayor that every citizen will feel proud of regardless of politics."

Apparently many others felt the same. During Baughman's term as mayor, natural gas was discovered in the Ponca city area by Charles G. Ruby. Gas mains were laid from the wells located northeast of the city, although initial acceptance of natural gas for domestic and commercial use was slowed by popular fears that the fuel could cause explosions and fires. Another hallmark of the Baughman mayoral years was Colonel Miller's staging of his Wild West Show at the 101 Ranch for the National Editorial Association convention, which drew 65,000 spectators for all of the performances.

At the time Baughman served as mayor, he was manager of the local Long-Bell Lumber yard. In 1908, R.P. and J. J. McGraw had started the American Lumber Company by purchasing the Pond Lumber Company of Chicago. The firm soon grew and in 1921 merged with F. D. Bearly Lumber Company of Oklahoma City and Norman to become the American Lumber Company, with Baughman as C.E.O. After R. P. Baughman's death in 1926, his son, Harper, became president of the company. Assisted by his two brothers, Harry and Karl, he renamed the company the Baughman Lumber Company, with operations in Ponca City, Kaw City, Bartlesville, Fairfax, and Hominy. Growing up in Ponca City, I used to visit the Baughman Lumber Company, with its bright yellow buildings with black trim, to purchase material for my summer projects. Although I might only need a few sticks of lumber and a handful of nails, I was always treated with the same courtesy by one of the Baughman brothers as if I had ordered a truckload of materials.

The R. P. Baughman house is located at 310 North Sixth Street. The massive frame structure with its wrap-around porch sits on an oversized lot, giving it a rather grand feeling. The exterior and interior detailing tells us that the house's design came from a mail order catalog often furnished by lumber yards. The living room extends across the front of the house with the staircase at the north end of the room. Behind the living room on the south end of the first floor is the dining room, with a high wood wainscot topped with a continuous plate rail that held Mrs. Baughman's collection of hand-painted chinaware. Sliding pocket doors separate the living and dining rooms, and a similar set on the north wall of the dining room opens into a small library. The second floor of the R. P. Baughman home has four bedrooms, each positioned on a corner of the house. All of the flooring and trim throughout the house is quarter-sawn white oak, and the detailing is in the Arts and Crafts style. — JBW

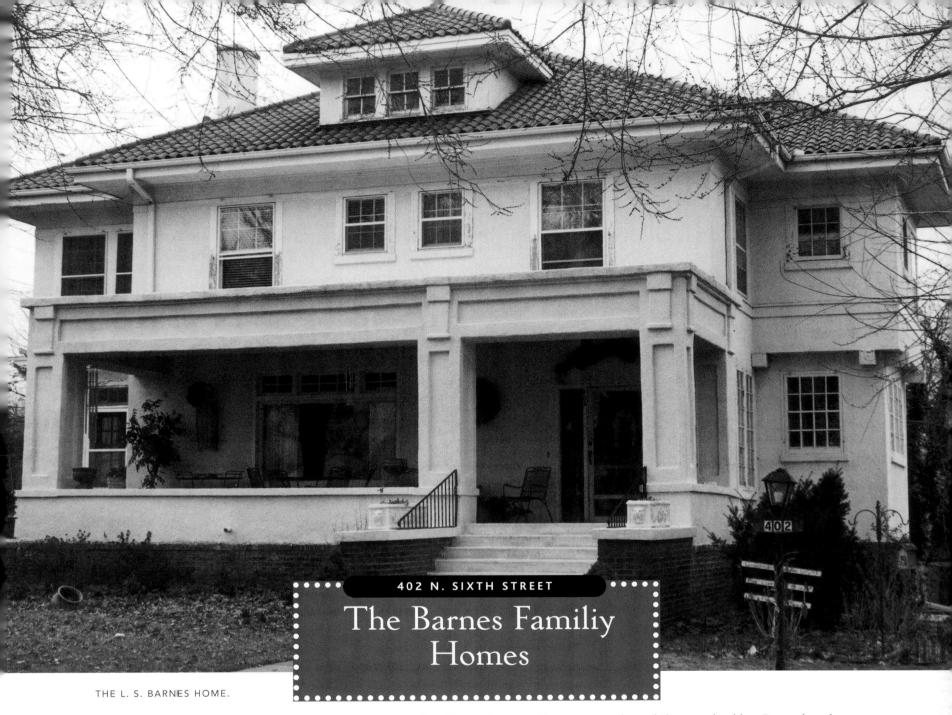

THE L. S. BARNES HOME.

402 N. SIXTH STREET
The Barnes Familiy Homes

When Burton Seymour Barnes made the run into the Cherokee Strip on September 16, 1893, he staked his land claim on what is now the southeast quarter of the city. Fifteen persons claimed the same land but Barnes bought or negotiated the other claims to became the parcel's owner. Through the efforts of B. S. Barnes, the township of Ponca City soon gained supremacy over the neighboring

HISTORIC HOMES OF PONCA CITY AND KAY COUNTY ~ 75

town of Cross. He hired surveyors to lay out the town and stake the four corners of each city lot. He also supervised the drilling of a water well in the business district, the grading of all streets, the building of crosswalks, the erecting of coal oil street lighting, and the employing of a city marshal.

On December 19, 1893, the township of Ponca City was incorporated, and B. S. Barnes became its first mayor. During his administration, the Presbyterian and Methodist churches were built, and the cornerstone for the Santa Fe depot was laid. A limestone school building was also completed on East Grand Avenue between Sixth and Seventh Streets. (For many years this was Ponca City's junior high school until it was replaced with today's East Middle School building.)

The B. S. Barnes family home was built around 1900. Originally located on the site of today's Civic Center on Grand Avenue, it was moved in 1916 when the Civic Center was built. Today this house with its wonderful Victorian architecture stands at 408 North Fifth Street.

THE L. S. BARNES HOUSE

Mayor Barnes's son, Louis, was twelve when he arrived in Ponca City with his family, and as a youth he worked on Saturdays and during summer vacations at the Ponca Cash Store, a grocery and department store located at 307 East Grand Avenue. After high school, Louis began working full time at the store and was able to purchase it from the owner, James Hutchison, in 1905. Six years later he sold the business. He was twenty-eight years old. Next he built a building to house the new Barnes Department Store, which opened its doors in September, 1911. The west side of the store was devoted to groceries and the east side to dry goods, notions, ladies' and men's apparel, and shoes. In 1924, Louis Barnes sold the business and took his family on an eight-month vacation. Through the years he would become a leader in civic and financial affairs including the Ponca City Savings and Loan Association and the Security Bank.

Louis Seymour Barnes and his wife, Mayme, built their home at 402 North Sixth Street. It was built by O. F. Keck and designed by the well-known Oklahoma City architectural firm Layton and Forsythe. The house's stucco exterior is in modified

Craftsman Style, and its massive proportions make it one of the dominant homes in the Historic North Sixth Street District.

The living room, across the front of the house, features a large, large picture window overlooking the long front porch. (As the Barneses' newspaper boy, I often visualized what would happen if I threw the paper into that picture window and broke it.) To the south of the long living room is the sunroom with its own mantelpiece and ceramic tile floor. In the 1940s, this room was furnished with wicker furniture that was moved to the adjoining veranda during the summer months.

The formal dining room is behind the living room, and its furnishings during the Barnes years came from the dining room of E. W. Marland's Grand Avenue home. This room has three sets of pocket doors leading to the sunroom, living room, and library. The cozy breakfast nook has the original built-in table and benches in the Craftsman Style. There are four bedrooms, one on each corner, at the second floor level. The master bedroom suite has a large walk-through closet connecting the master bedroom to the guest bedroom.

Louis and Mayme Barnes's son, Reg Barnes, once recalled, "After being exposed to life outside of Ponca, I one day suggested to Dad that the gas logs in the fireplaces should be removed and the fireplaces be converted to wood burning fireplaces. He smiled, patted me on the head and said, 'Son, if you had spent years chopping wood to heat the house, splitting kindling for the kitchen stove, and hauling ashes outside every day or two, you would love this gas fire as much as I do.'"

In *The Last Run* (published by the Ponca City Chapter of the Daughters of the American Revolution in 1939), Louis Barnes shares his early Ponca City memories in essays titled "The First Train Stop" and "Cross Moves to Ponca City." The day before he died in 1956, Barnes completed another article called "The Founding of Ponca City," which was later published by the Oklahoma State Historical Society.

FACING PAGE: TWO VIEWS OF THE L. S. BARNES HOME. RIGHT: THE G. S. BARNES HOME.

901 E. OVERBROOK

Louis was rather short in stature but a very friendly person. He would always offer a smile and nod when passing you on the street, and, as a young boy, I looked forward to those greetings.

Mayme Barnes was a very dignified lady and described in some circles as being a bit "uppity." On one occasion, she paid a social call on one of her neighbors (a friend of my family) and after being invited in, she took out her handkerchief and dusted off the chair seat before sitting down.

THE B. S. BARNES HOME.

THE G. S. BARNES HOUSE

Another son of B. S. Barnes was Gilbert S. Barnes, who became associated with his brother, Louis, in the grocery and dry goods business. Mr. and Mrs. Gilbert Barnes built their Acre Homes house in 1924. The classical stucco-facade home is located at 901 East Overbrook. Its well-proportioned exterior is enhanced with a small porch above the beautiful French entrance door with its matching side panels. The protruding brackets at the upstairs windows indicate that they once supported long second floor flower boxes. Off the living room is a delightful sun porch surrounded with many windows and below its roof line are a series of similar roof brackets. The home has a typical center hall floor plan with formal living and dining rooms at either side of the foyer. The second floor has three bedrooms.

Louis Barnes built his grocery and dry goods building in 1911. Located on the northeast corner of East Grand Avenue and North Third Street, the two-story structure was described as "Neoclassical in style, although greatly simplified in design." The general contractor was N. H. Welch, who also did the brick masonry on the building. The Barnes building was referred to as the "Daylight Store," for it had been designed to allow as much natural light as possible inside the building. It featured large plate windows on the front, smaller windows along the side, and unusually large second floor windows.

An early-day newspaper advertisement read:

The Barnes Grocery Store conducts the neatest, cleanest and best stocked grocery store in the city. If any housekeeper who reads these lines is puzzled as to what to have for dinner tomorrow, just call phone number 27, for it will always have quality food stuffs that just fits the bill.

The Barnes Grocery makes an effort to carry only the most reliable goods on the market such as Chase & Sanborn coffee, and, by buying directly from the producer, they are able to offer reasonable prices to both large and small buyers.

Two wagons are used for delivering foods and customers are always assured of having orders filled with accuracy and delivered promptly.

In 1924, Gilbert Barnes purchased the Barnes Grocery from his brother, Louis, and in 1933, he sold his grocery store and relocated to Tulsa, Oklahoma. —JWB

COUNTRY CLUB-HILLCREST

In March 1923, it was announced that a new housing addition would be built east of the Marland golf course. It was referred to as the Country Club Addition, although some also called it "Snob Hill"! The addition was to have fifty building tracts averaging an acre in size, with homes that would range in value from $15,000 to $50,000. Not surprisingly, Marland Oil Company executives purchased most of the lots. This area was developed at the same time as the Acre Homes Addition. Both areas were on land owned by E. W. Marland.

The Ponca City News described the Country Club Addition as promising to be "one of the most beautiful in the city. It is just east of the Marland golf links and from there an excellent view of the Osage hills is presented." — JBW

10 E. HILLCREST

Dillard Clark Estate

When completed, the Dillard Clark, Jr. house overlooked its own private polo field. Clark was an independent oilman who made his fortune in the Three Sands oil fields south of Tonkawa, Oklahoma. The house was designed by John Duncan Forsyth, and the landscaping was by Henry Hatashita, E. W. Marland's Japanese gardener. The Clark home is designed in the Colonial Revival style. Some have described it as a replica of George Washington's Mount Vernon, which I question. However, the house is oriented like many southern plantations, including Mount Vernon, with tall covered verandas overlooking a river or waterway (the Clark house overlooks the polo field) and their main entrances at the back of the house, accessible by foot or carriage. The front veranda of the home faces east, and its tall graceful columns extend two floors in height. One can imagine sitting on the veranda with drink in hand watching a polo match with Dillard Clark and young George Marland as two of the players. The exterior of the house is white painted brick and lap siding. The main foyer extends from the

FACING PAGE: WEST ELEVATION AS IT APPEARS TODAY. RIGHT: EAST ELEVATION OF THE ORIGINAL HOUSE. BELOW: THE CARRIAGE HOUSE.

front of the house to the rear motor court. During the Clark years, the formal living and dining rooms were of banquet size, and the game room was where Mr. Clark kept his gun collection. There was a walk-in refrigerator in the basement and, in addition to the large cooking range in the kitchen, a range in the utility room for preparing foods with an offensive odor.

The Clarks had a full-time staff that included a cook, chauffeur, gardener, and several maids. The rear motor court served the garage, with the chauffeur's apartment above it, adjoining a tall stone retaining wall. Penetrating the wall is a small wooden door leading to the wine cellar. This combination of architectural elements reminds one of an estate on the eastern Atlantic seaboard.

The second floor had six bedrooms and six baths. In 1949, the home was struck by lightning and was severely damaged. Two weeks later the house was once again struck by lightning (see, lightning does strike twice in the same place), and the second floor was completely destroyed. When they rebuilt, the Clarks deleted the second floor area.

In 1955, Dr. and Mrs. Curt Yeary purchased the Dillard Clark home. Dr. Yeary recalled that their first visit to the house was on a cool fall day, and Mrs. Clark had prepared a warm and inviting fire in the living room fireplace. Upon entering the living room, Yeary knew that he must own this wonderful old house.

The twenty-acre Clark estate included a beautiful horse stable also designed by John Duncan Forsyth. The Yearys' long-range plan was someday to convert the stable into their retirement house. This plan became a reality when several years later they commissioned architect Phil Fitzgerald to design the conversion.

The home is reached by a narrow winding road off Hillcrest Drive and is not visible from the street. In my high school days, my friends and I drove down the narrow road with the car headlights turned off—it was a scary trip. As we approached the house, we would turn on the headlights and sound our horn, awakening and hopefully scaring the Clark household. We thought this was great fun, but we were no doubt a "pain in the neck" to the Clarks.

Mrs. Clark drove a large Pontiac with back seat cushions slipcovered in white cotton. During World War II, she grew vegetables and raised chickens on the estate, and would deliver the vegetables and eggs in this "specially equipped" car. —JBW

HISTORIC HOMES OF PONCA CITY AND KAY COUNTY ~ 81

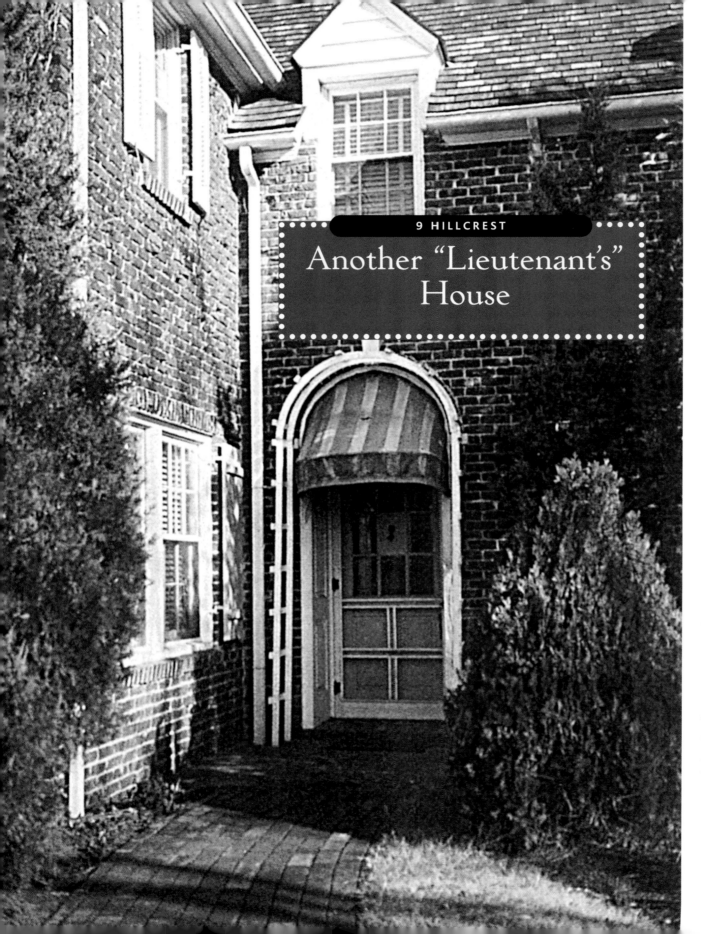

9 HILLCREST
Another "Lieutenant's" House

Seward Sheldon graduated from the University of Oklahoma in 1917 with a degree in business. By the time he became treasurer of Marland Oil Company, he had become one of E. W. Marland's trusted "lieutenants," and, as icing on the cake, he also played a good game of polo. Marland Oil's holdings in 1923 were estimated at $85 million, and the company was marketing its products in every state in the Union and seventeen foreign countries.

The October 23, 1923, issue of the *Ponca City News* headlined a story that said, "The new home of Seward Sheldon in the Country Club Addition [later called Hillcrest] is almost finished and the Sheldons are planning to begin moving in the latter part of this week." The article continued, "The home is a two-story brick structure and has nine rooms and a built-in garage." Seward Sheldon would continue as treasurer of Marland Oil until its merger with Continental Oil in 1929.

The next owner of the Sheldon home was William H. O'Connor, who also worked for Marland Oil and who later became purchasing agent for Continental Oil Company. O'Connor and his wife, Mary Ward O'Connor, had two sons, Bill and Allan, and a daughter, Mary Jane O'Connor Taylor.

The original first floor plan of the house had an entrance foyer, formal living and dining rooms, a breakfast room and adjoining kitchen plus a small den with a connecting half-bath on the front of the house. The second floor had five bedrooms and three baths. The attached garage had a concrete floor. (Mary Jane remembers learning to skate on the garage's concrete floor since the driveway and street were paved with bricks.) The architect is said to be John Duncan Forsyth, who was also the architect for the Marland mansion.

Mary Jane Taylor has many memories growing up in her family home:

Mary Elizabeth Thompson and I shared the same birthday so we always had our birthday parties together. Our backyard had a large dog pen, a huge garden, and an asparagus bed,

bordered by hollyhocks adjoining the gate that led to our neighbors, Dillard and Jane Clark.

"My mother was a very nurturing person and we always had a steady stream of visitors, especially during World War II with the English pilots from Darr School and also other servicemen who were friends of my brothers. They would appear at our front door and always be welcomed for a night or two or, as long as a month if they were recuperating from injuries. I don't know how mother fed all of us, what with food rationing, but she always seemed to manage. In growing up, my best friend was Hopie Cleary and the two of us kept a path worn between our houses.

FACING PAGE: A BIRTHDAY PARTY. MARY JANE IS IN THE BACK ROW, FIFTH FROM LEFT, AND MARY ELIZABETH THOMPSON IS TO HER LEFT. RIGHT: MARY JANE IN 1935.

After the O'Connors, the next owners were Louis Linch and his wife, Adeline Van Winkle Linch. It was during the Linch years that much of the landscaping and gardens were completed. Louis Linch was an avid gardener and always shared the fruits of his labor with friends and neighbors. He and Adeline spent many hours in their kitchen canning their harvest of fruits and vegetables.

The cover of a mid-1920s issue of *Better Homes & Gardens* magazine featured the Seward Sheldon home, and, almost eighty years later, this home could easily be featured once again. The reason? Because of its fine lasting design and because of the people who have lived in and have maintained this historic Ponca City home.

A footnote to the Seward Sheldon home: In growing up in Ponca City, this was my favorite house in Hillcrest. The reason it appealed to me was the very comfortable and "homey" feeling of its exterior. In later years, I was uncomfortable with its front entrance for it seemed too small and undecorated for the overall mass of the front facade. But after receiving early-day photos of the house from Mary Jane, I saw that the original arched trellised arbor and the curved canvas awning above the door are missing. Perhaps, in the not so distant future, these architectural features can be replaced. —JBW

HISTORIC HOMES OF PONCA CITY AND KAY COUNTY ~ 85

8 HILLCREST
The Lackey-Alcorn House

William Lackey was first vice-president and financial director of the Marland Oil Company from 1920 to 1925. In 1922, Lackey built his home at 8 Hillcrest, and in 1928 the house was sold to John Alcorn.

Alcorn began his ventures in the oil business in the Burbank field from 1915 to the early 1920s, when the Alcorn Oil Company was purchased by Marland Oil. Alcorn became vice-president of Marland Oil Company and a member of E. W. Marland's "brain trust," often called Marland's "lieu-

tenants." And to further make Alcorn a part of Marland's inner circle, he was an excellent polo player. The Lackey–Alcorn house was designed by the architect John Duncan Forsyth. It was published in Forsyth's 1937 book as "The home of John Alcorn, Esquire."

The style of the house is Georgian, with its symmetrical red brick facade and white trim. The detailing is not unlike that of homes by the famous English architect Sir Christopher Wren. The front entrance with its Doric columns and pilasters, its sidelights and fan transom panel are all in perfect scale. Today the house is listed on the National Register of Historic Places. Part of the nomination reads, "Marland and his Lieutenants continued to extend their operations during the 1920s, acquiring interests in the Garber, Billings, and Blackwell oil fields in Oklahoma, constructing additional storage tanks to accommodate the Tonkawa field production and to expand the Marland Refinery in Ponca City." The nomination concluded: "John Alcorn was a powerful figure in the Marland Oil Company during his residency in the nominated property."

To the left of the center entrance foyer is the formal living room and beyond is the ceramic tile floor in the sunroom. Surrounded by windows, including one in the Palladian style, the sunroom is on the south side of the house. A similar style Palladian window appears at the landing of the main staircase. To the right of the entrance foyer is the formal dining room and both the living and dining rooms have their own fireplaces. A third fireplace is located in the basement club room. The club room has knotty pine walls that held a secret panel for the storage of liquor—remember, these were the days of Prohibition. There was also a bell system in the room connected to the first floor. This device was to signal the card players with their alcoholic refreshments that the local law enforcement officers were at the front door.

One of the Alcorns' daughters, Joanne, who held the title of "Miss Oklahoma," married songwriter Pinky Tomlin. One of Tomlin's more famous songs was "The Object of My Affection," published in 1934. Those of us past the age of sixty-five can well recall that popular tune. I believe the first stanza goes something like this:

The object of my affection
Can change my complexion
From white to a rosy red
Anytime he holds my hand
And tells me that he's mine.

The words seem rather silly today but sixty-plus years ago we thought they were great!

One of the celebrities who visited the Alcorns was Will Rogers, for the dedication of the Pioneer Woman statue in 1930. Rogers had his noon meal in the Alcorn home, after which the noted humorist was keynote speaker at the dedication. It has been said that E. W. Marland was upset with Rogers's humorous speech, which kept the audience laughing at an occasion that Marland considered to be a very serious affair.

The next owners of the home were Dr. C. E. Northcutt, his wife, Marie, and their two sons. Dr. Northcutt was one of the founders of the Nieman-Northcutt Clinic and was a well-respected physician in the community. Mrs. Northcutt drove a green LaSalle automobile, and the story is told that she once entertained a group of her sons' Roosevelt School teachers at an after school party. Light refreshments were served, including alcoholic cocktails. It is also reported that the party soon got out hand.
—JBW

In Nathaniel Hawthorne's book *The House of Seven Gables,* he tells about a large New England house with seven gables in its roof line. This spooky mystery novel was written in 1851 and was a "must read" in our junior high English class.

Ponca City's "House of Seven Gables" is located at 13 Hillcrest. Built for John Cleary in 1926, the large rambling Colonial farmhouse design sat on thirty-five acres of land. In the 1936 book on the architecture of John Duncan Forsyth, the Cleary house and the Marland mansion are featured. However, the original drawings of the Cleary house show the architect to be John McDonnell of Tulsa, Oklahoma. The reason for this conflict of architects is that, in the early 1920s, John Duncan (Jack) Forsyth worked for McDonnell as his chief designer. In 1926, John McDonnell died quite suddenly, and his Tulsa office was soon closed. There are two other Tulsa houses in the Forsyth book whose drawings show McDonnell as the architect. Having known Forsyth personally, I believe he was the actual creator of these houses and ten years after McDonnell's death felt that he could list the houses as his own. And I probably would have done the same thing.

John Kearny Cleary and his wife, Helen Boswell Cleary, were both from the state of New York. They met when Helen was visiting a school friend whose father was a general in the United States Army stationed in Little Rock, Arkansas. At a house party there, young Lieutenant John Cleary was one of the guests, and it was love at first sight. Lieutenant Cleary served in the United States Army during World War I and was stationed in France. He and Helen were married in 1918, and in 1919 they moved to Ponca where John was employed by the Marland Oil Company. In 1921, Marland relocated Cleary to Tulsa, Oklahoma, where the Clearys built their first home. It was designed by John McDonnell, and I am certain that was when Forsyth had his first contact with John and Helen Cleary. Soon after

HISTORIC HOMES OF PONCA CITY AND KAY COUNTY ~ 89

EARLY AERIAL VIEW OF THE CLEARY ESTATE.

their Tulsa house was completed, John was called back to Ponca to head Marland Oil's land department, a position he held until the demise of the Marland Oil Company. In later years, Cleary would become a successful independent oil operator. The Clearys had three children, Constance, Bill, and Hopie.

The Clearys completed their "House of Seven Gables" in 1926. Its painted stone and wood facade with its seven roof gables is not only a masterpiece in Colonial design but the floor plan of this very large house is also the plan of a very comfortable home.

The very large central hall foyer has an informal appearance with simple but elegant detailing. To the right, one steps down into the long living room with its traditional mantelpiece. A pair of arched bookcases are at one end of the room and matching pairs of arched mirror panels are at the opposite end of the room. Beyond the living room is the glassed porch. This area had large divided glass windows on three sides of the room, and in the summer months these panels were removed making the space a screened porch.

To the left of the foyer is the dining room with its own fireplace. The dining room connects to the kitchen, butler's pantry, and two bedrooms used for the household staff. Behind the main staircase was the children's dining room which today makes an ideal library or study. Upstairs in the Cleary house is the master bedroom and five additional bedrooms, each with their own baths, plus a large playroom. During the Cleary years, the household staff included a butler, a cook, an upstairs maid (nanny), two housekeepers, a stable boy, and two gardeners.

When the Clearys left their "House of Seven Gables," it was sold and later it was resold again to Everett Parker and then to Wallace Edwards and his wife, Polly Black Edwards. Today, the Edwardses' daughter, Jane, and her husband, Tom Morris, live in her family home with their five children.

Joyce Patterson Dunham and her sister, Gloria Patterson Presley, remember spending many hours in the "House of Seven Gables" visiting Hopie Cleary. When in junior high school, Joyce and Gloria attended a summertime slumber party at the Cleary home. Later that night, the overnight guests decided to take a "chocolate dip" in the family pool. (I had never heard that expression— we always called it "skinny dipping.") According to the Patterson girls, the late night swim was great fun until some of the neighborhood boys showed up with flashlights. —JBW

THE ORIGINAL CLEARY STABLE.

36 HILLCREST

The "Seven Stables"

Atop the cupola on the John K. Cleary horse stable is a weather vane depicting his son, young Bill Cleary, being chased by a bull in the family pasture. This incident actually happened.

The stable was built in 1926, the same year the Clearys' main house, "The House of Seven Gables," was being built. The Cleary family humorously called their nearby stable, with its seven horse stall openings, "The House of Seven Stables." The Cleary stable included space for the children's ponies, a horsedrawn carriage, and other livestock, including the family cow. At the second floor level was a hayloft.

In 1948, the Clearys sold twenty-four acres of their land to Charles and Vivian Anne Morrill and the stable was included in

HISTORIC HOMES OF PONCA CITY AND KAY COUNTY ~ 91

TODAY'S CLEARY STABLE HOUSE.

the sale. The Morrills had three children, David, age five, and the twins, Anne and Mary, age three. Their plan was to convert the Cleary stable into the family home. They would also develop their twenty-four acre tract of land into a housing subdivision named "Enfield." The subdivision was named for a village in England and to honor Charles's English ancestor, Sir Edward Morrill.

Charles and Vivian Morrill started the conversion of the stable into their family home on a very limited budget. The interior of the stable received batt insulation at all of the exterior walls, and for the next four years, this insulation would be left exposed. A new downstairs bath was added, and the bathroom door was the only inside door in the house for several years. A staircase was constructed to the second floor hayloft and four large dormers were added for three future bedrooms and a bath. In the new living room area, they built a massive brick fireplace, and the original carriage room, measuring twelve by nineteen feet, became the dining room. Later additions to the house included a two-car garage, a bath, and a utility room. Eventually the garages would be converted into a family room.

Throughout the restoration of the Cleary stable into their family home, Charles and Vivian Morrill attempted to preserve the original integrity of the architecture that John Duncan Forsyth had created. And they succeeded. —JBW

47 HILLCREST

The Polo Barn

THE ORIGINAL HAYLOFT. PRECEDING PAGE: THE HAYLOFT TODAY. FACING: THE ORIGINAL EAST ELEVATION (BOTTOM) AND THE EAST ELEVATION TODAY.

E. W. Marland was responsible for bringing the sport of polo to Ponca City in the 1920s. He established three polo fields for practice and competition for the Ponca City polo teams played against polo teams from nearby cities such as Wichita, Kansas, and Tulsa. George Marland, E. W.'s adopted son, was a very accomplished polo player; E. W. himself, however, never played, but preferred to sit atop his horse, Tom James, and observe from the sidelines.

In the halcyon days of the Marland Oil Company, Ponca's prominent people were in abundance at the polo matches, for if you were not playing polo, you were watching the games in anticipation of the after-game parties.

Marland built a special barn on land he owned east of North Fourteenth Street in what became the Country Club or Hillcrest addition. Built around 1926, the 4,000-square-foot structure was designed by John Duncan Forsyth and overlooked one of the

original polo fields. Today the site of the polo field has become an attractive cotton field.

In the 1950s, Dr. Curt Yeary purchased the thirty-two acre Dillard Clark estate at 10 East Hillcrest, and the Marland polo barn was included in the transaction. Dr. Yeary's long range plan for the barn was to someday renovate it into his retirement home. In 1981, the Yearys commissioned local architect, Phil Fitzgerald, to design their "polo barn home," and, wherever possible, the existing rafters, beams, and posts were to be incorporated into the design of their new house.

The living room in the polo barn house was the original tack room, and the ponies lived in what is now the dining room where each stall had its horse's name plaque on the wall. The den in the Yeary barn home was

HISTORIC HOMES OF PONCA CITY AND KAY COUNTY ~ 95

once the grain storage bin, and adobe tile has replaced the original dirt floors.

The living room is to the right of the front foyer, and its tall stone fireplace separates the two spaces. Behind the foyer is a small den with its fireplace and a series of small windows that once were used to feed the animals in their stalls. These windows continue into the dining room area that connects to the kitchen and breakfast room. The master bedroom is at the south end of the first floor, and the original barn doors in this area have been replaced with sliding glass doors that overlook the swimming pool. The hayloft opening above is now a large skylight. The staircase in the foyer leads up to what was once the hayloft. The heavy wood beams and trusses in this space were an important element in Forsyth's original design of the barn. Today these structural members are still in place, making for unusual spaces for the second floor sitting room, the two bedrooms, and two baths.

During the Yeary years and prior to the renovation, the polo barn was a working barn. The Yeary children were active in the 4H Club, so their ponies, sheep, and goats were housed in the barn. As teenagers, the young Yearys hosted barn dances with their livestock observing the activities. A shed structure once used by the groom has become a cabana overlooking the swimming pool and the "chukker bell," which rang to announce the start of a polo match, still rests on its eight-foot post.

The Marland polo barn's roof is capped with a cupola which holds an iron weather vane. This unusual weather vane depicts a rider astride a prancing horse that seems to have frightened a large goose whose wings are spread for a hasty ascent into the sky. — KA

THE ORIGINAL POLO BARN.

ACRE HOMES

In March of 1923, an article in the Ponca City News told of a new housing development being created by oilman E. W. Marland. Marland called his development Acre Homes, and its slogan was "An Ideal Place for a Real Home." —JBW

"Acre Homes! What a picture these words conjure up in the minds of the city dweller. He immediately thinks of freedom and the opportunity to have flower beds, a small orchard, a chicken pen, and many other things that are impossible on a narrow fifty foot lot. Most people come from the farm and long for more room where neighbors will not repeat the morning after, the things a man said to his wife the night before.

Acre Homes has become a reality in this community by the development of the 200 acres just north of the city by E. W. Marland. The term Acre Homes is not quite accurately used as the tract has been divided into 209 home sites, some containing more than an acre and others less. There is also a reserve for a park and perhaps a school."

711 OVERBROOK
The Edward J. Sheldon House

John Duncan Forsyth was the architect for the home of Ed and Jessie Sheldon at 711 Overbrook, across the street from Forsyth's own Ponca City home. The Sheldon house was designed in the rural English cottage style, and the focal point of its facade is the steep pitched gable that is alive with casement style windows rising three windows in height. The exterior of the house is a mixture of lap siding and wood shingles, which gives an interesting contrast and play of materials.

Forsyth must have liked his design for the Sheldons' Ponca City house, for he repeated similar facades on several houses in Tulsa, including his own. The large grouping of windows on the front of the Sheldon house are in the living room. This room's high-vaulted and beamed ceiling helps to accentuate the window wall.

Behind the living room is the cozy dining room that connects to the kitchen and eating areas. The original Sheldon house had only two bedrooms, but a third bedroom and a bath were added at a later date.

Ed and his wife, Jessie Oglevee Sheldon, were married in Caldwell, Kansas, on Christmas Eve in 1921. Edward went to work for the Marland Oil Company in 1920 and continued with the company when it became Continental Oil Company. He retired from the post of assistant treasurer in 1956, after thirty-six years of service.

The Sheldons had a daughter, Ann, and a son, Edward, who was my age. I remember attending one of Ed's grade school birthday parties. The favors were balsa wood glider kits that required assembling. After much difficulty, I managed to get my glider put together and, on its maiden voyage in the Sheldons' back yard, it broke into several pieces.

LEFT: EDWARD J. SHELDON SEATED AT FRONT ENTRANCE ARBOR. BELOW: AN EARLY PHOTO OF THE HOUSE WITH HOLLYHOCKS IN THE FOREGROUND.

98 ~ HISTORIC HOMES OF PONCA CITY AND KAY COUNTY

After Jessie Sheldon's untimely death, Ed relocated to a house on North Seventh Street next door to my parents. The Sheldons' longtime housekeeper, Ethel, also became my mother's housekeeper. On several occasions, Ed Sheldon would get upset with Ethel and fire her. But Ethel never left. She would say, "You can't fire me for I promised Mrs. Sheldon I would always look after you."

In later years, my father and Ed Sheldon became good friends. Ed was a very punctual person, and each Saturday morning he would call our house at 10:55 A.M. and ask if he might come over for a visit. The doorbell would ring at 11:00 A.M. and at 11:59 A.M. Ed would announce that he must leave. My father often said that he could set his watch by Ed Sheldon's Saturday morning visits. —JBW

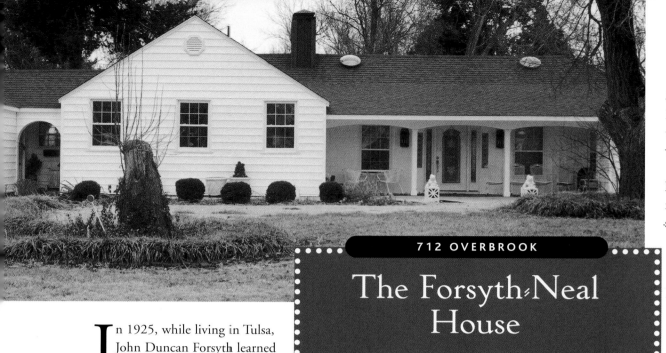

712 OVERBROOK

The Forsyth-Neal House

In 1925, while living in Tulsa, John Duncan Forsyth learned that oilman E. W. Marland was planning to build his "Palace on the Prairie." He immediately made a trip to Ponca City only to learn that Marland was vacationing in Colorado. Forsyth then packed up his wife and daughter in the family Chevrolet coupe (complete with a rumble seat). He stowed camping gear and a tent and headed for Colorado Springs, camping on schoolyards along the way. Upon arriving, he discovered that Marland had relocated to Estes Park, so, with gear still in tow, he followed Marland there. In Estes Park, his persistence paid off and he received the commission to design the Marland mansion.

Design started in 1925 and was completed in 1928. During this period, Forsyth moved to Ponca City and designed and built his Ponca City home. Located at 712 Overbrook, the Cape Cod cottage reflects Forsyth's diversity of design talents. In 1930, "Jack" Forsyth returned to Tulsa and reestablished his architectural practice there. During his stay in Ponca, Forsyth designed several beautiful homes that have become an important part of Ponca City's heritage.

THE DR. LAILE NEAL YEARS

In 1931, the Forsyth Ponca City home was purchased by Dr. Laile Neal and his wife, Vivian. Dr. Neal started his medical practice in Ponca in association with Dr. A.S. Nuckols. Eventually Dr. Neal established a private practice, which served the community many years (he was my doctor as I was growing up). He was president of his senior high school class in Blackwell, Oklahoma. After graduation Neal enrolled at the University of Oklahoma to study medicine. During his college years, he met Vivian Stewart while swimming at a local swimming pool, and it was love at first sight. "I am going to marry that girl," he told a friend. In 1926, Vivian and Laile were married in McAlester, Oklahoma, Vivian's home town. The Neals had two children, Sue (we were classmates from Roosevelt Elementary School through high school) and Richard, who would become an architect.

The Forsyth-Neal Ponca City home is a low, rambling structure reminiscent of Cape Cod. The simple but functional floor plan has a long living room with a matching screened porch across the back of the house. There was a breakfast room and kitchen, and two bedrooms accessible down a long, long hall. The family's single telephone was in the breakfast room. Sue recalls how her father would race down the hall in the middle of the night to answer an emergency phone call from one of his patients.

Dr. Neal loved to travel, especially by car. He insisted on doing all the driving and would only stop to refuel. Sue Neal Massey recalls being awakened one morning at 2:00 before a planned family trip. Her father had just returned home from delivering a baby, and he was wide awake. So the family dressed and started their planned trip to South Dakota. In another memory of a family motor trip, Dr. Neal, while speeding down the highway, turned to his wife and said, "That is really a very unbecoming hat, so why do you wear it?" Whereupon Vivian removed the hat and threw it out the window. The car continued to travel down the highway. —JBW

116 VIRGINIA AVENUE
The Loft House

Emmerretta Parthenia Wood (neither of her children knows whence her name originated) was born in Durant, Oklahoma, where she graduated from the Southeast Normal School of Durant with a degree in music. After graduation, M'Retta (her abbreviated name) became superintendent of music for the Madill, Oklahoma, public schools.

William Earl Sexton was born in Bokoshe, Oklahoma, and graduated from Oklahoma State University. Bill and M'Retta were married on June 15, 1924, at the home of the bride's sister in Tulsa, Oklahoma. The newspaper article described the bridal dress as "a small tailleur of pearl gray charmeen, a silk cloche embroidered in the pastel shades and accessories to match her gown." (The only item of apparel that I can

HISTORIC HOMES OF PONCA CITY AND KAY COUNTY ~ 101

decipher is the "cloche," which was a style of hat.)

Bill Sexton worked for Marland Oil and Conoco until his retirement. In 1926, Bill and M'Retta signed a contract to build their Ponca City home at 116 Virginia Avenue. The contract described the home as "a one-story, five room modern house, with a detached garage, together with a chat driveway and rustic bridge." The charming cottage-style facade of the Sexton home is matched by an equally charming interior. Upon entering a small vestibule, one steps down into the living room with its knotty pine walls and rustic stone chimney breast. To the left of the living room is the front bedroom that connects to a hall, bath, and back bedroom. (A third bedroom and screened porch were added later.) Behind the living room one steps up into the pine paneled dining room and beyond is the kitchen and breakfast room.

The Sextons' son, Bill, was my age. When the movie *Snow White and the Seven Dwarfs* came to Ponca, John Hutchins, a fellow classmate, and I were going to the late matinee performance after school. When we told Bill Sexton of our plans he wanted to go too. Since he did not have the ten cents admission, John and I decided to forego our five-cent sacks of popcorn so that Bill could attend. The problem with this arrangement was that Bill had neglected to tell his parents. Halfway through the film a neighbor, Mrs. Westfall, came walking down the aisle accompanied by a policeman to ask if young Bill Sexton was in the theater. Bill was taken

M'RETTA SEXTON HOLDING HER SON BILLY.

from the theater and returned home immediately. I often wondered if he ever saw the last half of *Snow White and the Seven Dwarfs*.

Sue Sexton Jester Bynum recalls growing up in her family home with its "rustic bridge" across the small ravine in the front yard:

When the creek flooded, it covered part of our yard. We would put on our bathing suits and swim in the murky waters. What fun. When the creek was dry, we followed its trail under a viaduct and then east under Virginia Avenue. That was creepy.

In our house you could stand in the living room at the fireplace wall and look straight into the dining room and beyond to the kitchen. One evening when our parents were out and we had a babysitter Billy shot his BB gun from the living room through the dining room and into the kitchen cabinets. It scared the poor sitter so much she hid in a closet until our parents arrived home. Billy was in a lot of trouble. During World War II, Daddy often rode a bicycle to work at Conoco to save on gasoline.

In 1943, M'Retta saw the need for a place where teenagers could gather and socialize. With the help of her husband and a committee who planned the inception of the project, "The Loft" became a reality. Located on the second floor of the Barnes Building at the northeast corner of Grand Avenue and North Third Street, The Loft soon became the hangout for many of Ponca City's young people. M'Retta solicited other parents to serve as chaperons for the teenagers, who had to be within a certain age range and had to sign in and out (only once an evening) and abide by the rules.

At The Loft, you could socialize with your friends, eat snacks, drink pop, and dance to the music of a jukebox. We all lovingly called M'Retta Sexton "Emmie." Her family nickname was "Happy," for she always made people laugh.

Emmerretta Parthenia "M'Retta" "Emmie" "Happy" Sexton certainly lived up to all of her titles. —JBW

215 VIRGINIA AVENUE
Clyde Muchmore House

Clyde Muchmore was from Kiowa, Kansas. His article in the book *The Last Run* tells of his remembrances as a young boy during the Cherokee Strip Land Run of 1893:

For weeks men and women had been making preparations for the Run along the Kansas border when the promised land of Oklahoma would be available for homesteaders. Times had been hard, work scarce and wages low. Any change that promised improvement was doubly welcomed.

Father had used his homestead rights but a good friend, who had no horses, asked father to make the Run with him. September 16, 1893 came—hot, dry and dusty, with crowds moving down toward the Kansas state line. Mother took us children in the farm wagon and we managed to get a place of vantage on the line road. Soon a shot was heard and the tightened line surged forward as a unit and then began to expand as slow equipment gave way to faster ones.

Mother slowly drove the wagon back to Kansas where we eagerly awaited word from father. Along toward the night of the second day, father drove in. He was smiling and we knew they had made a claim.

The first year after the Run we experienced a terrible drought and many a homesteader gave up and returned to whence he came. But rains in the second years made for late crops such as turnips. With the abundance of turnip greens, turnips and jackrabbits the persistent ones survived. For many of them did stick and would remain to conquer a wilderness that today we call Oklahoma.

The *Ponca City News* was introduced to its readers on November 18, 1918, by its publisher, Richard Elam. The new daily was printed on a twelve-page Duplex, a flatbed press which was slow, rickety, and undependable but still capable of turning out more and bigger papers faster than the sheet-fed presses of its competitor, the *Courier and Democrat*. Elam's newspaper venture was financed by oilman Lew Wentz, who was interested in seeing an improved newspaper promote the interests of Ponca City. However, it turned out, Elam was not successful in running the newspaper, so in 1919, Clyde Estes Muchmore became editor. Muchmore had acquired his taste for journalism at an early age. He was born July 20, 1884, in Liberty, Nebraska. Later his family moved to Kiowa, Kansas, where his first introduction to the newspaper business was inking forms for a Washington handpress on the *Kiowa Review*.

The groundbreaking for the Muchmore home was October 21, 1927, and its completion was only eighty days later on January 1, 1928. The Muchmores had two sons, Gareth and Allan, and a daughter, Marjorie. In 1947, they sold their home to Dr. Robert Moore, a local dentist, and his wife, Pauline. The real estate transaction was handled by Lee Drake, and according to Pat Drake this was the first house that Lee had ever sold. Today the Moores' granddaughter, Ann

HISTORIC HOMES OF PONCA CITY AND KAY COUNTY

Moore Jackson, and her husband, Scott Jackson, live in the home.

The native stone and shingle exterior of the Muchmore-Moore house contains elements of Dutch Colonial with touches of country English. The gambrel roof line is penetrated with a continuous dormer at both the front and rear elevations. Upon entering the house you are in the formal living room with its traditional wood mantelpiece and green tile surround. Behind the living room is the dining room, which opens onto a screened porch overlooking the expansive back yard. To the left of the front door is a small study that has also served as a music room. Off the living room is the open staircase, with its turned balusters, and a coat closet that houses a hidden gun closet. Adjoining the dining room is a breakfast nook and kitchen which connects to another screened porch. The second floor of the house has three bedrooms.

An interesting feature in the dining room is its chandelier which was installed during the Moore years. While stationed in Europe during World War II, Dr. Robert Moore would periodically send back packages containing glass items he had found in war-torn southern France. These bits and pieces of glass included beading, prisms of all sizes and shapes, and crystal candle cups (bobeches) in various colors from clear to cranberry to aquamarine. Also among his findings were metal parts from fine chandeliers. After the purchase of the Muchmore home, Dr. Moore began assembling his finds into a grand chandelier that today hangs in the dining room, along with a smaller version hanging in the ceiling of the stairwell.

Dr. Moore entered the United States Army in 1944. He served in southern France until July, 1945, when he was transferred to the Pacific. While serving in France, Dr. Moore received a presidential citation for dental work he had performed on German prisoners-of-war. In doing this dental work, Moore soon learned that the German population, as a whole, gave their teeth little care and attention. "It is not uncommon to see a twenty-five year-old German man who has lost all of his teeth," he said.

Robert and Pauline Moore had two sons, Everett and George, who both became doctors. George Moore recalls how he and his brother would throw "water balloon bombs" out their bedroom window onto the neighbor's "kids" who were playing on the driveway below.

Much of the charm of the Muchmore-Moore home is its spacious back yard. When Acre Homes Addition was platted, each house was to sit on one acre of ground. On their acre, the Muchmores planted an orchard that included apple, pear, persimmon, cherry, and crabapple trees. Beyond their property was a trotter horse race track and beyond the track was Marland's polo field. Also included in the rear yard was an elaborate swing set complete with a teeter totter plus a ten-foot-square "buried greenhouse," where Mrs. Muchmore planted seedlings for her spring and summer flower beds. —KA

204/210 VIRGINIA AVENUE

The Tom Irby Houses

The two houses built by the Tom Irby family sit side by side on Virginia Avenue. The first was built in 1929 and is located at number 204. Its next door neighbor, which the family referred to as the "Rock House," was completed in 1940. Its address is number 210.

Thomas L. Irby was born in Grenada, Mississippi, in 1898. He enlisted in the United States Army in 1917 and served as sergeant and company commander in the 140th Field Artillery in France. Irby completed his undergraduate work at the University of Mississippi and received his law degree from the University of Oklahoma in 1923. In that same year young Irby opened his law office in Ponca City. In 1924, he married Marion Tolley, of Denver, Colorado, the daughter of George and Harriet Tolley, natives of England. Marion held a Bachelor of Music degree from the University of Oklahoma and had come to Ponca City in 1921 to teach music in the public school system. She went to work in her husband's law office and soon developed an interest in the practice of law. After much studying on her own, Marion was admitted to the Oklahoma Bar in 1925.

HISTORIC HOMES OF PONCA CITY AND KAY COUNTY ~ 105

TOP: THE HOUSE AT 204 VIRGINIA AVENUE. BOTTOM: THE HOUSE AT 210 VIRGINIA AVENUE.

The first Irby home was built as a duplex but was designed so that it could easily be converted into a single family dwelling. Its white lap siding exterior has a Dutch gambrel roof with a long continuous dormer across the front and back of the structure. The Irbys lived in the second floor unit, which had two bedrooms and a bath. Later they added a third bedroom addition on the back of the house above a first floor breakfast addition. In 1937, Marion's mother came to live with them and a second addition was added on the south end of the house above the first floor sunroom. This addition became the fourth bedroom with its own bath and a kitchenette so Grandmother Tolley could make her afternoon tea.

In 1939, the day England declared war on Germany, the British merchant ship *Athenia* was sunk by a German torpedo, causing heavy loss of life. Marion's mother was aboard that fateful ship, en route home to America after visiting her English relatives. She was not one of the survivors. The captain of the ship reported that "After the torpedo was fired, the German submarine rose to the surface and shelled the ship. One shell carried away the main mast and was evidently aimed at the wireless room, but missed its mark."

In 1940, the Irbys built their second house just to the north of the first one. It was designed by Marion Irby, and her husband, Tom, served as the contractor. Their daughter, Margaret, would later recall: "They hired a stone mason to lay the rock work and workmen to pour the foundation and frame the structure. My father and my brother, Tom, did much of the interior work such as the plastering and laying the floor. And we all did the painting."

An interesting feature of the house was the stonework around the front door. It was a series of cut stone figures that the family had collected on their numerous trips to Mexico. These trinkets were purchased from small boys selling to tourists near the pyramids, claiming they had been found in the ruins and in neighboring farm fields. A later owner of the Irby "Rock House" had all of these stone figures removed from around the door claiming they were "heathen idols." I remember the carved wood mantelpiece and the matching carved wood exterior door custom-designed and fabricated in Mexico—I had never seen anything

The British merchant steamship Athenia (above), with 1400 passengers aboard, was torpedoed off the Hebrides, west of northern Scotland. The vessel, bound for Montreal from Glasgow, was 526 feet long and was built in 1923 at Glasgow.

TOM L. IRBY
1898 - 1964

This book was given to the
PONCA CITY LIBRARY
by friends in memory of
Tom L. Irby

like them. The "Rock House" had one of the first residential dishwashers installed in Ponca City. The Irbys had seen a demonstration of one at the 1939 New York's Fair and thought it was the coming thing. In 1945, the Irby family sold their two Virginia Avenue houses and purchased a home at 206 North Sixth Street.

Tragedy struck the Tom Irby family once again in 1945. On December 21, 1945, their only son, Tom, Jr. was killed in a toboggan accident in New London, New Hampshire, while enjoying a weekend holiday from his university studies at the Massachusetts Institute of Technology. He was thrown from the sled into the path of an approaching car and died beneath its wheels. His sister, Margaret, Irby Koenig, and I were in the same class at school and Tom was two years older. Although I did not know him well, I remember Tom Irby as a friendly and very intelligent young man.
—JBW

HISTORIC HOMES OF PONCA CITY AND KAY COUNTY ~ 107

When driving down Virginia Avenue and admiring all the beautiful homes, I would always take a second look at the house whose yard was once enclosed with a white picket fence. Today that white picket fence marks only the north and south property lines. Located at 221 Virginia Avenue, the home was one of the first built in Acre Homes, platted in 1924. It was built by Vernon Sills, whose daughter, Peggy, would recall, "I spent many happy hours playing in the bright sunroom off the living room and will always remember the many gatherings of family and friends playing croquet on our lawn."

When the Sills family moved to Houston, Texas, in 1940, the house was purchased by Charles Duffy. Duffy had established a Ponca City law practice following graduation from the University of Oklahoma School of Law in 1922. He would serve in the Oklahoma Senate for twelve years, from 1934 to 1946. Senator Duffy had aspirations of becoming governor of Oklahoma, but power king Robert S. Kerr, said, "No, he is too honest a man."

The Sills-Duffy house is Colonial Revival in design. Its white clapboard siding exterior is penetrated by a protruding entrance vestibule on the front of the house. This vestibule's pediment and pilasters say "Georgian Revival" in their detailing. The center hall plan of the house has a traditional staircase leading to the second floor. To the right of the foyer is the living room whose mantelpiece is flanked by two arched openings leading into the sunroom. To the left of the foyer is the dining room and at the rear of the house is the kitchen and a rather large breakfast room. The original second floor plan had three bedrooms, but the Duffys created a fourth master bedroom over the downstairs breakfast room.

During World War II, when Ponca City's Darr School trained RAF pilots from England, Charles and Vala Duffy often entertained these homesick young men in their home. Every Sunday afternoon they would drive out to the school, pick up British boys and take them home for a Sunday afternoon visit and food. The Duffys became well acquainted with many of the boys and corresponded with them upon their return to England. Some of their houseguests were killed in the war, and Charles and Vala kept in touch with their families and later visited them in England.

The Duffys had two daughters, Virginia Duffy Edgington and Dorothy Duffy Work. Dorothy Work recalls that "During the war years, we had dances in the basement club room with its knotty pine walls and concrete floor. We practically wore out our collection of Glenn Miller, Tommy Dorsey, and Harry James records. We also loved the new singing entertainer, Frank Sinatra." She continued, "Both my sister and I had our wedding receptions in our yard with its beautiful green grass and many large trees."

Vala Solf Duffy was born in a sod house. Her father, Edward Solf, had made the 1893 Land Run. Charles Duffy died in 1979, and his wife, Vala, died in October of 1984. The Duffy girls celebrated Christmas in 1984 at their family home, ending a forty-year tradition. On March 22, 1979, the Oklahoma State Senate passed a resolution honoring the late Senator Duffy for an "extraordinary career of public service that merits the praise of all Oklahomans." —JBW

717 EAST OVERBROOK

Casey-Skidmore House

On April 23, 1937, the Marland estate issued a warranty deed to W. H. Casey for the purchase of a lot in the Acre Homes Addition. Located at 717 East Overbrook, the Addition's restrictions stipulated that the cost of the structure be no less than $5,000 and that the house must set back seventy-five feet from the Overbrook curb line. The Caseys completed their new home in 1938, and in December of 1939, Casey and the other owners in the block formed a homeowners group to set addi-

tional restrictions on construction. They included allowing the use for residential purposes only and limiting the dwellings to two and a half floors in height with a private garage for not more than three cars.

The Casey home was constructed with elements of Colonial Revival and Georgian styling, including limestone field stone at the first floor and wood siding at the second floor level. The first floor consisted of the living and dining rooms, kitchen, half bath and a den. Off the living room was a screened porch, and the basement included a knotty pine club room with its own fireplace.

The Casey family included three sons, Hal, Bob, and Charles, and two daughters, Doris and Velma. Mr. and Mrs. Casey used the first floor study as their bedroom while the boys shared the north second floor bedroom. The girls' bedroom was originally designed to be the master bedroom, and the third bedroom became the guest bedroom, though rarely used, and never by family. It was always ready for guests.

W. H. Casey was a game ranger. He raised chickens in the back yard and built a brick smoker where he smoked meat that he would sell to friends and customers. Today, that fine smoker still remains a part of the back yard.

The Caseys' eldest daughter, Doris (now called Casey) Von Iderstein, recalls, "The huge yard where my brothers played football, and the woods beyond the back yard where I would run with my dog and fish for crawdads in the tiny creek, is now covered with 'new' houses. I loved the staircase, where as a child I would thrill at starting at the top and running down the curved staircase all the way to the basement—over and over again."

The Skidmore Years

The Herb Skidmore family purchased the Casey house in 1958 and lived in it for over thirty years. The Skidmore children, Steve and Ann, have many happy memories of life in their Overbrook home. Steve's bedroom was on the north, and he recalls an east window that he could climb out and onto the porch roof. He also remembers the ping pong table in the basement club room and the indentations in the ceiling caused by a ping pong paddle when he would take out his frustrations with the game.

The basement area of the house is divided into two sections, the knotty pine club room and the dark, "spooky" utility room. Both Charles Casey and Steve Skidmore remember, as children, being frightened of going into the utility room.

Ann Skidmore was married in the family home and remembers the large mirror at the bottom of the staircase. She also recalls the feeling she had swirling from the second floor down the two flights of the curving staircase to the basement.

Both the Casey and the Skidmore children remember the large flat rock in the back yard. Charles Casey would mount his father's horse from atop the rock and Steve Skidmore recalls using it as "home base" for ball games with other neighborhood children. Ann Skidmore remembers getting her "haircuts" while seated on the rock. —KA

131 ELMWOOD
Drs. Browne and Neal House

Howard Storm Browne was born in 1886 on a farm in Illinois. Later his family would move to Guthrie, Oklahoma, where Howard graduated from high school. When he was eighteen, his family moved to Kay county, where his father had purchased a 160-acre farm. In 1909, Browne received a degree in pharmacy from the University of Oklahoma, and in 1911, he married May Melvin. While studying for medical school at O. U., he was assistant dean of pharmacy until transferring to the University of Illinois, where he received his Doctor of Medicine degree. Browne returned to O. U. to become the dean of the School of Medicine before opening his private medical practice in Ponca City.

The Brownes completed their Ponca City home in 1926. They had three children, two older daughters, Jane Elizabeth and Barbara, and a younger son, Howard Browne, Jr., who would follow in his father's footsteps as a doctor of medicine. Dr. Browne loved the sports of shooting and golf. He built a putting green made of sand and oil on the vacant lot next to his house. Dr. Howard Browne would spend many hours practicing his pitching and putting there.

Dr. Howard Browne, Jr. has flashes of events when growing up in the 131 Elmwood house: "A couple of weeks before the Fourth of July, our fathers would take us to buy fireworks. We would accumulate arsenals of lady fingers, firecrackers, cherry bombs, and the sissy stuff like sparklers and Roman candles. On the big day we would arise at dawn, light our first punk, then sit on the curb and light the crackers and blow up ant hills. After dark, everyone would pool their rockets, Roman candles, and pinwheels, and have a great fireworks display in one of our yards. People entertained a great deal in those days. My parents would have bridge parties in our home and I was allowed to pass among the guests with a silver tray containing cigarettes and chewing gum. Once Gordon Geddes taught me a dirty rhyme which I in turn repeated to Mary, our maid. She told my father and he sternly lectured to me about the rhyme but never explained the meaning of it."

In 1935, the Brownes sold their family home and moved to 220 Virginia Avenue.

THE DR. LAILE NEAL YEARS

In 1941, the Dr. Laile Neal family relocated to 131 Elmwood, the former home of the Dr. Howard Browne family. Their new Elmwood home was a welcome relief from their former rather compact cottage at 712 Overbrook. The Elmwood house has a central entrance foyer with a staircase leading up to the second floor and, at its landing, is a back stair down to the kitchen. The living room is to the left of the foyer and I still remember its fireplace. It was an Art Deco fireplace mantel that was a complete contrast to the traditional architectural detailing throughout the house. I am certain the mantel was a later addition for it was rather long with the ends curving back to the wall. The unusual part of the mantelpiece was the fact it was covered in a brown tightly woven carpet material trimmed out with horizontal wood strips making the piece cry out "Art Deco, Art Deco." The description of the mantelpiece makes it seem somewhat out of place but its simple straightforward design seemed to compliment the traditional furniture in the room. (A bit of trivia on the term Art Deco: This description was not created until the early 1960s when an English historian referred to the modern style of architecture from the 1920s into the early 1940s by that term.)

The second floor of the house has four bedrooms and two baths, one with a tub and the other with a shower. The exterior facade is faced with dark red brick accentuated with white trim and topped with a red barrel clay tile roof. In 1942, the Neals closed their family home and moved to Alexandria, Louisiana, where Laile was stationed before being sent to the South Pacific during World War II. After the war they returned to their Elmwood home, and in 1951, their daughter, Sue, and her husband, Jack Massey, were married in the living room of the home.

The Browne-Neal house has a full basement which included a very large club room. This room not only had its own fireplace but also a long built-in bar extending the length of one wall. An unusual feature of the bar was its access opening from the utility room only three feet in height. One almost had to crawl through it. In 1941, the Neals hosted a party-dance for Sue's sixth-grade classmates in their basement club room and I do not think there was an absentee from the class. During the party the club room bar served as a jungle gym as we crawled through the low doorway, pretended we were bartenders, and then climbed over the bar and started the game once again. A phonograph played music for dancing, and I had been instructed by my mother to ask Mrs. Neal for a dance. Apparently Bob Baughman and Charles Gibson had received similar instructions for the three of us entered into a long discussion on the subject during the party. I

FACING PAGE: AN EARLY PHOTO OF THE BROWNE-NEAL HOUSE. BELOW: YOUNG HOWARD BROWNE, JR., SITTING IN THE SPARE TIRE OF THE FAMILY CAR.

ended up dancing with our hostess and as I was leaving the party, Dr. Neal's mother approached me to say that I was a very polite young man for asking Mrs. Neal to dance.

Little did she know that I had drawn the shortest straw. —JBW

146 FAIRVIEW
The Last Tribal Chief's House

Ernest Emmett (E. E.) Thompson was the last elected chief of the Kaw Indian Tribe. He was born on the Kaw reservation located in Kay County across the Arkansas River from old Kaw City. Emmett attended the Indian Agency school in Washunga, Oklahoma, and his family lived nearby in one of the "settlement" houses provided by the Agency. He was one of the last members of the Kansa (Kaw) tribe to be placed on the Allotment Rolls. This allotment gave Emmett 160 acres of land, close to the soon-to-be discovered Burbank Oil Field, in nearby Osage County. The discovery of oil on his allotment in 1921 made E. E. Thompson a wealthy man overnight.

Thompson used the proceeds from his oil interests to relocate to Ponca City, and soon afterwards he married Olavene Bellmard. He became a successful Ponca City businessman and founded the National Loan Investment Company. But he never forgot his Kaw Indian heritage and was always quick to provide medical care, groceries, and other necessities to the Kaw community. During the years of the Great Depression, Thompson had an open account with the Monsour Grocery Store to provide groceries to any Native American who would say they had been sent by "Emmett." He sponsored a yearly powwow on his 320-acre farm in rural Kay County.

Friends and businessmen from Ponca were invited to attend and become honorary members of the Kaw Tribe. These new members were expected to bring flour, sugar, coffee, and other foodstuffs instead of money as gifts for the tribe.

Emmett and Olavene Thompson purchased their house in Acre Homes Addition in 1928. They had three children, John, Joe, and Mary Elizabeth. Joe was born in the family home in 1929. The Thompson house is located at 146 Fairview. It is a single story-structure designed in the English cottage style and was built by the DeWitt family. The house has a large living room, formal dining room, a library, and four bedrooms. The full basement housed the laundry room, a large recreation room, and a card room. Near the card room was a closet used for "aging whiskey." (Those were the days of Prohibition.) In the living room, sitting atop the Steinway grand piano, was a photo of an old family friend, Charles Curtis. Curtis was vice president of the United States during the Herbert Hoover administration. He was also a member of the Kaw Indian Tribe—hence his autobiography was titled *From a Kaw Tepee to the Capital*.

The Thompsons' household staff included a full-time cook, a gardener, and a housekeeper. Emmett Thompson kept in close contact with his Kaw family and friends, many of whom were less fortunate than he. This extended family always felt welcome when they dropped by the Thompson home, be it for breakfast, lunch, or dinner. The garage at the rear of the property had an attached servants' quarters and a large screened sleeping porch across the back of the building. The sleeping porch could easily accommodate ten people, and son Joe recalls that it was "often filled with guests who had arrived for dinner and then decided to spend the night."

FACING PAGE: CHIEF ERNEST THOMPSON AND HIS WIFE OLAVENE. BELOW: JOHN, MARY ELIZABETH, AND JOE.

Emmett Thompson died in 1938 at the very early age of thirty-six, from a heart condition derived from his battle with rheumatic fever as a young boy. At his funeral, the First Presbyterian Church in Ponca City was filled to overflowing with family, friends, and dignitaries from throughout the country. More than 150 more mourners stood outside.

In 2000, Emmett Thompson's children, Joe Thompson and Mary Elizabeth Thompson Bryan, presented the Gilcrease Museum in Tulsa, Oklahoma, with the Emmett E. Thompson Collection. This outstanding collection consists of nearly 100 important Native American artifacts. — JBW

113 GLENSIDE
The John Whitehurst Family Home

John Whitehurst and Charlotte Linch were married on September 14, 1921, on the Linch family farm. The bride's father, Perry Linch, built a white flower-covered arbor for the couple to stand under during the wedding ceremony.

John Whitehurst was raised in Salida, Colorado, and after graduation from the Colorado School of Mines spent five years as superintendent of a gold and silver mine east of Mazatlan, Mexico. After investing in the Marland Oil Company, John came to Ponca City to visit a fellow investor, Dr. A. S. Nuckols. Charlotte Linch was working for Dr. Nuckols, and it was "love at first sight" for John. Despite the fact that Charlotte was engaged, John told her, "I'll come back to marry you." Later John would write many letters to convince Charlotte to marry him, knowing "the results of good hard efforts will not be too long in coming."

John and Charlotte had four daughters, Charlotte Virginia (born in Shreveport, Louisiana), Margaret Louise (born in San Diego, California), and Barbara and Kathryn, both born in Ponca City. By 1927, John had established the Whitehurst Construction Company and had built several houses in the Acre Homes Addition. One of these was the Whitehurst family home. Later his company was employed by Continental Oil Company to construct additions to their refinery and Conoco's many service stations.

The Whitehurst family home is located at 113 Glenside. Built in 1927, the house was designed and built by John Whitehurst and was originally designed as a two-story structure. At some point, the plans were altered to a single-story house showing a bit of Mediterranean influence with its peach-colored stucco facade and clay tile roof. The interior rooms consisted of living and dining rooms, a kitchen and adjoining breakfast room, two bedrooms, and a bath.

On April 17, 1935, a devastating hail storm hit Ponca City with hailstones the size of baseballs or even larger, and many roofs were destroyed—in particular clay tile roofs. The Whitehurst tile roof was one of them. After the disaster John decided the time had come to add his proposed second story. He told Charlotte, "We'll have that second story up soon." John's second story addition was not completed until early 1938.

With this addition to the house, the first floor back bedroom became a music room

FACING PAGE: CHARLOTTE LINCH WHITEHURST ON HER WEDDING DAY AND THE ORIGINAL HOUSE. BELOW: KATHRYN, CHARLOTTE, MARGARET, AND BARBARA IN THEIR WADING POOL.

CHARLOTTE, MARGARET, BARBARA, AND KATHRYN. ABOVE: THE GIRLS READY FOR A SUNDAY DRIVE.

that now opened into the formal living room. The music room had knotty pine walls and a back staircase leading to the second floor. The second floor had three bedrooms and two baths. The two girls' bedrooms were referred to as the pink and blue bedrooms, for obvious reasons. The master bedroom's mantelpiece was probably the most unique feature in the house. Above the fire box opening are three large scenic inlaid Mexican tiles flanked by two vertical bands of glass block. At the corners are more vertical glass block panels with rounded edges. This unusual mantelpiece was even more unique when a light switch was turned on above the bed headboard. Behind the glass block panels are colored Christmas tree lights that give a warm "Christmas glow" all year long. I remember my first view of this unusual mantel. I was so fascinated by its design I would often incorporate it into my imaginary house designs in my "growing up" years in Ponca City.

The Whitehurst kitchen cabinets were painted in tones of gray accentuated with green glass knobs. There were two small pullout bread boards used for Charlotte's homemade bread making (she was a marvelous cook) and also a miniature pullout board to accommodate a meat grinder.

The additional lot on the three-quarter acre homesite had a chat-covered tennis court with canvas-taped markings. (This was sometimes called a deck tennis court.) Every spring, the Whitehurst girls' first chore was to pull weeds so they could play the game of tennis. The tennis court was Mrs. Whitehurst's idea since she and her siblings had played tennis on the Linch family farm located just south of the I.O.O.F. Cemetery. In the summer of 1942, the Whitehursts' eldest daughter, Charlotte Virginia, became a counselor at a girls' camp near Sparta, Tennessee. Her family decided to surprise her and have the chat tennis court converted to concrete. Sadly, their beloved Charlotte was struck and killed by lightning just two days before she was to return home.

But the new concrete tennis court continued to play an important part in the Whitehurst family life for roller skating, birthday parties, graduation dinner parties (I can still recall the abundance of baked ham that was prepared by Thad Tucker) and even

CLOCKWISE: THE FAMILY HOME TODAY. HAND-DECORATED TILE IN THE BATHROOM; FIREPLACE IN THE MASTER BEDROOM WITH GLASS BLOCKS LIGHTED WITH COLORED LIGHTS AND DECORATIVE TILE INSETS; HAILSTONES (WITH GOLF BALLS THE SAME SIZE), APRIL 17, 1935.

a wedding reception for the Whitehursts' granddaughter, Annie Douglas, in 1981.

Mrs. Whitehurst lived in the family home until her death in 1984. She was a gifted quilter, learning the art at the age of nine. Charlotte Linch Whitehurst completed more than ninety quilts during her lifetime. They are now owned by her children, grandchildren, and great-grandchildren. What a treasured inheritance to leave to one's family.
—JBW

132/134 GLENSIDE AVENUE
The Pat's Potato Chips Houses

Long before there were Lays and Pringle Potato Chips, Ponca City had Pat's Potato Chips. And they were delicious. The company was founded by L.B. Patterson, whose two sons, Claude (Pat) and Harry Patterson, were also in the food service business. The October 26, 1926, issue of the *Ponca City News* told of the two Patterson brothers opening their candy shop in the recently completed Poncan Theater Building. To be known as the Poncan Candy Shop, the new eatery was described as "A room paneled throughout in solid walnut with booths, tables, magazine racks, and showcases trimmed in the same material. The most modern fountain has been installed for the preparation of fancy drinks and light lunches, and a good line of candies and the usual line of tobaccos will be carried." The article concluded: "The Patterson brothers hope their new establishment will appeal to girls and women too."

The Patterson brothers were raised in Guthrie, Oklahoma. Pat arrived in Ponca in 1916 and Harry two years later. The brothers' other venture in the food business in Ponca City was the Theater Candy Shop that adjoined the Murray Theater just one block away from the Poncan Candy Shop. This establishment soon became the meeting place for downtown businessmen and was referred to

A BIRTHDAY PARTY AT 134 GLENSIDE.

HISTORIC HOMES OF PONCA CITY AND KAY COUNTY ~ 119

GLORIA, ROSALIE, AND JOYCE IN FRONT OF PAT'S ENGLISH INN. BELOW: JOYCE AND GLORIA BUILDING A SNOWMAN AT 132 GLENSIDE.

simply as "Pat's." In the late 1920s, Harry Patterson won first place in a newspaper contest as most popular Ponca citizen. He even beat out E. W. Marland and Lew Wentz.

In the early years of the Great Depression, the Patterson brothers were forced to give up their theater candy shops, but soon ventured into another type of eatery service called "Pat's English Inn." Located at the intersection of Virginia and Overbrook Avenues in Acre Homes, Pat's English Inn was an instant success. Housed in a small English style cottage that had been built by E. W. Marland as the sales office for his Acre Homes sub-division, its address was 301 Virginia Avenue. The original architecture was perfect for an English Inn.

Pat's English Inn's specialty was barbecue, and the *Duncan Hines Directory for Good Eating* listed it as the best barbecue in this part of the country. The Patterson brothers commissioned a local artist to paint two murals on the sloping ceiling wall panels. One depicted a rural English country scene and the other (my favorite) featured silhouettes of Pat and Harry seated opposite of each other at a high-backed booth, not unlike those in the inn. This scene was viewed as if you were standing outside and looking through a multi-paned window.

In later years, Harry Patterson would take over the Pat's Potato Chips enterprise and the making of its fine product. I firmly believe that at one time there was not a single Ponca citizen who had not tasted a Pat's Potato Chip.

Pat and his wife had one daughter, Patsy Patterson Steanson, and Harry and his wife, Viola Flannery Patterson, had three daughters, Joyce, Gloria, and Rosalie. Viola was an accomplished violinist. Before moving to Ponca City, she played with the Oklahoma City Symphony. She continued her music career in Ponca, playing for various civic and club organizations and later becoming president of the northwest district of the Oklahoma Federation of Music Clubs.

The Patterson houses are both located on Glenside Avenue. The one at number 132 was the first house and the second one was next door at number 134. In later years Harry and Viola Patterson built a home on East Whitworth in Acre Homes.

Joyce Patterson Dunham and I were in the same grade at Roosevelt Elementary School. We enjoyed our drawing sessions together, during which I would design an imaginary house and she would draw its furnished rooms. —JBW

GATHERING FOR THE HUNT, NEW YEARS DAY, 1927.

904 E. OVERBROOK
Master of the Hounds House

When E. W. Marland brought the sports of polo and fox hunting to Oklahoma, they soon became the favorites of Ponca's "elite set," often referred to as Ponca's "horsey set." Major Donald L. Henderson was Master of the Hounds for Marland's fox hunts and also acted as referee for Marland's polo matches.

One of Major Henderson's responsibilities was to instruct the hunters on how to conduct themselves during a fox hunt. First you sent out the fox, next you released the hounds, and then the riders were to follow the hounds. Unfortunately, many participants never quite understood the procedure. They would often override the hounds and end up chasing the fox instead.

The small red foxes that were hunted were not indigenous to this part of the country and instead were brought from Pennsylvania by Marland. Today, there are many descendants of the "Marland foxes that got away" still living in the area. It also was reported that these early-day foxes would raid the local farmers' chicken houses and whenever a bill for the lost chickens was presented, it would be paid immediately. Bob Baughman remembers hiking in the fields north of the Marland mansion that were part of the Marland game refuge: "There were areas separated by barbed-wire fencing. But these rows of fencing would be interspersed with a panel of wood fence where the horses and their riders could jump the fence without the danger of being entangled in the barbed wire."

After the takeover of the Marland Oil Company by Continental, Marland's successor, Dan Moran, immediately fired Major Henderson. Until Henderson could find another position, E. W. and the Polo Association continued to pay his salary.

Don Henderson and his wife, Edith, left Ponca City, never to return again. The second owner of the "Master-of-the-Hounds house" was Robert E. Clark, one of Marland's executives who continued to work for the Continental Oil Company. Bob Clark and his wife, Ruth, would live in their home until 1943, with their sons, Bob, Jr. and Nate. Bob, Jr. recalls the fun of growing up in the Acre Homes neighborhood. The boys and their friends would dig caves on nearby vacant lots, build tree houses, and have monumental water-gun fights.

Behind the Henderson-Clark house was the original Lakeside Polo Field that extended from Elmwood to North Fourteenth Street. The polo field received its name from the Lakeside Refinery that once bordered the polo field on North Fourteenth Street. The polo games would continue during the early Clark years in the home, and Mrs. Clark would often serve lemonade to spectators on their rear terrace.

The Henderson-Clark home, built in 1928, was designed by Marland's chief architect, John Duncan Forsyth. For many years, its English cottage style architecture retained the original exterior color scheme, dark brown painted shingles at the second floor and native fieldstone at the first floor level. Today, with the many additions and its heavy cedar shake shingle facade, the house's exterior shows little resemblance to the 1928 original.

Bob Clark, Jr. remembers his family home as a gathering place for many leaders of Ponca City: "E. W. Marland spent many evenings in our home, along with Dan Kygar, Grover Blackard, Bill McFadden, and Harold Osborn. They would discuss local and national politics and the economic events of the day. It was the years of the Great Depression, so there were no frivolous discussions and no poker games." —KA

920 OVERBROOK
Lincoln-Gibson House

Bert H. Lincoln was a graduate assistant when he taught chemistry at the University of Colorado, and Sara Alice Blackburn was one of his students. After a teacher-student romance, Bert and Sara were married in 1927. The Lincolns relocated to Ponca City where Bert would serve as chief chemist for the Continental Oil Company. Bert and Sara Lincoln had three children, Gilbert, Sara Ann, and John, and in 1938 they built their dream house located at 920 East Overbrook.

In the designing of her home, Sara used architectural drawings and details from books and articles showing the restoration of Colonial Williamsburg, Virginia. These sources were the inspirations for the design of her home. Tall, stately columns greet you at the front entrance, and the red brick facade, with its Flemish bond pattern and white painted trim, gives the Lincoln home a special look. This combination of style and materials definitely says "Georgian architecture," which is the basic style of many buildings in Colonial Williamsburg. The Georgian style was developed in England during the reign of the three King Georges, King George I, King George II, and King George III.

Sara Lincoln was noted for her charm and hospitality. Through the years she filled her home with antique Victorian furniture, including many pieces belonging to her family. Dr. Bert Lincoln specialized in chemical research and, after studying the practice of law on his own, became a patent attorney in 1933. During his years with Continental Oil Company, Lincoln gained 164 patents for Conoco. In 1954, he was made a fellow in the English Royal Society of Arts and, from 1958 to 1968, he was head of the Department of Chemistry at Arkansas State University in Magnolia, Arkansas.

Sara Alice Blackburn Lincoln died on April 18, 2003. She was ninety-seven. When recalling her years in Ponca City, Sara often said, "Never let it be forgot that once there was a Camelot—called Ponca City."

The Dr. Bob Gibson Years

In 1959, the Lincoln home was sold to Dr. Bob Gibson and his wife, Marian Cuzalina Gibson. Bob and Marian, both lifelong residents of Ponca, had two children, a daughter, Toni, and a son, Bobby. In 1950, Dr. Bob joined his father's medical practice in Ponca City.

Through the years, Dr. Bob Gibson practiced family medicine the old fashioned way. From his practice, he developed a loyal following of patients who were appreciative of his "country doctor" ways. He was taught by his father, Dr. R. B. Gibson, to listen to the patient and use his skills to help whether he used medicine or just kind words. House calls and the willingness to stay with a patient through the night, if necessary, became Dr. Bob's hallmark.

Although trained as a medical doctor, he was a great believer in alternative holistic medicine as it related to general practice and to the treatment of cancer. This unwillingness to accept only conventional methods contributed to his forced "early retirement" at the age of seventy-six. Dr. Bob Gibson died on September 13, 2002. At his funeral, a fitting epitaph was sung at the conclusion of the service. It was the well known song, "I Did It My Way." —JBW

133 WHITWORTH
The Harper Baughman House

In 1951, Harper Baughman, the son of former mayor R. P. Baughman, was also elected mayor of Ponca City. During his administration as mayor, the Po-Hi Marching Band performed in Washington, D. C.'s inaugural parade for President Dwight Eisenhower. A new terminal building and concrete runways were also dedicated at the Ponca City airport, and Lydie Marland left Ponca.

Harper and Betty Baughman built their dream home in 1938. The Colonial Revival-style house is located at 133 Whitworth, a street that is filled with beautiful homes in various styles of architecture. The original floor plan for the Baughman house was conceived by a house featured in the *American Home* magazine. From this concept came the couple's dream home.

The exterior of the house is clapboard siding painted white. The gabled wing on the front of the house has a large bay window with diamond-shaped leaded window panes. It is interesting to note that the steep pitch of this gable matches the pitch of the nearby large dormer window. The front entrance of the house leads into the foyer that extends to the living room across the rear of the house. French doors in the living room open onto a screened porch that overlooks the spacious back yard. To the left of the front entrance is the formal dining room with its beautiful front bay window. Between dining and living rooms is the staircase rising to the second floor. This wonderful pine staircase looks down into the pine-paneled living room. In fact, the Harper Baughman home is ablaze with pine wood paneling that reflects Harper's love of wood. On the right side of the entrance foyer is a small hall that takes one to a small den and beyond to the first floor guest bedroom. The kitchen is on the front of the house and connects to the double car garage. The second floor contains the master bedroom and the son, Bob's, bedroom. Bob's bedroom had a pine wainscot with a shelf to display his collection of miniature dogs.

Bob Baughman and I were in the same class at Roosevelt Elementary School. Because his last name started with a "B," Bob always sat on the front row. And because my last name started with a "W," I sat on the back row. How I envied Bob his preferential front row seat.
—JBW

124 ~ HISTORIC HOMES OF PONCA CITY AND KAY COUNTY

121 ELMWOOD

House on the Street of Many Children

In 1925, builder and lumberman T. R. Boggess borrowed $9,000 from the Ponca City Savings and Loan to build a house at 121 Elmwood. He sold it to J. M. Barker for $11,000. In 1941 the house was sold to Oakley B. Lloyd. Actually, the Lloyds first moved into the house in 1930, and lived there until 1935, when Lloyd was transferred by Continental to Chicago. In 1938, they returned when Lloyd was appointed general sales manager for Continental Oil Company, a position he held until his retirement in 1956.

Oak Lloyd and his wife, Kathryn Forsyth Lloyd, had a daughter, Patricia Lloyd Deisenroth (Pat), and a son, Oakley B., Jr. (Bill). Pat remembers that twenty children lived on her long block on Elmwood and its adjoining block on Overbrook, all within three years of the same age.

"We rode bicycles down to the 'woods' (the uninhabited wooded block with its deep ravine on the west side of Elmwood). We played Pony Express, which included the use of our cap guns, and ping pong and archery in our back yard," Pat remembers. She also tells of "how we watched for the ice man who gave us shards of ice that he chipped off a block of ice." She also recalls that the boys in the neighborhood dug dark and scary caves on a nearby vacant lot.

The Oak Lloyd home is a two-story frame house in the Colonial Revival style. Its symmetrical facade had as its focal point a classical front entrance complete with sidelights and an arched wood fan panel above the door. At each front window were dark wood painted shutters sized to fit the openings. (Today most shutters come in one size regardless of the window width.) The center entrance foyer was flanked by the formal living and dining rooms, and at the end of the hall was a small breakfast room connected to the kitchen. In 1952, this space was enlarged into a family room. Off the living room was an open porch that held a porch swing, and at its corners were two trellis panels covered with fragrant honeysuckle. Later this porch would be enlarged to adjoin the family room and become a screened area ideal for eating and entertaining. The second floor had three bedrooms.

The deep back yard had thirty-three lilac bushes that eventually became the size of trees. When a late spring frost was forecast, the family went out with clippers and scissors in hand, cutting armfuls of blooming lilac and placing them in the basement laundry sinks. The next day many beautiful lilac

THE HOUSE IN 1959. BELOW: THE BARBECUE PIT IN THE BACK YARD, NOW BEING RESTORED TO ITS 1940S CONDITION.

bouquets were distributed to friends and neighbors.

The rear section of the back yard holds an outdoor stone barbecue, hand-built in 1940 by Oak Lloyd. Lloyd enjoyed cooking out, and his family recalls the many long trips from their distant kitchen with trays of hamburger and supplies for a meal in the back yard. Today this barbecue is being restored to its original 1940s state.

Another memory was of the time a neighbor's pet skunk escaped. The Harold Osborn family was noted for unusual pets, such as a burro and a de-scented skunk named Odie. Mrs. Osborn called her neighbors asking them to look out for Odie, who had wandered away. Later neighbors called saying that Odie was hiding in their garage. The Osborn's house man, Roscoe, was sent to retrieve the family pet from its hiding place. It was not long before Roscoe discovered the skunk he was holding in his arms was not Odie.

The many children of what was once the "street with many children" have grown up, and the house at 121 Elmwood is much changed too, with narrow plastic shutters and its classical front entrance covered with a small front porch. —JBW

128 ELMWOOD
The Johnson-Pitts House

In 1927, the L. F. Johnson house cost $10,500 to build. Located at 128 Elmwood, the home was designed by Mr. and Mrs. Johnson and built by a well-known contractor of the day, Richard Sherbon. The exterior walls of the house are of "clinker brick" from a brick plant in Shawnee, Oklahoma.

Clinker brick was once a throwaway mistake, bricks placed too near the flames in the kiln when firing. The bricks would become overheated, fuse out of shape, and often bond to each other. But with its unusual shapes and colors, it became popular and was often placed as accents in a regular brick wall or even used to cover an entire wall, which is the case in the Johnson house facade. With today's modern technology, clinker brick is a thing of the past except when it is desired for additions or special effects. When this is the case, clinker brick can be produced, but at a greater cost than regular brick.

The massive chimney on the front of the Johnson house is of native limestone with smaller pieces of the stone placed at random in the brick walls. The driveway, front walk, and porch are the original bluestone paving.

The interior detailing of the Johnson

house is typical 1920s except for the rough stucco living room chimney breast. With its clinker brick surround at the fireplace opening and the massive custom made wrought-iron screen, the fireplace has a very southwestern look. One enters directly into the long rectangular living room. At the north end of the room are French doors leading into the library. At the opposite end of the living room is the formal dining room, and beyond is the small breakfast nook with its original corner china cabinet. Behind this space is the galley-type kitchen. All of the original light fixtures have been preserved, including a Czech glass pendant chandelier in the dining room and a five-arm wrought-iron fixture decorated with painted leaves and berries in the library. This latter fixture reminds me of the massive chandeliers and wall sconces on the lower level of the Marland Mansion but on a less grand scale.

In 1967, Richard and Connie Pitts purchased the Johnson house. Dick was employed by Frontier Federal Savings and Loan in 1956 as an accountant. Upon his retirement in 1986, he held the office of president and chief operating officer of the American Bank. One afternoon after hearing the family dog's continuous barking, Connie Pitts investigated and found an owl cornered in one of the basement window wells. She called her neighbor, Jack Barrett, who was ninety-two years old at the time. Jack was an ornithologist and soon identified the bird as a Barred Owl. After Jack had rescued the injured owl he delivered it to the O.S.U. School of Veterinary Medicine in Stillwater, Oklahoma, for treatment and release.

It was just another case of being a good Samaritan. —KA

824 N. FOURTEENTH STREET
C. W. Arrendell House

Dr. Cad Wallder Arrendell was born in Trade, Tennessee. His first and middle names honored a physician who saved his father from a leg amputation after a train wreck. The local doctors wanted to amputate the leg, so Cad's father traveled to the Mayo Clinic for a second opinion. A Mayo Clinic physician, Dr. Cadwallder, saved the injured leg, and so when his next son was born, he was given the name Cad Wallder Arrendell.

Dr. Cad Arrendell graduated from Tulane Medical School in 1905. In 1906, he opened his medical practice in Ponca City. Cad married Edna Wheeler, a native of Missouri, whose family had relocated to Pawhuska, Oklahoma. The Arrendells had two sons, Cad, Jr. and Gene. Both would follow in their father's footsteps and become medical doctors.

Cad and Edna purchased their Ponca City home in 1925. Located at 824 North Fourteenth Street, the Mediterrean-style house had been built by E. W. Marland for one of his executives. The moving date for the Arrendells to their newly acquired home was April 15, 1925. The exterior of the house is stucco with a cut stone surround at the front entrance. Matching cut

HISTORIC HOMES OF PONCA CITY AND KAY COUNTY ~ 131

stone windowboxes appear at two of the second floor windows, and the wide roof overhangs are supported by a series of decorative brackets.

Upon entering the home, you are in the long living room with its heavy rough plaster walls. These walls carry the Mediterranean theme throughout the house. Adjoining the living room on the front of the house is the dining room that is separated from the living room by a graceful curved arch. At the south end of the living room was an open porch surrounded by arched openings. In later years, the Arrendells converted this space into a sunroom. A rear entrance hall houses the staircase to the second floor with its three bedrooms. (Actually this rear entrance served as the primary entrance to the Arrendell home.) A servants' quarters was added off the kitchen. One of its occupants was Thad Tucker, who many will remember as the owner of Thad's Blue Moon Barbecue, on South Avenue in Ponca City.

Dr. Gene Arrendell remembers his father as a kind and generous man and a very loyal servant to his patients, for he also considered them friends. Gene remembers his mother as a clever and artistic person who enjoyed gourmet cooking. He also remembers lying in front of the fireplace on a wintry Saturday afternoon listening to the Metropolitan Opera on the radio.

Young Gene was a member of the "cavalry troop" of Colonel Henderson (Marland's Master of the Hounds). They would go out on Saturday mornings and ride their horses west of where Lake Ponca would be located. There they would divide into troops and practice cavalry maneuvers and have sham battles. Afterwards the troop would stop at a nearby farmhouse for hot cocoa and doughnuts.

There were two riding clubs, one for boys and one for girls. In 1928, the two groups were invited to a children's riding party at the Marland Mansion. It was held in the recreation room (now known as the inner lounge), where a miniature sterling silver loving cup with a guest's name engraved on it marked each place. Thad Tucker prepared the meal, which included fried chicken and homemade biscuits. Afterwards the young guests were entertained on the east lawn of the mansion with a miniature circus complete with trained dogs, Shetland ponies, and monkeys.

But the crowning glory of the party was dessert—molded sherbets in the form of riders on brown horses, each jumping over a green hedge. —JBW

YOUNG GENE ARRENDELL LEAVING FOR A MOTOR TRIP TO TEXAS, WASHINGTON, D.C., ANNAPOLIS, AND NIAGARA FALLS.

THE MARLAND ESTATE

Inspired by a trip to Florence, Italy, where he visited the Davanzati Palace, E. W. Marland hired the architect John Duncan Forsyth to design a new mansion for him. It was constructed in 1925-1928 at a cost of $5,500,000. Marland lived in his new dwelling for less than eighteen months before he lost control of Marland Oil Company and was forced to move out of the mansion and into the nearby artist's studio.

Though he would never gain back his old wealth, Marland became a successful politician and was elected to the United States House of Representatives in 1932, later becoming Oklahoma's tenth governor.

The Marland Mansion was sold to the Carmelite Fathers in 1941, who in turn sold the property to the Sisters of Saint Felix in 1948. In 1975, the city of Ponca City purchased the E. W. Marland mansion and opened the estate to the public. — JBW

901 MONUMENT ROAD

Marland Mansion

In our research for this chapter on E. W. Marland's Mansion, we came upon two articles that are of great interest to the history of the mansion. The first article, from the *Daily Oklahoman* newspaper of May 10, 1930, recounts a visit with E. W. Marland in his recently completed mansion. The second article, written in the 1950s, describes a return visit after a twenty-year absence, by John Duncan Forsyth, the architect of the Marland Mansion. I had been familiar with the John Duncan Forsyth article about his return to the Marland Mansion for several years but my first reading of the *Daily Oklahoman* story occurred while doing research for the chapter on the Marland Mansion. While reading this historical and descriptive article for the first time, I got goose bumps.

These articles, both presented below, offer a wonderful insight into E. W. Marland's "Palace on the Prairie." —JBW

From the *Daily Oklahoman*
May 10, 1930, Ponca City, Oklahoma:

If ever the State of Oklahoma builds an art museum, it will scarcely surpass the Marland Mansion.

Ernest Whitworth Marland did an unprecedented thing when he threw his home open to the thousands that flocked to see the unveiling of the Pioneer Woman Statue, which Marland gave to the State of Oklahoma.

Other thousands couldn't come, but the next Sunday saw them riding into the estate so thick that headlights touched bumpers, and the kindly host, quite surprised by the crowd, slipped into a tuxedo and went to a friend's house for tea. The home will not be open to the public again, but the reception, fine as it was in spirit, met with a worthy response, for despite the priceless tapestries, pottery and Aubusson rugs that lay about in the mansion, not a piece was disturbed by the Oklahomans who came to visit that day.

So now the dreamer-half of oilman E. W. Marland tells us why he planned his house as he did: 'You see, I have always liked to look off in the distance, down a vista,' Marland explained. 'That is one of the features of the gardens of Hampton Court in England that are so beautiful, so I thought I would try it here. When you view the Avenue with the Pioneer Woman Statue it looks across to my old home. (Marland's intent was not to have a road on this vista, but make a park open to the public.) The one straight ahead is a copy of the gardens of Versailles that Marie Antoinette loved. And the one to the left is just a soft hall of trees that leads off into the woods.' Marland's eyes gleam as he views the beauty of the scene. It seems as if he doesn't own it, but is just an art-lover that has dropped into an art museum for some pleasure.

As you enter the entrance hall there are two flights of stairs rising from the dull red and blue tiles on the hall floor. You also look down a flight of fifteen steps, through a long corridor, hung with rich, rose-colored Persian rugs, into the famous Marland banquet hall. Sitting low in the house, the rear view of the room overlooks the large swimming pool.

To the right in the entrance hall is a small parlor, paneled in soft, brown woods, used to receive callers' hats. And to the left is the formal dining room, also in wood paneling. If you ascend the stairs from the entrance hall, the arches with the Japanese murals form a hall running the length of the parlor floor, and revealing through their pillars double sun parlors that are a picture from every angle, for the arches are creating depth and variety. Sunlight can fall into these comfortable, informal parlors at any time of the day, but the furniture and colors seem to help the gay feeling of the rooms. The right parlor is filled with groups of dull gold furniture, upholstered in black, that seem to breathe a challenge to bridge players. The left parlor has great, comfortable cane chairs, covered in bright colored chintz that say, on the other hand, 'Oh you're too weary for cards. Get a magazine and read.' And all around pots of ferns, cerise bougainvilleas, and ivy vines make the rooms look more like gardens than interiors.

The arched hall leads on to the jewel of all the rooms—the Music Room (Ball Room), a serene, soft gold and ivory room that holds such art objects as many museums do without. It is easy to see that Marland loves the beauty. He goes over to one Louis XV chair. It is part of a large grouping—a dainty, dull gold frame covered with tapestry. 'These aren't exactly antiques,' Marland explained. 'The new frames were put on about 150 years ago. But this is genuine Aubusson,' and he points to the tapestry on the chairs. 'And those?' he asked. He looks to the simple white stone walls where two pairs of wall tapestries hang over either side of wrought iron doors. The tapestries are ivory background with rich rose patterns—the one touch of sprightly color in the room.

'Oh those are not so old,' he explained, 'But how do you like the canvases?' By the tone of his voice you know you have reached the center of the house for him. For on either side of a high, white stone fireplace, beautifully carved, are two long colorful canvases, one of George Marland, the adopted son—roguish, at ease in a yellow polo shirt and white trousers. The other canvas is Mrs. Marland, caught in a swing of the tarantella, wearing a white Spanish dance costume.

VIEW OF THE SOUTH SALON, MARLAND YEARS.

LEFT: SOUTH END OF THE BALLROOM
BELOW: A VIEW OF THE SALONS, MARLAND YEARS.

Between the two portraits is a gesture that would be difficult to find in any other millionaire's home—but typical of 'E. W.' There is a stern kindly bronze head of a woman on the fireplace that is none other than 'Mother Jones,' the famous Socialist leader, a friend of Marland's and a character he admires. Two pedestals at one end of the room hold the Bryant Baker model of the Pioneer Woman that won the contest and the Lynn Jenkins model that was placed second. At the other end, two other pedestals hold the well-known 'Bacchanate and Child,' and a beautiful torso by Jo Davidson, one of the sculptors who also entered the contest.

On the top of the fireplace in Marland's upstairs study are two fine bronze heads, one of E. W. and one of George. They sit on either side of a painting of Infanta Isabella, done in the Middle Ages, and found for the home by a French concern that was at work for two years gathering the Marland art collection. Marland has chosen soft green walls, toning into a velvet rug in a darker green for his study. At each end are double bookcases with conch-shell patterns, forming arches over them. Naturally, red should give emphasis to such a room, and it enters in fine bookbindings, in the pattern of Crewel embroidery used

LEFT: FIREPLACE IN E. W. MARLAND'S BEDROOM. NOTE THE CARVED HORSE HEADS AND POLO GEAR. ABOVE: THAD TUCKER SERVING COFFEE IN THE HUNT KITCHEN OFF THE GREAT WINTER ROOM.

to throw over a day lounge, and in the tapestry of heavy drapes. From the chair at his desk, Marland can look down onto the swimming pool, or out to another lake set in a frame of Lombardy poplars and elms.

In another room there are a pair of unusual book ends done by Bryant Baker—bronze models of Marland's hands that stand upright to hold the books. They bear the inscription: 'Workers, not alone of materialistic things, but of beauty, these hands of the builder of parks and shrines, and of the dreamer who tried to understand and better the lot of his fellow men, cast from life May 8, 1928, and presented to E. W. by his friend, Bryant Baker.' [I discovered these bookends in an antique shop in Oklahoma city several years ago, and they were not for sale. I recently checked on them and they had been sold. I believe the Marland silver tea service is still in one of Ponca's bank vaults. The deceased owner of the tea service also owned the elaborate silver centerpiece bowl with its Marland monogram which was also in the same location. I am told the centerpiece bowl is missing. Do you think it might be sitting on a Ponca City dining room table?]

The three vistas seen from the sunrooms also can be seen from Mrs. Marland's bedroom. And such a room! It seems waiting for Marie Antoinette. All of the details are done in the Louis period. Alencon lace covers the bed. Pure white Cararra marble forms the carved fireplace. The dresser is dull green and gold over which hangs a long French mirror. The deep orchid rug is perfect to set off the luxurious day couch of pink satin, heaped with silk cushions. A dainty screen with panels of hand embroidered pink satin is topped with beveled glass panels.

The banquet hall on the lower level features the entire history of the southwest on its painted beamed ceiling. The colors look, even now, as rich as the yarns in an antique rug. But they are expected to grow even more beautiful with age. At one end, over an immense inglenook and fireplace hang two pictures of the southwest in its early days that hung in England from 1791 to 1929, when Marland bought them. They were originally painted for an English earl who was so taken by our Southwest that he brought an artist to America to execute the two oil paintings. On another wall hangs a tapestry, a copy of a painting at the nation's capitol building in Washington, D.C. Called 'Westward Ho,' this tapestry could only be created after Congress

ENTRANCE TO THE MARLAND
MANSION.

took a special vote permitting the copy. [Today, this tapestry hangs at Frank Phillips's Woolaroc near Bartlesville, Oklahoma.]

An adventure lies in the long baronial table and the court chairs flanking it in the banquet hall. Marland comes of an English family and naturally he wanted some English furnishings in his home. He found an authentic Charles II walnut banquet table and two matching chairs. Then he had a wood carver make a matching table and an entire set of matching chairs. Now only Mr. Marland can tell which pieces are the originals.

Only an airplane can give one an idea of the entire setting for the Marland Estate. Lakes, darted with islands and covered with solemn looking squadrons of wild geese, circle the house on three sides. Soft flanks of dark green trees, natural as any very old wood, make a setting for the swimming pool on the back of the mansion. But to its front a parade of soft elms and evergreens border the drive to the house. The studio is another stone structure behind the mansion which Marland has built to house whatever painter or sculptor who wished to use the building as their workplace.

The final resting place for the twelve Pioneer Women who traveled the United States for half a year, for the public to see and vote upon, stand on dull, wooden pedestals, at regular intervals along a patio like porch that connects to the studio." [Now also at Woolaroc. They were purchased by Frank Phillips.] —JBW

FIREPLACE AND INGLENOOK AT THE LOWER LEVEL OF THE "WINTER ROOM";
BELOW: A SCENE NEAR THE SWIMMING POOL DURING THE CARMEL PRIORY YEARS.

NOTES ON THE RESIDENCE
OF THE LATE E. W. MARLAND
BY ITS ARCHITECT

The existence of an abandoned stone quarry originally used as a crusher depot by the Santa Fe Railroad became the determining factor in the location of the Marland mansion. Its deep excavations were used for the magnificent swimming pool that was in place long before any design was started on the mansion. Because of the abundance of stone at the nearby quarry, it was decided that this material would be used for the exterior of the house.

The selection for the style or period of architecture for the mansion was largely determined by Mr. Marland's ideas as to the function and purpose of his new home, which

Thursday, Feb. 17, 2005

ROBERT S. CROSS / Tulsa World

Beverly Schafer (left), John Brooks Walton and Susan Ducato will gather at the Skelly Mansion on Feb. 24 for a special evening for patrons of this year's Moveable Feast event.

Moveable Feast to feed nonprofit center, library

Get ready to travel along with a Moveable Feast.

The Oklahoma Center for Nonprofits and The Tulsa Library Trust will have the feast from 6:30 to 9 p.m. March 4 at the Hardesty Regional Library.

The evening will feature authors, food, music and wine.

Event patrons also will be invited to a special evening Feb. 24 at the home of Jeff and Susan Ducato — the historic Skelly Mansion. John Brooks Walton, author of "Tulsa's Historic Homes," will be a special guest and will speak on the history of the mansion.

Authors at the feast will include William Bernhardt, P.C. Cast and Michael Johnson, who will read from and discuss their books. Don Ryan will provide the music.

Participating restaurants will include Johnny Carino's at 41st Street and Sheridan Road, Mazzio's, Organic on Brookside, Billy Simms' BBQ, HoneyBaked Ham Co. and Cafe and others.

Old Village Wine & Spirits, Select Wine & Spirits, and Grape Ranch of Okemah are providing wine.

Proceeds will go to raise money and awareness of the programs of the sponsoring agencies.

The Oklahoma Center for Nonprofits develops the professional skills of all nonprofit organizations. Services include consulting with nonprofit boards, volunteers and staff of nonprofit organizations. Adult

people & places

The Gelvin Foundation is once again the presenting partner of the event.

For more information, call Karen Fraser at the Oklahoma Center for Nonprofits at 579-1900.

Danna Sue Walker 581-8342
dannasue.walker@tulsaworld.com

Thursday, Feb. 17, 2005

patient with hypertenison

can they seek further help?

Reader: This question is way [beyond] my capabilities because I [cannot] determine, from your brief [description] the cause of the neurological [abnorm]alities. In fact, these puzzling [cases] seem to have challenged spe[cialists] in several cities. In my expe[rience] with patients who have trou[blesom]e diagnoses, I've often found [soluti]on if they are examined and [seen] in tertiary medical centers [where] super-specialists and sophisti[cated] equipment abound.

[There]fore, with a profound apolo[gy for] saying, "I don't know," I sug[gest th]at the patients investigate the [possibi]lity of seeking help in a med[ical s]chool atmosphere. Which one [the de]cision I'll leave to your broth[er's pr]imary care physician.

[I sh]ould add that while difficult [ca]ses are a welcome challenge [to mo]st doctors, really difficult diag[noses] can be a frustration beyond

belief. Despite the marvels achieved by medical science, we don't have all the answers and our limitations are no more evident than in the vignette you supplied. Clearly, your brother and his friend must be frightened and confused about their lack of diagnosis. This is the reason that I am suggesting further, expert analysis, instead of being content with inconclusiveness.

To give you related information, I am sending you a copy of my Health Report "Medical Specialists." Other readers who would like a copy should send a long, self-addressed, stamped envelope and $2 to Newsletter, P.O. Box 167, Wickliffe, OH 44092. Be sure to mention the title.

Newspaper Enterprise Association
Write Dr. Gott c/o United Media, 200 Madison Ave. 4th floor, New York, NY 10016

THE STARS

BY JACQUELINE BIGAR

THE STARS SHOW THE KIND OF DAY YOU'LL HAVE:
5★—dynamic 4★—positive 3★—average 2★—so-so 1★—difficult

Feb. 17, 2005

Happy birthday for Thursday: This year you are a powerhouse that cannot be stopped. Others respond to your imagination and musings. Schedule a workshop or some other type of intellectual or spiritual pursuit to contribute to your life. The quality of your life needs to be your major concern.

♈ ARIES (March 21 - April 19) .... 5★
Times change. Moods change. You can be very happy with others' attitudes. At this point, you'll easily clear obstacles that you have previously hit. Others you run into seem unusually cheery and happy. Tonight: Hook up with a friend.

♉ TAURUS (April 20 - May 20) .... 4★
You're on top of your game. You might find it hard to stop what is going on in your daily life. A project or plan seems to take on a life of its own. You accomplish more than a lion's share. Tonight: Figure out how much discretionary income you have.

♊ GEMINI (May 21 - June 20) .... 5★
With the moon in your sign, life finally becomes copacetic and easy. Isn't this more like it? Make calls and schedule a trip in the near future, perhaps a weekend getaway. Tonight: All smiles.

♋ CANCER (June 21 - July 22) .... 2★
Take your time, especially when dealing with a very special person in your life. You particularly enjoy your home and family. Why not do something special for someone incredible? Tonight: Keep plans private.

♌ LEO (July 23 - Aug. 22) .... 5★
Friends and associates prove to be a delightful distraction, one that helps you realize more of what you want from your daily life. Your style and way of communicating separates you from others. Tonight: Follow your friends.

♍ VIRGO (Aug. 23 - Sept. 22) .... 3★
What others cannot do has a way of dropping on you. If you're involved with a community project, you might feel as if you are the CEO, with so much to do. Deflate any tension by focusing on a possible purchase. Tonight: Reward yourself.

♎ LIBRA (Sept. 23 - Oct. 22) .... 4★
Reach out for more information. For some, your quest might be signing up for a seminar and/or talking to an expert. Whatever you choose will expand your life and opportunities. Just don't lie back. Tonight: Buy tickets to a concert or play.

♏ SCORPIO (Oct. 23 - Nov. 21) .... 4★
Your intuition guides you with a special partnership. Treat this person as you would like to be treated. Working as a team, you gain and allow the bond to grow even closer. Share your feelings more frequently with those in your life. Tonight: Be a duo.

♐ SAGITTARIUS (Nov. 22 - Dec. 21) .... 5★
Opportunities tumble into your lap. You might wonder what to do with your good fortune. Visualize more of what you want. Through this process you will come up with a strong set of directives. Tonight: Go along with someone else's plans.

♑ CAPRICORN (Dec. 22 - Jan. 19) .... 3★
You could easily feel overwhelmed with all the work you have. The [ef]ficiency will boost your image. Be careful when [handling y]our finances or paycheck, especially if there is [...]ake a walk after dinner.

[AQUARIUS (Jan. 20]- Feb. 18) .... 5★
[...] way that helps others open up to you. Where [...]sitant to reveal themselves, you make it down[...]nce away.

[PISCES (Feb. 19 - M]arch 20) .... 3★
[...]m home. You will get a lot more accomplished [...]ble. Others want to pitch in. A partner or asso[ciate brings] greater success and strength. Seriously con[sider the] home front. Tonight: Anchor in.

[Websi]te: www.jacquelinebigar.com

must not only serve for abundant living and entertaining, but as a background for the display of Mr. Marland's collection of 'Objects of Art.' The selection of a style for the exterior was narrowed down to the formal styles of Mediterranean, although the exterior of the building has no definite approach to any particular style. However, the Italian Romanesque influence may be observed not only on the exterior but also on the interior of the building.

Approaching the Porte Cochere on the west, attention is called to the stone corbels supporting the roof. Stone carver, Pelligrini, created the uncanny likeness of Mr. Marland's four dogs, carved in place without the use of drawings or clay models. Upon entering the grand Entrance Hall, one must notice its workmanship and scale that reflects the simplicity in grandeur similar to the designs of the Davanzatti Palace in Florence, Italy. The decorative ceiling in the Entrance Hall was executed by Vincent Maragliotti, a Florence mural artist of international reputation, who over a period of one year executed all of the many decorative ceilings throughout the building. Maragliotti along with his three assistants, slept, cooked and ate in the basement of the mansion.

To the left of the Entrance Hall is the Dining Room, designed in the Elizabethan Style and executed in English Pollard Oak, a rare and sought-after wood. The ceiling being of decorative plaster, was cast at bench level and then hoisted to its ceiling position and wired into place. The wall sconces in English silver are of particular beauty. To the right of the Entrance Hall is the Reception Room, with its floor to ceiling walls in American walnut. This room was executed in the style of Sir Christopher Wren, England's Georgian Period architect. As you ascend the pair of stairs to the upper gallery, you see the work of Pelligrini who created the two stone night owls whose eyes light up brilliantly when all of the other lights in the mansion are darkened. Another piece of fine stone-carving at the outside face of the northeast terrace is the cantilevered stone staircase with its stone brackets of mythological grotesque animals and birds carved in the manner of the great Chateaus and Palaces of Europe.

Mention should be made of the Garden Vista from the mansion leading down to the Pioneer Woman statue that has been assumed by many as the main approach to the house. Such was not the intent of Mr. Marland, for his plans were that the center portion of this long Vista would be in grass with a suitable landscaped border and walks on either side leading close to the main entrance gate of the house and returning back again. This would become a park type Vista open to the public at all times. The drive from the gate would turn to the west and terminate at the gate house on East Fourteenth Street.

The second floor of the Marland Mansion was occupied by Mr. and Mrs. Marland's separate suites, E. W.'s library and several guest suites and bedrooms. Mrs. Marland's beautiful Boudoir was designed and executed in the style of Louis XV with the walls being in lime wood paneling. Mr. Marland's Bed-Sitting Room has oak wainscoted walls in a restrained English Tudor manner.

Construction work on the Marland Mansion was started in the summer of 1925, and completed in 1928. However, the Garage and the Stables had been completed at an earlier date. The Artist Studio was completed about the same time as the Mansion.

John Duncan Forsyth, A.I.A.
Architect

1720 CHRISTMAS TREE LANE

Marland Stable

Built as part of the Marland game refuge, the Marland Stable is located to the north and west of the mansion. It was designed by John Duncan Forsyth and its facade is an integral part of the overall architecture of the mansion and its surrounding "dependencies" structures.

In the early 1930s the stable and its land were sold to Felix and Billie Duvall. Duvall was a prominent Ponca attorney whose clients included oilman Lew Wentz, the Miller brothers of the 101 Ranch, and the Vanselous ranching family. It was Billie Duvall who supervised the remodel of the "Stables." With her keen eye for design and detail, Billie made a "barn" into a lovely and livable home that has many wonderful details such as hand-wrought door handles to match those in the mansion.

The six horse stalls were converted into the living room, dining room, kitchen, and a bedroom. The tack room became the utility room while the feed and storage room became the master bedroom. The gallery that extends the entire length of the structure was once an open runway for Marland's prized steeds. Its dirt floors have been covered with stone and red bricks. The kitchen's exterior Dutch door was one of the original stable doors. One of Mrs. Duvall's major renovations was having the stone arched entrance removed and replaced with a window wall of glass that extends upward to the high vaulted ceiling in the living room.

In 1972, the stables were purchased from the Duvall estate by Charles and Betty Thompson. The second floor groomsman's apartment—a living and dining room, kitchen, and bedroom that had been used by the Duvalls as a guesthouse—was remodeled into two bedrooms. Its only access was an exterior stone staircase, but after one winter with two of the Thompsons' three children occupying these bedrooms, a graceful interior wrought-iron circular staircase was installed at one end of the long gallery. Created by Tulsa craftsman Ernest Weimann, this work of art certainly became a feature of the home's ground floor. Weimann also designed the fireplace accessories, which include the decorative grate, the screen with a horseshoe for its latch, and the coal shovel with a matching horseshoe for its handle.

Located at 1720 Christmas Tree Lane, adjoining a housing development created in the 1960s, the Marland "Stables" is listed on the National Register of Historic Places. Fortunately both the Duvall and Thompson families have carefully cared for and maintained the structure, and perhaps someday this historic structure and the ground it sits upon may once again become a part of the original complex and be owned by the citizens of Ponca City. —JBW

747 N. FOURTEENTH STREET

Marland Gatehouse

Designed by John Duncan Forsyth, the Marland gatehouse was to be the primary entrance to the Marland Estate. According to the master plan, the area between the Pioneer Woman statue and the entrance gate was to be a grassy mall open to the public.

Located at 747 North Fourteenth Street, the Marland gatehouse was the office of John Duncan Forsyth and his staff of draftsmen and architects while their drawings for the mansion were underway. The photograph of Forsyth's reception room shows several small chairs and a cupboard that were designed by Forsyth. The bronze statue atop the cabinet was executed by Jo Davidson, one of the sculptors selected for the design competition of the Pioneer Woman. Davidson was not awarded the commission but was asked by Marland to execute the statues of E. W. seated in a chair (now at the west end of City Hall) and statues of Lydie and George (now on display in the Marland Mansion.)

Another Jo Davidson commission is the large bronze statue of Oklahoma humorist Will Rogers located in the Will Rogers Museum in Claremore, Oklahoma. Forsyth was the architect for the Will Rogers memorial building and because of his long friendship with the sculptor, we may guess that Forsyth was indirectly responsible for Davidson receiving that commission. Forsyth and Davidson were both students at the Beaux Arts School in Paris.

Also located in the Marland gatehouse was the very private office of E. W. Marland. The passageway leading to Marland's office contained a hand-forged wrought-iron gate. According to legend, when the gate was closed, E. W. was in his office and not to be disturbed.

One of the best known owners of the Marland gatehouse were Laura Streich and her husband, John. Laura was a leader in historic preservation and she loved her unusual home. It was after I met Laura that my interest in Ponca City and the Marland mansion again resurfaced.

My hope and dream for the Marland gatehouse is that someday it too will be a part of the Marland Mansion and, perhaps, become a visitors' information center for the city and even the state. This conversion might include a brick drive leading off North Fourteenth Street through the gates and into a park-like setting with a motor court and picnic area. All of this would be beautifully landscaped with flowering plants similar to those that bloom around the entrance to the Marland Mansion today. — JBW

THE GATEHOUSE CONFERENCE ROOM.

The following is a story created by WBBZ Radio for one of their programs. It has been speculated that parts of this article are fiction and other parts are nonfiction.

So who knows? —JBW

901 MONUMENT ROAD
Invitation to a Party at the Marland Mansion

E. W. Marland is throwing a party at his recently completed mansion, and you are on the guest list. You arrive in your shiny new Ford at the impressive wrought-iron gates and are greeted by a uniformed attendant who asks to see your engraved invitation. With a curt, "thank you," he hurries to the gatehouse phone to inform the mansion of your arrival. As you arrive at the front entrance, a driver takes your car to be parked.

The massive doors open, and you are greeted by a gentlemen wearing a tuxedo, who greets you by your name. (Learned from the phone call at the gatehouse.) Inside, the mansion is filled with sounds of music from a chamber orchestra. You are helped with your wraps and then led to the ballroom where another man announces your arrival.

The ballroom is filled with beautiful artwork, tapestries, paintings and sculptures. In one corner of the room is a well-stocked bar of imported liquors and wines and as you cross the room, you step on deep Persian carpets.

It soon becomes evident that your host is more interested in his guests enjoying themselves than he is in the luxurious decor of his mansion. During dinner in the English Tudor dining room, a debate ensues over the size of the huge recreation room at the lower level of the mansion. Someone remarks that it would hold twenty Fords, but Marland believes it to be larger. After dinner, E. W. Marland leads his guests downstairs and, to your amazement, you see your Ford parked in the middle of the recreation room surrounded by many others. You are asked to count the cars. "Thirty," you announce. And Marland's reply, "I told you it was big."

So ends your evening at the mansion for it is time to retire to your private guestroom. You will need your sleep. Tomorrow will be your first Royal Fox Hunt.

John Duncan Forsyth

The following is a paper I gave at a seminar sponsored by the National Trust for Historic Preservation on small towns in America, held in Ponca City. I was asked to present this paper having served with Forsyth during part of my architectural apprenticeship years. —JBW

I would like to start the biography of John Duncan Forsyth with a quote from one of his daughters:

"My father was one of the world's 'Great Story Tellers.' He was full of anecdotes which he told with great skill to fit any occasion."

So with that introduction, Jack Forsyth was born on July 23, 1887, and although his birthplace has been listed as Edinburgh, Scotland, and Florence, Italy, it was probably Kingkettle, Scotland, a small hamlet near Edinburgh. For a brief period he attended the Ee' Ecole Des Eeaux Arts in Paris studying to be a portrait painter, but was soon discouraged in this endeavor and architecture was recommended as a profession by his professors. He next was apprenticed to Alexander McCulloch, an architect in Edinburgh. In later years, Forsyth would reflect how his father probably paid for his apprenticeship to cover his son's many mistakes. Jack Forsyth also attended the Harriot-Wall Engineering School and later did additional studying at the Edinburgh Royal College of Arts.

John Duncan Forsyth arrived in New York City in 1908 and worked for the firm of Hoppin and Cowan, Architects. Later he was associated with the architectural firm, Warren and Whitmore, but his great mentor was John Russell Pope, whom he worked with for several years. Pope was known for his many magnificent public buildings including the Jefferson Memorial, the National Archives Building and the National Gallery, all located in our nation's capitol.

During World War I, Forsyth enlisted in the British Royal Flying Corps in Toronto, Canada, but was soon given an honorable discharge due to a leg injury occurring when he fell out of an airplane (fortunately the plane was on the ground when the accident occurred). Upon returning to New York City, Forsyth worked for the architectural firm of Murphy and Dana and in 1918 was sent to Shanghai, China, to establish a branch office. The firm's first commission in Shanghai was a school for "Yale in China," sponsored by Yale University. They also built several banks and an office building for the "Dollar Steamship Lines" in Hong Kong.

In 1921, Forsyth and his family returned to the United States and relocated in Tulsa, Oklahoma, where he became associated with the architect, John McDonnell. During this association he was instrumental in the design of the Tulsa home of John K. Cleary at 1224 East Nineteenth Street. Several years later Forsyth was to design a Ponca City home for the Cleary family. Located on a thirty-five acre estate the address is 13 Hillcrest.

In 1925, John Duncan Forsyth received the architectural commission to design the E.W. Marland Mansion in Ponca City. The Forsyths moved to Ponca City where Jack received several commissions prior to starting the Marland Mansion. After the completion of the Marland Mansion in 1928, Forsyth returned to Tulsa in 1929 and, during the 1930s, John Duncan Forsyth would design many of Tulsa's finest homes and mansions.

At the start of World War II, architects Frederick Vance Kershner, William Wolaver, Joseph Koberling, and Forsyth received the commission to design the Army Air Force base near Ardmore, Oklahoma. Upon completion of this project, Forsyth moved to California and for the remainder of the war worked for the United States Navy in the Sea Bees division, designing and building warehouses.

Forsyth returned to Tulsa in 1948, and attempted to reopen his architectural practice, but soon returned to California and established a practice in San Clemente. In the early 1950s, he returned once again to Tulsa and this time was successful in establishing his practice there. Former clients were ready to build new retirement homes and many of their children wanted to build their first homes not unlike the homes they had grown up in.

In 1908, Jack Forsyth married Ella Denison, an artist whom he had met while they were working together in New York City. They returned to Scotland for a brief period where one daughter, Ellen Forsyth Bellingham, was born. During this time period the family lived in Loch Gilpied, where Forsyth designed a church project. In 1928, he married Ann Top who died in January of 1939. They had one daughter, Anne Lindsay Forsyth. Jack's next wife was Peggy Williams with their wedding being held in the John Cleary home in Ponca City. During this marriage they were divorced and then remarried twice. In 1949, Forsyth married his fourth wife, Mary, who died in 1959. And in 1961, Jack Forsyth

married his fifth or sixth wife (depending on whether you count the number of divorces), Edith Ache.

John Duncan Forsyth died on October 5, 1963, at the age of seventy-five or seventy-seven depending on which newspaper you read. This difference in age was probably created by the Great Storyteller himself.

ARCHITECTS AND THEIR HOUSES

Ponca City has been fortunate to have had many talented architects who helped create its many beautiful homes. Several of the early-day Ponca architects include Harold Flood and George J. Cannon. C.N. Terry of Wichita, Kansas, designed the DeRoberts-Calkins mansion on West Grand Avenue and Elmer Boillot of Kansas City designed the Pickrel-Casey home on North Tenth Street. Boillot also designed several of Tulsa's fine homes and mansions.

Probably the two most significant architects were Solomon Layton of the Oklahoma City firm of Layton, Smith & Forsythe, who was the architect for Marland's Grand Avenue home, and John Duncan Forsyth, who was the "in-house" architect for the Marland Mansion. Two other architects who designed many beautiful and interesting Ponca City homes were William Caton of Winfield, Kansas, and Robert Buchner of Tulsa.

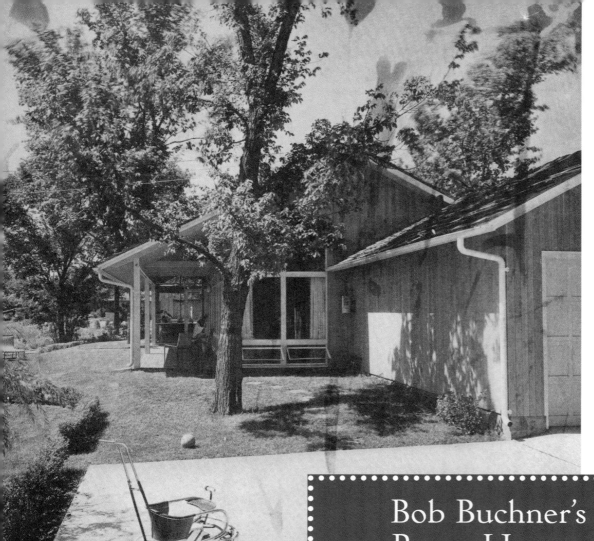

REAR VIEW OF THE FRENCH RESIDENCE, 117 NORTH TWELFTH STREET.

Bob Buchner's Ponca Houses

Bob Buchner was born in Tulsa, Oklahoma, of pioneer parents, and graduated from the University of Michigan with a degree in architectural design. After serving in the military, he worked for architects in Kansas City and New York City, and in 1950 returned to Tulsa to establish his own architectural practice. Bob Buchner soon became well known for his contemporary style of architecture. His designs had aspects similar to those of Frank Lloyd Wright and Bruce Goff. Goff was one of the designers of Tulsa's Boston Avenue Methodist Church. But Buchner's architecture definitely makes a strong statement. It clearly says "Bob Buchner, Bob Buchner."

In 1951, Buchner designed his first Ponca City home, for Mr. and Mrs. Phillip R. French. Located at 117 North Twelfth Street, the French home was an exercise in good, clean design with its steeply pitched roof and large window walls at the rear of the house. Because of its fine 1950s design, the French home was selected by the National Cedar Shingle Association to appear in many national magazines. The June 28, 1954, issue of *Time* Magazine featured a full-page article which included the French house. Titled "The Value of the Architect," the article noted that "Tulsa architect Robert E. Buchner turned the back of the house to the street, which cuts down traffic noise and makes it possible to locate the living and dining areas away from the neighbors on either side. This makes it possible for the picture windows to frame real 'pictures'."

Bob Buchner's next Ponca City house was for Mr. and Mrs. John Cleary. The Clearys had built their large country estate home in 1926. Designed by John Duncan Forsyth, that home still remains one of Ponca's grand houses. But the year was 1952, and people were moving away from large homes with staffs of servants to simpler ones with a single housekeeper. Casual living was in vogue and formal dining rooms were a "no, no." The Cleary house, located at 45 Hillcrest, sits on sloping land that was once part of the original

Cleary estate. The tri-level design has the master bedroom one level above the living room area. The Clearys had requested a ramp rather than steps up to the master bedroom. I remember "inspecting" the Cleary house near its completion and still recall the large circular fireplace opening in the living room.

In 1953, Buchner designed a home next door to the Cleary home for the Clearys' daughter, Constance Cleary Clark, who still resides in her Buchner house. In describing the two Cleary houses Buchner noted: "The

THE MERLE LONG RESIDENCE LOCATED AT 1500 PIONEER ROAD. ABOVE RIGHT: THE LIVING ROOM IN THE LONG HOUSE.

Cleary-Clark house at 41 Hillcrest was a very low budget design but I enjoyed the challenge. There were no budget restrictions on the John Cleary home, and I would describe it as being a garden-style design with lots of glass and designed for its sloping lot."

After the Cleary family houses came the Merle Long house at 1500 Pioneer Road. Built in 1954, the original design featured open "fin-like" elements extending out from the apexes of the elongated living room. Unfortunately these designs elements are no longer a part of the house.

Another Buchner-designed Ponca home was for S. V. McCollum. This house is located on Monument Road. After living in it for just a few years, McCollum was transferred to Houston, Texas, by Conoco. Upon their relocation to Texas, the McCollum family asked Buchner to design their Houston home, which was almost a duplication of their former Ponca City house. Today the McCollum house is surrounded by tall landscaping. A carport has been added and, as with the Merle Long house, some of the original exterior design elements have been removed.

The last Ponca City Buchner house is located at 900 East Overbrook. It was created for William and Cleo Bruce. Bruce was a retired Conoco vice-president. Buchner describes the Bruce home as "one of the best houses I ever designed." —JBW

CLOCKWISE FROM UPPER LEFT: LIVING ROOM OF THE JOHN CLEARY HOUSE AT 45 HILLCREST; EXTERIOR FACADE OF THE JOHN CLEARY HOUSE; NIGHT VIEW OF THE CONSTANCE CLEARY CLARK HOUSE AT 41 HILLCREST.

RIGHT: EXTERIOR DETAILS OF THE CLEARY HOUSE.

Architect Robert E. Buchner

This design by Robert E. Buchner for a compact house features related space areas rather than more traditional room separations. Conceived for a young couple with a small son in Ponca City, Oklahoma, this "friendly" house of contemporary design was built for ease of maintenance and direct circulation of all rooms.

FACING PAGE: THE WILLIAM BRUCE HOME AT 900 EAST OVERBROOK. BELOW LEFT THE CONSTANCE CLEARY CLARK HOUSE. BELOW RIGHT: ORIGINAL EXTERIOR OF THE S.V. MCCOLLUM HOUSE AT 1560 MONUMENT ROAD. LEFT: ARTICLE FROM *TIME* MAGAZINE, JUNE 28, 1954.

William N. Caton was a well known regional architect who practiced his profession in Winfield, Kansas, from 1923 through 1965. He once described his work as "a complete practice of architecture but specializing in fine small homes." The town of Winfield, Kansas, has many Caton-designed houses, primarily located through the older neighborhood and, in particular, from the college down to the business district. W. N. Caton also left his mark on Ponca City beginning with his first Ponca house built in 1927, for George Miller, son of Colonel George Miller.

Other Caton-designed Ponca City homes include:

John Vance residence, 825 North Seventh Street

Jean Brisco residence, 819 North Seventh Street

Jay French residence, 145 Fairview

George Gay residence, 153 Fairview

Earl Pfeffer residence, 129 Whitworth

Lloyd Bird residence, 216 Virginia Avenue

H. Edwards residence, 1904 Lake Road

Stewart Clark residence, 124 Elmwood

M. M. Evans residence, 906 East Overbrook

Glen Clark residence, 117 Elmwood

Lea Clayton residence, 92 Elmwood

R. S. Ross residence, 127 Elmwood

In 1939, the Marland Estate Incorporated sold a lot, located at 825 North Seventh Street, to John and Ruth Vance. In the spring of 1940, the Vances completed their William N. Caton-designed home. The Vance house was constructed of concrete block walls with stucco veneer, giving the house a blend of English country and rural French feeling.

The floor plan of the house has often been described as that of a ship, for every space in this small compact house has been used to its utmost. The pine front door opens into a foyer with its limestone floor and small diamond patterned leaded glass window. Opposite the front door is another not-so-high pine door that leads into the powder room. The powder room has anoth-

William Caton's Ponca Houses

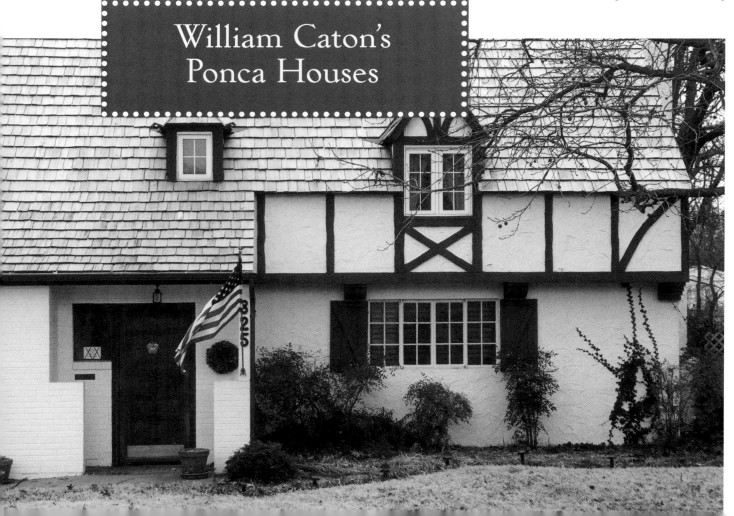

THE VANCE-RALEY HOUSE AT 825 NORTH SEVENTH STREET.

CLOCKWISE FROM TOP: THE GEORGE MILLER HOUSE AT 160 WHITWORTH; THE R.S. ROSS RESIDENCE AT 127 NORTH ELMWOOD; THE JAY FRENCH HOUSE AT 145 FAIRVIEW.

er similar small door that opens into the compact utility room. Under the staircase in the foyer is an even smaller door opening to a very compact coat closet. To the right of the foyer is the living room with its knotty pine walls and oversized fireplace that dominates the south wall of the room. Beyond the living room is the dining room and a small "ship's galley" style kitchen. Across the back of the house was a long screened porch that was later converted into a sunroom. The second floor of this delightful Caton-designed home has two bedrooms and a bath.

In 1996, John Raley, Jr., purchased the house. Raley had arrived in Ponca in 1969 to become a partner in the law firm of Northcutt, Raley, Clark, and Gardner. Prior to practicing law, he had served in the United States Navy. Following active duty, he continued to serve his country in the reserves for thirty-four years. In 1982, he retired with the permanent rank of captain. Raley also served his community—as mayor

HISTORIC HOMES OF PONCA CITY AND KAY COUNTY ~ 155

of Ponca City from 1980 to 1983. During his term in office, DuPont purchased all of Continental Oil Company's stock, making it a wholly owned subsidiary. Mayor Raley's term also saw the restoration to its original design of the facade of the Masonic-Security Bank building at South Third Street and Grand Avenue. John Raley is now Judge Raley, municipal court judge for the city of Ponca, and one of his favorite pastimes is participating in Civil War reenactments. —KA

TOP: THE LLOYD BIRD HOUSE AT 216 VIRGINIA AVENUE.
ABOVE: THE GEORGE GAY HOUSE AT 153 FAIRVIEW.

RURAL PONCA

An entire book could be written about the farms and ranches of Kay and Osage Counties. In Osage County in my youth you could travel down any of a number of interesting narrow lanes that led to large ranch homes built in the 1920s with Osage Indian government head-rights and oil money. It is said that the wealthy Osage owner of one of these fine houses purchased a very large and expensive antique dining room table on a trip to New Orleans. The shop made careful arrangements to deliver the table to Oklahoma. When the courier arrived at his destination, he came upon a large impressive ranch home many might call a mansion. The whole family was sitting under a tree in the front yard. When asked where they wanted the dining room table they said, "Just put it here under the tree where we will be using it." A classmate of mine lived in such a house, with a two-story stucco facade and red clay tile roof. At the attached porte cochere was the former owner's gas pump, just like the ones at service stations in downtown Ponca. The J. G. Paris ranch, just across the old Arkansas River bridge, was another interesting ranch in the Osage. Its large stone barn and two-story house were located along the old highway. My friend Halsey Davis and I used to take overnight campouts on the Paris Ranch. On one of these excursions, we arrived after dark. The next morning we discovered that we had set up camp in a small fenced pasture holding two very mean looking bulls. We left as soon as possible. —JBW

When Colonel George Miller founded his 101 Ranch in 1879, he built a semi-dugout structure on the south bank of the Salt Fork River that was used for the ranch's headquarters. In about 1890, the first permanent ranch house was built on the north side of the Salt Fork River but it was destroyed by fire several years later. In 1909, a new ranch house was built. It became known as the "White House" because of its white stucco exterior. The new Miller family home was fireproof with its steel and concrete structure and roof of asbestos shingles, for only the doors, flooring, and ornamental detailing were made of wood. Built at a cost of $35,000, the 101 Ranch White House soon became known as a showplace throughout the southwestern United States.

This seventeen-room Victorian-Colonial style mansion was steam heated and lit by its own power plant, and all of the furnishings were luxurious, including costly objects of art and fine paintings that decorated each room. A large collection of early-day curios, guns, and Indian costumes were also displayed throughout the home, and Indian rugs covered many of the polished wood floors.

The first floor of the White House was designed for entertaining, with its large reception hall and grand staircase leading to the upper floors. Off the reception hall were drawing rooms, a parlor and the large formal dining room. Nine bedrooms, each with its own bath, were on the second floor, and there were enough four-poster beds in the house to sleep 100 guests during the rodeo season. The grand staircase continued up to the third floor ballroom. Affectionately called "the attic," its walls adorned with pictures of buffalo and cattle.

The White House was kept cool in summer by thick white stucco walls and large windows positioned for good cross ventilation. Guests relaxed on the wide, shady porches and verandas where they could view the surrounding Salt Fork River Valley. The White House lawns were enclosed with a wrought-iron fence whose gates were always open to welcome the many visitors.

The 101 Ranch "White House"

Probably no other home in the Southwest had as many guests as the Miller's White House. From United States presidents and European royalty to the Indians and cowboys that worked on the 101 Ranch, tens of thousands of visitors came to view the operation of the world's greatest agricultural empire.

The White House guest book, always open on a library table, carried names of great political and social leaders. Many of these distinguished guests donned colorful cowboy regalia during their stay in the White House. Admiral Byrd of exploration fame had a tremendous thrill when he rode the elephants at the 101 Ranch. Another guest, bandmaster and composer John Phillip Sousa, was made a member of the Ponca Indian tribe and given the name "Chasing Hawk." Walter Teagle, president of Standard Oil company, sat on the floor in the White House holding a bust of the Indian Chief Geronimo while he and officials of the Gypsy and Humble Oil Companies discussed the price of crude oil.

Probably the most famous guest was humorist Will Rogers, whose public career had begun with the Miller Brothers' Wild West Show in Madison Square Garden. Rogers sang cowboy melodies all one night in the White House with Mrs. Gordon Lillie, wife of the famed Pawnee Bill, accompanying him on the piano.

Other visitors included Presidents Theodore Roosevelt and Warren G. Harding and presidential candidate William Jennings Bryant, who shook

MILLER BROTHERS AND GUESTS BEING SERVED DINNER BY THE WHITE HOUSE CHEF. BELOW: THE SITTING ROOM.

hands with Tony, the ranch's pet bear. John D. Rockefeller, Jr., John Ringling of circus fame, William Randolph Hearst of the Hearst Newspaper Syndicate, and Senator Charles Curtis (later Vice-President of the United States) were also visitors to the ranch. This famous house whose front door was never locked became the hub of a self-sufficient city that grew to a population of 3,000 citizens.

The 101 was broken up into acreages by the United States Government in the late 1930s, and the once grand White House was taken down in 1943.
—KA

160 ~ HISTORIC HOMES OF PONCA CITY AND KAY COUNTY

The Big V

From a *Ponca City News* article dated September 19, 1976 comes this account:

One of the most colorful figures of the Cherokee Outlet and also one of the best mule traders in the United States was William H. Vanselous, owner of the Big "V" ranch, located seven miles west and four miles south of Ponca City, Oklahoma. Born in 1863, in Three Rivers, Minnesota, Bill came to Kansas in 1877, when his father moved the family to a claim twelve miles west of Wellington, Kansas. Later the family moved to Belle Plaine, Kansas, and it was there Bill met Viola Frances Love. The couple were married in 1893.

In February of 1894, the couple moved to Oklahoma Territory where Vanselous purchased a settler's rights and filed on the claim which was two miles southwest of Blackwell. A poorly built shack was the sole improvement on the claim. Viola stayed alone to protect their rights against claim jumpers while Bill went back to Belle Plaine to bring their farm implements and household supplies.

Corn and cane were their first year's principal crops, but Bill also planted thirty acres of onions. When the onions were harvested, they were traded for supplies and groceries on trips he drove with a good team and wagon to Enid, Arkansas City, Ponca City, and Newkirk.

In 1895, the Vanselouses built a six-room house on the claim. The materials were hauled by teams from Newkirk, the nearest railroad drop-off. Viola was now living in luxury with her built-in sink and a zinc-lined bathtub. Three of the Vanselous children were born here, Beulah Zoella, Grace, and a son, Kay, named for Kay County. In 1907, another son was born and in honor of Oklahoma's statehood that year, he was named Okla.

Vanselous began leasing Ponca Indian land, and when a law was passed whereby land could be purchased from the heirs of tribesmen, he bought up adjoining land as fast as they would sell, until he had acquired 10,000 acres. The Vanselous family moved from the Blackwell area to the Big "V" ranch in 1904.

THE BIG V RANCH HOUSE, BUILT IN 1903, IS TODAY LISTED ON THE NATIONAL REGISTER OF HISTORIC PLACES.

Vanselous gained notoriety by buying an entire herd of 500 highly desirable, unbroken range mules at a San Angelo, Texas, auction. Looking over the mules prior to the sale, he decided they were the best he had ever seen. Dealers bidding on the best four or five mules were given the option of buying as many more as they wished from the herd at the same price. A stranger to most of those present, Vanselous threw the auction into an uproar when he announced he wanted to buy all of the animals in the herd and would pay by check. The sales company wired the Blackwell bank for confirmation and the check was accepted.

Vanselous built a 200-by-800-foot barn, complete with branding and breaking chutes and an outside breaking pen. He hired the toughest bronc busters available and following several weeks of breaking and training the animals were on their way to the St. Louis, Missouri, markets for shipping all over the United States. Mules with the Big "V" brand became the most popular in the nation.

Another product of the ranch had even greater distribution. In 1906, Big "V" produced 130,000 bushels of white "Wonder" corn. To handle the corn while getting ready to ship to parts of the country, Big "V" had two cribs, 500 and 600 feet long, with a capacity of 110,000 bushels.

Early in the 1890s, Vanselous turned a profit and prevented disaster for a number of surrounding farms. Neighboring farmers had grown large crops of hay and corn, but by harvest time there was no market for their products. Vanselous offered the farmers day wages to cut their own crops. Owning virtually all the crops harvested that year in the locality, he was able to sell $30,000 worth of hay and feed the next year to Kansas farmers, when their own crops failed.

The Big V ranch house was built in 1903. It is a large two-story white frame structure with two spacious porches. Rising above its flat terrain, the house in early day photos reminds one of a stage set out of *Lonesome Dove.* It is said that when the Miller brothers built their first house on the 101 Ranch it was patterned after the Big V ranch house. —KA

LOST PONCA

Like other Oklahoma towns, Ponca City has lost many fine and interesting houses over the years to growth and progress. Let us visit one of Ponca City's early-day homes and Ponca's first brick yard. They are now gone but should not be forgotten. —JBW

305 S. FIFTH

The George H. Brett Mansion

The George H. Brett mansion, which was truly the grandest house in early-day Ponca City, was taken down in 1976 to provide a parking lot and drive-in facility for the Ponca City Savings and Loan Company. The sad demise of this fine home also included the removal of its longtime neighbor to the east, the original Saint Mary's Catholic Church. Located at 305 South Fifth Street, the Brett mansion's grounds extended from East Oklahoma to East Walnut Avenues.

George Brett and his wife, Eleanor Thayer Brett, built their fine home in 1901, and it was the talk of the town. The front veranda had at its apex a covered porch supported by six Ionic columns extending two stories in height. The massive front door, with its leaded glass side panels and transom, led into a small tile-floored vestibule often called a "windbreak," for it prevented the cold wind from entering into the main parts of the house. From this small space, one entered through another door into the main foyer. In this very large room, a grand staircase with highly polished mahogany fittings rose to the upper floors. Behind the foyer was a cozy room with its own fireplace that was called the fireplace parlor. To the left of the foyer was the long living room extending the full depth of the house. At the far end of the living room was another fireplace, and on the front of the house at the opposite end of the room was a large glass "picture window," a very expensive luxury at the turn of the twentieth century. Above this window spanned a seven-foot-long fan-shaped transom panel in beveled glass done in the spider-web pattern. A matching window and transom panel were in the dining room on the opposite end of the front facade. (I own one of these beautiful transoms and would like to return it to Ponca when an appropriate place is found.)

To the right of the stair foyer was the formal dining room with its large bay window overlooking the south lawn. Pairs of massive mahogany pocket doors were used at the living and dining room entrances. A butler's pantry and kitchen completed the first floor of the Brett mansion. The second floor contained four spacious bedrooms, each with a very large closet, another novelty of the day. Three of these bedrooms had their own fireplaces. The attic was left unfinished but could have served as a ballroom, as attics often did in grand houses of that era.

The exterior of the Brett home consisted

164 ~ HISTORIC HOMES OF PONCA CITY AND KAY COUNTY

of cut limestone walls at the first floor and porch railings. The second and third floor walls were covered with wood shingles stained dark brown with white trim. A small balcony above the front door added to the ambiance of the front entrance.

George Brett made the run into the Cherokee Strip from the south and staked a claim near Perry, Oklahoma. But the next morning he found that two others had staked the same claim so Brett gave up his rights and left the claim for the others to fight over. Soon afterwards he came to Ponca and participated in the drawing for city lots. George drew two lot sites on which he built a two-room house with a shed kitchen at the rear. It was on this site that George and Eleanor Brett would later build their Ponca City mansion.

Brett was a very industrious merchant and rancher. He operated implement stores and harness shops in Ponca and Newkirk and also owned three cattle ranches in Osage and Kay Counties. He built several downtown Ponca City buildings, including the Kress Building, and was also one of the partners who created the Poncan Theatre structure. Many of his customers were Indians who called their merchant friend "Blue-Eyed George." Through the years, the Brett family would often return home to discover an Indian and his family sitting on their front porch waiting to talk to "Blue Eyed George."

The Bretts had four children, Harold (George), Ellen, Ruth Brett Parker, and Albert. The family's Sundays were spent in church and Sunday school at the First Presbyterian Church. The remainder of the day there was no work or entertainment of any kind. All cooking was done the day before and even their clothes were to be selected and laid out on Saturday. The family's household staff included Moses, the gardener, and his niece who served as cook.

I played my first game of "Post Office" in the dining room of the Brett home. George Brett's twin granddaughters, Helen and Ellen Parker, who grew up in the Brett mansion, were my junior high school classmates. These identical twins could only be identified by the small gold brooches they wore that spelled "Helen" and "Ellen." Another means of identification was to say, "Smile, Twinny," for Ellen had dimples. This particular game of "Post Office" happened on a late fall Sunday afternoon when a small group of us had ended up at the Brett home. The twins closed the large pocket doors for privacy, and we sat around the dining room table waiting for our name to be called. I cannot remember the rules of the game but I do remember when it was my turn to go into the kitchen with a selected member of the opposite sex. I cannot recall what actually happened but I do remember staring at the large kitchen range for a long, long time. —JBW

GRANDMOTHER BRETT WITH HER TWIN GRANDDAUGHTERS, HELEN AND ELLEN PARKER (OR IS IT ELLEN AND HELEN?)

Ponca's First (and only) Brick Yard

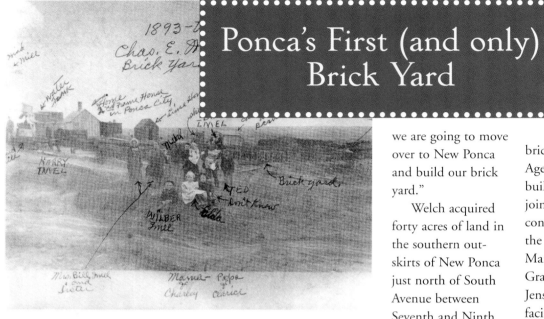

Charles Elvin Welch was born in Nemeha City, Nebraska, in 1857. His family would eventually relocate to Independence, Kansas, where they operated a brick yard and also engaged in masonry contracting. Charles and his two brothers would furnish the brick from the family brick yard and build the original mill on Caney River for Mr. Bartles on the site that today is Bartlesville, Oklahoma.

On September 16, 1893, Charles and his young son, Ted Welch, made the Land Run from the south border. He established a brick yard in Perry long enough to fire two kilns of brick and then would move on to the new township of Cross. Charles intended to build a brick yard in Cross, but one day he traveled to "New Ponca." Upon his return, Charles told his wife, Mary Thayer Welch, "There are a group of promoters over there and they will have a big town someday. The town of Cross will be dead, so we are going to move over to New Ponca and build our brick yard."

Welch acquired forty acres of land in the southern outskirts of New Ponca just north of South Avenue between Seventh and Ninth Streets. This became the site of the city's first (and only) brick yard. Clay for the bricks was dug from a creek that ran through the area and lime was hauled by wagon from a limestone quarry about four miles northeast of the brick yard. On his forty acres, Charles built his family a permanent house which stood at 702 South Ninth Street for many years. A newspaper article told of the Welch Brick Yard and their family home:

C. E. Welch began Monday to burn another kiln of brick. It contains 100,000 brick and he expects to be even more successful than in his former kiln, having been hampered less by continued wet weather. Among the brick are several thousand of fancy design which was a special order. He will soon commence the erection of a brick house for his own occupancy. One story in height, the stones for the foundation are already being hauled and mason work will begin at once. It will be a nice architectural design, and a credit not only to its builder, but to Ponca City. The distinction will be accorded it that it is the first brick house in the Strip.

The Welch Brick Plant shipped brick to the Ponca, Otoe, and Osage Agencies to be used in their headquarters buildings. Charles Welch's five sons would join him in the brick making and masonry construction business. Their work included the original Municipal Auditorium, the Marland Refinery, and E. W. Marland's Grand Avenue home; other projects were the Jens Marie Hotel and the Empire Refinery facility, which later became Cities Service. Many early day homes in Ponca used brick from the Welch plant.

Ponca City had a barter economy in its early years, and Charles Welch was very involved in the system. Farmers and workmen who needed groceries and supplies from the Polk Adams Mercantile would work at the Welch brick yard earning ten cents an hour (a decent wage at that time) which gave them one dollar for a ten-hour workday. They took their pay in "script money," which was accepted at the Adams store, and Welch would pay off Adams with brick he was using for the new Adams Mercantile building.

Today the site of Ponca's first (and only) brick yard is now Garfield Park. —JBW

NEWKIRK

Kay County was known as "K" County at the time of the 1893 Land Run. The U. S. Secretary of the Interior had designated the land where Newkirk is located as the county seat of "K" County and set aside four acres there for a county courthouse. The townsite was first named Lamereux in honor of the commissioner of the U. S. General Land Office. Less than a year later its name was changed to Santa Fe by a vote of the town's citizens. The town's first newspaper, the *Lamereux Democrat,* published only one edition—the following week the paper became the *Santa Fe Democrat.* But the Santa Fe Railway Company refused to accept that name for its railroad station, and so, for the third and final time, the people voted to change their town's name, to Newkirk.

Newkirk is noted for the fine native limestone buildings lining its Main Street. It is said to have the largest collection of these turn-of-the century style buildings in Oklahoma. —JBW

225 N. ACADEMY
Newkirk's First Hospital

In 1907, a Mr. Pochell from Iowa built a Victorian style house in Newkirk. Located at 225 North Academy, the Pochell property was "out in the country" when it was first completed.

Dr. Herman O. Gowey came to Oklahoma as a young physician in 1908, having graduated from Keokuk Medical College in 1907. Upon his arrival in Newkirk, he soon saw the need for a hospital. He purchased the Pochell house and converted it into Newkirk's first hospital. The curved foyer with its built-in window seats became the waiting room. During its hospital days, the ground floor housed the doctor's private office and his family's living quarters. The second floor's five bedrooms were reserved for patients and the nursery. Another room at the second floor level was surrounded with windows on three sides plus four gas lights. This was the hospital surgical area. The third floor of the house was used as the nurses' quarters.

Dr. Gowey retired in 1958. Through the years he had helped to increase the population of Newkirk by delivering scores of babies and keeping them healthy. Unfortunately, the good doctor enjoyed only a few years of retirement before he died in 1960. His widow became somewhat of a recluse, living primarily in the upstairs master bedroom. The yard became overrun with bramble bushes and weeds while the structure of the house deteriorated due to neglect. After Mrs. Gowey's death in 1975, the house stood vacant until 1978. Through the years various owners of the "old Doc Gowey place" have done continuous restorations on the house that was once Newkirk's first hospital. —JBW

415 S. ACADEMY

The Anton Horinek House

At the age of four, Anton Horinek immigrated with his family from Ousosi, Moravia, to America. The year was 1882, and the Horineks settled in Fairfield, Nebraska. They would soon relocate to Atwood, Kansas, and a year after the opening of the Cherokee Outlet in 1893, the family would settle in Kay County near the town of Mervine.

Anton married Frances Vrbas on January 10, 1905, in Lincoln, Nebraska. The newlyweds' farm was seven miles southeast of Newkirk. In 1917, Anton and Frances moved into Newkirk so that their five daughters, who spoke Bohemian, could attend Saint Francis Academy. Through the years, the Horineks would have five other children.

The Horineks purchased several lots in the Academy Addition, where they built their family home. The living room of the one-and-a-half-story house faces east and runs the entire length of the structure. The dining room features a built-in china cabinet with leaded glass doors. There was also a downstairs bedroom and behind the kitchen was a pantry and a bath. This original downstairs bath was divided into three rooms, the tub room, the lavatory, and the water closet room, with a connecting hall. The second floor had one large bedroom, shared by the Horinek sisters, and two other bedrooms for their brothers. As in many houses of this era, there were no bedroom closets. The exterior of the home had a stucco facade which today is covered with lap siding.

Anton Horinek died in 1965, and the house remained empty until one of his grandsons, Fred, and his wife, Joanne, moved into the family home in 1968. With this move, their children, LaDonna, David and Tracey, became the fourth generation of Horineks to live in the house built long ago by Anton and Frances. —JBW

HISTORIC HOMES OF PONCA CITY AND KAY COUNTY ~ 169

The Chappell Houses

Guilford A. Chappell and his father drove by horse and prairie schooner from northwest Missouri down through Kansas and into Oklahoma Indian Territory from Caldwell, Kansas. From there they traveled through what is now Medford, Pond Creek, Enid, Hennessey and finally south to Oklahoma City. Their return trip took them to what is now Ponca City, Newkirk, and Arkansas City. They followed the Santa Fe Railroad tracks through the Ponca Indian Reservation where they saw a large group of young Indian men coming toward them. Fearing trouble, they pulled out their guns only to discover it was some Indian students returning home from the Chilocco Indian School near the Kansas state line.

When they arrived at the present sight of Kildare, they found government surveyors platting the county seat site for the future Kay County. However, Chief Bushyhead of the Cherokee Nation had filed an allotment of land in the amount of 160 acres adjoining the townsite being surveyed, but the federal government objected to his taking an allotment adjoin-

228 W. NINTH STREET

170 ~ HISTORIC HOMES OF PONCA CITY AND KAY COUNTY

201 S. MAGNOLIA

ing the Kildare townsite. Because of this encroachment, the United States government elected to move the county seat to the present townsite of Newkirk making it the official county seat for Kay County.

Guilford Chappell and his father made the Land Run of 1893. G. A. would later recall that "After the gun was fired at twelve o'clock noon, we arrived in Newkirk at twelve-thirty and staked our claims. At that time, I was said to be the youngest Pioneer in Kay County."

Chappell was admitted to the bar in 1902. In 1903, he was elected mayor of Newkirk and he held the office of city attorney from 1905 to 1909.

The first Chappell house is located at 228 West Ninth. It is a single-story modest frame house that today has been restored with much attention to its original detailing. The Chappells started construction on their new home in August of 1928. The two-story brick-veneered home was completed in 1929. Upon its completion the nine room modern home with a two-story matching double garage was built at a cost of $20,000. The architect was George J. Cannon of Ponca City. The Chappells lived in their family home until after World War II when it was sold to another local attorney, John Warren. In 1980, the home was sold to Raymond and Kathleen Simons. The Chappell home has remained virtually unchanged throughout the years, even retaining the original downstairs wall coverings with their hand-stenciled designs.

The September 16, 1937, issue of *The Newkirk Herald* quoted from an interview with Guilford A. Chappell: "What a change forty-four years have wrought. Eggs were selling for five cents per dozen, butter for ten cents a pound and corn for ten cents a bushel. Then we had a horse and buggy, a team and wagon, sod house shacks, hitching racks, open saloons and axle grease. Today, we have paved roads, automobiles, flying machines, radios, high taxes, mortgages, old age pensions and grasshoppers." —JBW

207 S. MAGNOLIA
The Native Limestone House

Today, downtown Newkirk, Oklahoma, is recognized for its abundance of native limestone buildings. The first one was completed in 1893, the year of the Land Run. The others date from shortly afterwards to about 1911. The stone for these structures came from three quarries located east of Newkirk, and many "oldtimers" could tell which quarry the limestone came from by its color.

A northern Civil War veteran named Nehemiah Tubbs served as both architect and contractor for many of Newkirk's limestone buildings. Tubbs was contractor for the county's first court house and also the architect for Kay County's second court house and the He also built the Eastman National Bank Building located at 100 South Main. During its construction, Nehemiah fell from a two-story scaffold and broke both his legs. In 1905, Tubbs was traveling to Langston University to be interviewed as the architect for one of their campus buildings. Unfortunately, he died of a heart attack while lodging in a hotel in Guthrie, Oklahoma.

One of Newkirk's early-day limestone houses is located at 207 South Magnolia and was built in 1901. (Perhaps the house was built and designed by Nehemiah Tubbs.) The owners were the M. E. Scofield family who owned a local clothing store. The Scofields sold the home to Belle Stewart in May of 1905, and a member of the Stewart family lived in the house until 1920. There were three other owners until the property was purchased in 1977 by Jim and Diane Crossland. Some remodeling had been done to the original house in the early 1970s, and, as a result, the only original light fixture remaining in the house is in the living room.

The first floor of the Scofield-Stewart house had five rooms including an entrance foyer, living and dining rooms, kitchen and bath. At some point the original back porch was enclosed into a breakfast and utility room. The third floor of the home was originally the ballroom.

At the north side of the house there was once a porte cochere, for the Stewart family owned Newkirk's first automobile. —JBW

215 S. MAGNOLIA
The Lancet Dome House

According to my *Dictionary of Architecture* by Henry H. Saylor, a lancet is "a sharply pointed Gothic arch formed by a radius equal to the span of the opening."

Newkirk's lancet dome house was built in 1902 for J. K. Lacy, manager of the famous Kay & Kaw Mercantile. Lacy owned the property until 1909. The house is a wonderful example of Victorian architecture and probably featured a great deal of gingerbread trim when first built.

The focal point of this unusual house is its circular tower that is capped with a lancet dome roof. The circular room on the first floor is the living room with its fireplace and tiled hearth. The formal dining room features a bay window with stained glass transoms and window seat. Beyond the dining room is the kitchen. The second floor's circular room is the master bedroom. There are three other bedrooms and a bath on the second floor with perhaps the bath having once been a storage room. An interesting feature of the circular room's windows is that not only are the sashes curved to match the radius of the room but also the glass window panes are curved. There are two stained-glass windows at the open stairway landing which may have served as a sitting room in this Victorian era house.

John and Karen Hobbs purchased the Lacy home in 1974. During the restoration, the square front porch columns were discovered to be a later addition and the original turned-cypress columns were still intact beneath them.

In my opinion, Lacy's lancet dome house is not only the most unusual Victorian house in Newkirk, but it is the finest example of that style of architecture in Kay County. —JBW

HISTORIC HOMES OF PONCA CITY AND KAY COUNTY ~ 173

229 N. MAPLE
The P.W. Smith House

When P. W. Smith was elected temporary treasurer of Newkirk, his acceptance speech was given in his usual smiling manner. He assured the audience that he would do his best to care for the city's money and, "would not reserve more than 20 percent for his own use."

On September 23, 1873, P. W. Smith married his twenty-year-old bride, Sarah B. McIntyre, in Galios, Ohio. Before the wedding ceremony, P. W. presented the minister with a five-dollar gold piece. The minister thought the gold coin was only a two-cent copper coin and almost refused to perform the ceremony. However, the minister's wife explained to her husband that the coin was gold, and he quickly apologized.

Three days after the marriage, the Smiths located on a claim near what would become Udall, Kansas. Smith would become one of the founders of Udall as the townsite was located on part of his land. His wife, Sarah, gave the town its name, Udall. P. W. and Sarah Smith had five children, Alta R., Georgia Mae, W. Floyd, J. Wendell and M. Florine.

On September 16, 1893, Smith traveled to Arkansas City, Kansas, and via a special Santa Fe train, went on to Kirk, a small stock-shipping station, located one mile north of the present Newkirk. He next staked a lot in the business district in nearby Newkirk and, less than one month after the Land Run, he had built a frame structure and opened the first bank in Newkirk, the Kay County Bank.

In 1900, Kay County Bank's name was changed to The First National Bank. A federal law had been passed which provided that national banks could be capitalized for $25,000, and The First National Bank of Newkirk was the first bank in the United States to be chartered under the terms of this new statute.

The Smith house is located at 229 North Maple. An early-day photograph shows the original roofline to have a flat area at its apex. What appears to be a small metal or wood railing surrounds the flat roof making it an adaptation of a New England "widow's walk." Accessible from a trapdoor in the attic, the purpose of these widows' walks was to allow the wives of sea captains to be able to watch the horizon in search of their husbands' homebound ships. Unfortunately, many of the early day sailing vessels never returned, making the sea captain's wife a widow.

Today the Smith house is in great shape with all of its original "gingerbread" trim at the porches and upstairs bay window gable still intact. —JBW

174 ~ HISTORIC HOMES OF PONCA CITY AND KAY COUNTY

415 W. NINTH STREET

A Colonial Revival

Colonial architecture includes the classical Georgian style of architecture and also designs such as Cape Cod cottages, New England saltbox houses, and Pennsylvania Dutch farmhouses. These various Colonial styles experienced a popular revival in the United States in the late 1920s and through the 1930s.

Newkirk's Colonial Revival house was built in 1937. The Depression was finally coming to a close when Frank S. Midgley Sr. completed his lovely two-story family home. According to Earl Davis, manager of Hufbrauer & Son Lumber, "The Midgley house was the only new construction in Newkirk that year."

Frank Midgley had the original house on the site taken down, and the family lived across the street while their new home was being completed. Ross Ammand was the contractor for the project, and Harold Flood was the architect. The first floor of the house has a living room with a fireplace, dining room, study, and large country kitchen with a breakfast nook. The study walls are covered with knotty pine paneling, and there are a matching pair of corner china cabinets in the dining room. (Probably made by the old Curtis Millwork Company.) The second floor has four bedrooms and two baths. A laundry chute carried soiled linens to the basement laundry room. There is a playroom in the basement with a fireplace, where Frank, Jr. and his friends enjoyed playing. In later years, the playroom was where Santa Claus and his helpers sacked candy for Newkirk's annual Christmas parade. Frank Midgley Jr. also recalls dropping the kittens down the laundry chute where they would land in the laundry basket in the basement.

Originally there was a fish pond in the back yard where, many years ago, Frank Sr. planted an acorn from the Midgley Ranch east of Newkirk. There was just enough seepage from the pond for that acorn to flourish and today, it has become a magnificent oak tree.

The cornerstone from the Newkirk Elementary School, built in 1896 on North Main Street, now sits in the shade of that same oak tree. The carving on the cornerstone lists George (Frank, Sr.'s father) as a school board member. Another stone memorabilia in the Midgley yard sits atop the stone wall on the east side of the house. It is the "Midgley" stone from atop the building constructed on Main Street by George Midgley in 1900. — JBW

109 W. NINTH STREET

The Israel Tipton House

The Israel Tipton house was built in 1907, the year of Oklahoma's statehood. The home remained in the Tipton family until 1944, when Coe Davis McClellan purchased the property. Coe was the first woman to hold the office of county clerk in Kay County.

The wood frame house features wood fish scale shingles at the gables above the second floor dormer windows, and there is a large bay window at the first floor level. The downstairs has a parlor, living room, dining room, kitchen, and first floor bedroom. Upstairs there were three bedrooms. In later years, one of these bedrooms was remodeled into a bath. In 1928, an addition to the house enlarged the dining room and kitchen and added a new back porch.

In restoring the Israel Tipton house to its original grandeur, Les Burke utilized architectural artifacts from a nearby house. This nearby house was built in 1894 as the Midgley Mercantile store. In 1898, the Midgley Mercantile building was divided into two separate houses by architect, Nehemiah Tubbs. One portion of the structure was moved across the street while the other was left on the original lot. —JBW

609 W. NINTH STREET
The Sam K. Sullivan House

Mr. and Mrs. Sam K. Sullivan completed their lovely two-story home in 1923. The house was described in the March 2, 1923, *Republican News Journal:* "One feature of the living room was the fireplace of variegated colored Bachelder tile and black mortar. The mezzanine (staircase landing) added another attractive feature to the home, which was planned for ease and comfort and was modern throughout." Sam Sullivan was an attorney who practiced in Newkirk

Over the years, few changes have been made to this attractive home. The first floor of the Sullivan house contains the living and dining rooms, library, breakfast room, and kitchen. The second floor level consists of two sleeping suites, each containing two rooms and a bath. The basement has a furnace room, a bath with shower, a laundry and drying room, and a fruit room. The exterior of the Sullivan house cries out "Prairie Style, Arts and Crafts," with its massive vertical stone columns at the entrance, its low-pitched hip roof, and the horizontal band at the exterior consisting of stone at the first floor and lap siding at the second floor level.

The architect for the Sam K. Sullivan house was Frank Brown of Ponca City and the interior decorators were Henry LaMar of Kansas City, Missouri, and Frank Venable of Ponca City. —JBW

516 W. NINTH STREET
The Home of the Judge and Miss Mittie

Claude E. Duval was born on February 6, 1877, near Glasgow, Kentucky. He arrived in Newkirk in 1902, where he became associated with the W. S. Cline law office. In 1906, Claude Duval married Anna Page, and in 1907 he filed a deed for his recently completed home at 516 West Ninth Street. The design of the Duvall home could be described as an "American Four Square," and it is assumed that the original house was remodeled in the early 1930s to its present appearance. In 1909, Claude's wife, Anna, died. On May 1, 1918, Duval married the former Alma Bell.

Claude Duval was elected city attorney in 1903, and in 1908 he became the first county judge elected in Oklahoma after statehood and served in that capacity for a number of years. Over the next thirty years Duval spent his life on one side of the judicial bench or the other, and one of his most famous court cases was presiding over the foreclosure hearing of the famous Miller Brothers' 101 Ranch conducted in the 1930s.

During the 1920s, Mittie Gunn worked as housekeeper and cook for the Duval household. In 1993, at the age of 101, Miss Mittie was interviewed by a staff writer, Judy Landry, for *The Ponca City News*.

On a hot summer night in August, I met Mittie Gunn while she was out walking with her seventy-three old son, Leo. As they passed in front of the Duval home they paused to 'reminisce' as Miss Mittie put it. Gunn, twice widowed and the mother of thirteen children, was born in 1892, in Narasota, Texas. She, along with her parents, spent many years as sharecroppers picking cotton and doing odd jobs to make ends meet . Miss Mittie arrived in Newkirk with her family in 1923, working for several families in the area, which ultimately led to her long-standing employment with Judge Duval.

Although she never learned to read, Miss Mittie did not hesitate to talk about her life with the judge so others might read about him. 'I remember the Judge was a very kind man and he was always very nice to me.' A big grin appeared over her face when she revealed the Judge's favorite meal was 'fried chicken and hot biscuits.'

Mittie Gunn left the Duval household soon after the Judge's death in 1940. When asked what advice she would like to give to the young people today, Gunn said, 'They should try to make things better by their own living styles and by erasing violence, carousing, drinking and drug use. If they do these things they will be able to live as long as I have.— JBW

178 ~ HISTORIC HOMES OF PONCA CITY AND KAY COUNTY

Amanda E. Shanholtzer was a feminist ahead of her time. In 1904, she purchased a lot in Newkirk, and in 1905 she and her husband, Edwin, completed their lovely two-story home and did so without putting a mortgage on it. Amanda was not only an attractive woman but was also intelligent and frugal.

The Shanholtzer home boasted of four bedrooms, indicating that a family was forthcoming, but Amanda and Edwin would have no children. Other improvements to the Shanholtzer property included a carriage house, a barn, and a cistern. Edwin, or "Shan," as he was called, was a rural mail carrier. He died in 1957, and Amanda went on living in the family home until her death in 1965. After her death, a search of the home and her safety deposit box revealed no will. At the time of her death, there was only one known relative, Eletha M. Tuttle, a first cousin. However, before the probate of her estate was completed, the list of relatives became a two-page document. It would take three years to settle Amanda's estate and after much legal wrangling and appeals, the court found that her surviving relative was this cousin who was the sole heir entitled to inherit her estate. Upon Amanda Shanholtzer's death on February 24, 1965, her estate value was:

Real Estate, Oil and Gas Leases	$13,500
Stocks and Bonds	$73,834
Personal Property	$32,612
Estate Outside of Oklahoma	$16,000
Total Gross Estate:	$135,946

From 1965 to 1975, there were three subsequent owners of the Shanholtzer property. These owners replaced the old plaster with gypsum board and started a bathroom addition. However, the house was not livable until the next owners, Mickey and Deanna Cantwell, completed the restoration. In 1993, Reagan and Maggi Hutchason purchased the property. Today, the Shanholtzer's 1904 house is alive with the laughter of the Hutchason children, Luke and Meghan. Amanda Shanholtzer would be pleased. —JBW

429 N. CEDAR
Amanda's House

521 N WALNUT
The J. P. K. Mathias House

One of the grandest houses in Newkirk when it was built, the J. P. K. Mathias home is a large two-story structure built in 1907 on city lots that James Mathias had staked during the opening of of the Cherokee Outlet in 1893. In 1899, Mathias purchased an adjoining lot that was to be included in his building site. The house was located in one of the key residential areas of the day, across the street from what was then the North City Park, today Lion's Park.

The woodwork throughout the Mathias home is white oak. The downstairs room arrangement consisted of the front hall, living and dining rooms, sunroom, and kitchen. The upstairs rooms included three bedrooms, a maid's room, and a bath. All the rooms are quite large. The front hall has a built-in settee, and there is a built-in china cabinet in the formal dining room. The large third floor attic with its dormers and narrow staircase was ideal for storage.

James Mathias sold his North Walnut Street home to Joe Thomas, the owner of the City Drug Store. The next owner of the property was the Mahoney family who had relocated to Newkirk from Tonkawa, Oklahoma. — JBW

BLACKWELL

Blackwell, one of the Cherokee strip township allotments, was given to Andrew Jackson Blackwell. As the prime mover of the town, Colonel Blackwell platted the original townsite and shortly after the opening of the "Strip," held a drawing for the lots, which were fifty feet wide. In advertisements for the drawing for the lots, Blackwell was promoted as a "Garden Spot City," which apparently drew considerable interest. More certificates were sold than there were lots. Thus, as in the old saying, "The goods had to be cut according to the cloth," so the fifty-foot lots became twenty-five-foot lots in order to meet demand.

When the local post office was founded in 1893, the town's name was changed to Parker, for a small hamlet located across the river to the east. But the arrival of the railroad in Blackwell and an increasing threat of flooding caused the Parker hamlet to disappear, and so after two months the post office was renamed Blackwell. —JBW

402 E. BLACKWELL
The McKee-Becker House

Walter McKee was one of the developers of the Three Sands oil field. He began building his oil baron family home in Blackwell in 1935 and moved his family into it on his birthday, April 1, 1936.

Located at 402 East Blackwell, the McKee house is one of the city's outstanding homes of the period. Sitting on a corner lot, the two-story structure with its beautiful sloping roof has a facade of soft brown bricks. The two-story garage is at the rear of the lot.

Dr. Don Becker and his wife, Joyce, purchased the McKee house in 1955, and in 1970, they added a two-story addition to the rear of the house that connects to the garage. This addition includes a large family room at the first floor level and two bedrooms and a bath at the second floor. The original second floor of the house has three bedrooms and two baths.

The front porch floor of the McKee-Becker house is in a decorative quarry tile pattern while the massive front door has a pair of long brass strap hinges. The "peep hole" in the front door is an ornate metal grille through which one can see "who's that knocking at my door."

One enters directly into the living room of the McKee-Becker home and on the opposite wall is the finest example of an Arts and Crafts tile fireplace mantel that I have ever seen. The decorative tiles are in shades of muted browns and tans, and an almost Art Deco panel of flowers and plants is featured above the firebox opening. The same type of tiles continue onto the hearth with its raised curbing.

Above the mantel hangs a beautiful oil landscape painting and on another wall is a still life painting. Both of these fine pieces of art are from the McKee years. On the fireplace wall is a curved arch opening that leads to a small staircase hall. The opening between the living and dining rooms carries a similar design. Behind the dining room is the breakfast nook and kitchen.

The basement staircase leads down to a wonderful club room with a terrazzo floor. The focal point of this room is the unique fireplace's chimney breast. There are seventy-two types of stones represented in this wall, each a different color and size, and all were collected by Walt McKee from the Black Hills of South Dakota. Another interesting item is in the basement utility room. It is two of the original cabinets from the upstairs kitchen. Each unit is six foot in length; one houses the stainless steel sink and drainboard, and both are constructed of metal with white porcelain panels that sit atop metal legs. These cabinets have a commercial kitchen look and they are great. These seventy-year-old cabinets would fit right into today's "modern tech" kitchens.

One final note on the McKee-Becker house. It was very gratifying for me to see an addition on such a fine home that blends so well with the original architecture. One can scarcely tell that it is an "add on" of the 1970s. The architect for this addition was M. D. (Doc) Timberlake of Ponca City. In my opinion, Timberlake's design certainly enhances the original architecture of this fine home that we call the McKee-Becker house. —JBW

BASEMENT CLUB ROOM FIREPLACE WITH ITS SEVENTY-TWO SPECIES OF STONE COLLECTED FROM THE BLACK HILLS OF SOUTH DAKOTA.

AN EARLY-DAY GEORGE WASHINGTON'S BIRTHDAY CELEBRATION. GREENE DOWIS IS SECOND FROM RIGHT, FIRST ROW.

216 W. PADON

The G. E. Dowis House

In *The Last Run,* Mrs. Greene E. Dowis wrote of her early day memories in an article titled "Early Days as I Saw Them." "September 16, 1893—noon—found me sitting atop a straw stack somewhere between Hunnewell and Caldwell, Kansas, waiting for the soldiers out there to tell the anxious mob on the line to 'go get it.'"

Her husband, G. E. Dowis, was in the line making the race for his mother, who was a soldier's widow and entitled to a homestead.

In 1900, Mr. and Mrs. Dowis came to Blackwell from Wellington, Kansas, and, as Mrs. Dowis wrote in her article, "The First National Bank came with us." The founders of the bank were Ola Goodson, W. H. Burks, C. R. Felter, Charles Day and G. E. Dowis.

The Dowis home was built in 1920 at 216 West Padon. According to the original plans, the architect was Frank Wilmont Brown of Ponca City. The two-story frame structure is typical of many houses of that era. Upon entering the front door, you see

NAN DOWIS WITH NEIGHBORHOOD TWINS GWENDYNE AND GWENDOLYN MCCULLEY.

that the interior is alive with beautiful quarter-sawn white oak trim and cabinetry, and, would you believe, none of it has ever been painted.

Upon entering directly into the large and spacious living room, to your left you see the oak mantelpiece between two pairs of French doors with their beveled glass panels. The first pair of doors lead into the library on the front of the house. The west wall of the library is filled with oak bookcases with glass doors. The other pair of French doors opens into the formal dining room with its oak china cabinet wall and an oak plate rail just below the ceiling line. Behind the living room is the stair hall and a downstairs bedroom and bath. Off the dining room is a breakfast room and a kitchen that connects to the stair hall. Upstairs are four bedrooms, a bath and a "trunk room." Off the kitchen is a back porch that connects to an existing "wash house" with a sleeping porch above. According to the architect's plans, this existing structure was part of the original house that once stood on the lot. When the Dowises built their home, the old house was taken down except for this wing which became part of the new structure.

Mrs. Nan Dowis was known for the many teas she hosted in her home. Some of her teas honored the graduating senior high school girls and, through the years, became one of the social events of Blackwell. In her article about the early years in Blackwell, Nan Dowis recalls, "There were nine saloons open day and night, with player pianos running full blast, which kept the main street in a very disagreeable atmosphere for most people. We were glad when statehood was voted on by the people whose ideals were above the things that were bringing sorrow and shame to some of our citizens." —JBW

321 E. BRIDGE
The Denton House

James Fountain Denton had two sons, Willy and Wally. Both sons made the 1893 Land Run and both homesteaded on claims south and east of Blackwell. The brothers came from Howard, Kansas, where they had purchased a wagon in which to make the Run. The Denton boys' full names were William H. and George Wallace Denton, and their father, James, followed his sons to their claims with a wagon loaded with supplies.

George Wallace (Wally) Denton and his wife, Myrtle Florence. had five children, four sons and a daughter. In 1928, Wally and Myrtle built their beautiful Mediterrean style home in Blackwell. Located at 321 East Bridge, it was (and still is) one of Blackwell's outstanding residences. Its beautiful buff brick exterior is accentuated with cut limestone and decorative glazed terra cotta trim. The front facade of the Denton house has a small protruding front porch with a flat arched opening trimmed in cut stone. Across the front of the house is a long veranda that connects to the open porch on the east side of the house. The two living room windows flanking the fireplace chimney have beautiful arched transom panels done in glazed ornately embellished glazed terra cotta. Smaller versions of these arches are found at the side porch openings and the small window in the study. A barrel-shaped Spanish tile roof sits atop the second floor level of the house.

The front door of the Denton house is surrounded with leaded frosted glass sidelights and a matching transom panel. The entrance foyer, with its tall-case clock that once stood in Guthrie's Masonic Temple, leads to the kitchen and an almost enclosed staircase rises up to the second floor. To the right of the front door is the small study or office, and to the left of the front entrance is the long living room extending across the front of the house. At the end of the living room is a small alcove with French doors leading to the side porch. Also in the living room is a glazed terra cotta fireplace in a decorative pattern. Behind the living room is the dining room with rounded plaster corners. A custom-built corner china cabinet is designed to fit one of the curved corners. To the left of the dining room is a small bedroom hall leading to a first floor bedroom and bath. This room was designed for Grandfather James Denton and has its own outside entrance.

Off the dining room is the kitchen with its original cook stove

and beyond is the breakfast room. All of the light fixtures in the Denton house are original, and the fixture in the breakfast room is most unusual. Suspended from its chain, the shade is a cylinder of frosted glass with a hand-painted bird motif. At the top of the shade are two brass arms in a Chinese design and from each arm hangs a silk tassel. (I wish I could draw you a picture of the fixture.) The second floor of the Denton home has five bedrooms and two baths. One of the upstairs bedrooms has an interesting Art Deco style rug on the floor.

One of Wally and Myrtle Denton's sons, William Delmer, met his future bride, Margaret Owen, at a University of Oklahoma football game. They were married in 1934. For many years, Margaret Owen Denton taught English and drama in the Blackwell Public Schools and she was said to be an excellent teacher. The Dentons had one son, David Denton, who is a local attorney. In 1968, Bill and Margaret Denton moved into Bill's family home.

My first visit to the Denton home was in early 2004, and it was like walking into a time capsule. In 1928, Myrtle Denton and her daughter had traveled to Kansas City to work with a decorator and to select all of the furniture for their new home. Today, all of these original elegant furnishings are still in the home. (When taking my first tour of the Denton home I was tempted to put a few small items in my pocket but, every time I looked up, David was watching me.)

After Wally and Myrtle completed their grand home on East Bridge Street, they hired E. W. Marland's Japanese gardener, Henry Hatashita, to design and install the landscaping. Their grandson, David Denton, still has the original $12,000 invoice for the landscaping.

That was a lot of money in 1928. — JBW

311 W. BRIDGE

Mrs. Daisy Riehl's House

Mrs. Daisy Anderson Riehl came to Blackwell, Oklahoma, as a bride in 1895. To make the journey to Blackwell, it was necessary to take a train to nearby Kildare and make the remainder of the trip by stagecoach. Daisy was born in Emporia, Kansas, and after completing her formal education, she taught school in Florence, Kansas, for six years.

She came to Blackwell as the bride of B. M. Anderson, a local lumberman. With the loss of her husband in 1909, Daisy elected to remain in Blackwell and continue her work toward building a new community in a new state. In 1911, Daisy Anderson was united in marriage with John A. Riehl, who in the early days was employed with the Wells-Fargo Express. John would later become Blackwell's chief of police and a municipal judge.

The Chautauqua Club and its lectures furnished most of the entertainment in early-day Blackwell, Oklahoma. Through this organization, the establishment of Blackwell's local library came into being. Mrs. Riehl's home was the scene of the first "book shower" for the Blackwell Public Library.

In the late 1940s, Daisy Riehl learned that she was a descendant of Charlemagne, Emperor of the West, and was invited to become a member of the Order of the Crown. Her ancestry on her mother's side could be traced back to King Edward II of England and on her father's side to the nobility of Germany.

The Anderson-Riehl home's exterior is a melody of graceful roof lines and unusual and spacious windows. The focal point is the beautiful staircase tower with its stairstep and oval shaped window treatment. Originally all of these windows were of leaded and stained glass. However, today, only the small oval windows remain in this decorative glasswork. The porch at the east side of the house overlooks the spacious east lawn. The porch columns are unique in that they curve upward and downward from the top and bottom to the mid-point of the column. The graceful bay window at the porch area adds to the beauty of the Anderson-Riehl home.

In a 1949 interview with the *Blackwell Journal*, Miss Daisy reflected: "I have had a full life, and certainly, it would be hard to find anyone who has led a more active one."
—JBW

303 E. OKLAHOMA

The Sylvester Jack Walton Home

Sylvester Jack Walton and his wife, Virgie Greene Walton, built their house in Blackwell, Oklahoma in 1926. Located at 303 East Oklahoma, the two-story frame bungalow structure was designed by a Wichita, Kansas, architect.

Sylvester Jack worked in the Texas oil fields at one time. An attractive young roustabout who was one of his crew would later become the well-known movie star Clark Gable. Jack Walton also served on the Blackwell police force.

Located on the front half of a corner lot, the Walton house has a rather unusual floor plan for the wraparound porch features a large brick chimney breast on the north wall flanked by two pairs of French doors. One of these pairs of doors serves as the front entrance to the long living room with its decorative brick fireplace and bronze chandelier and wall sconces. An oak Craftsman style staircase at one end of the room leads to the second floor of the house. A graceful arched opening connects the living room to an even longer formal dining room. Behind the dining room are the kitchen and downstairs bedroom and bath. The second floor

THE MANILLA APARTMENTS AS IT LOOKED BEFORE THE 1955 TORNADO.

has four bedrooms plus a smaller bedroom that was originally the sewing room.

The back half of the lot has a two-story red brick apartment house built by the Waltons' daughter, Manilla Walton Kopisch, and her husband, Edward W. Kopisch. The cut limestone panel above the front entrance reads, "Manilla Apartments." (She was named by her grandmother after reading about the Battle of Manila. But her name was spelled with two "Ls.") The original apartment house, whose address is 120 North B Street, had attractive front porches for each unit but when the tornado of 1955 did extensive damage to the structure, these porches were removed.

Jack and Virgie Walton's other daughter, Dott, never married. The Waltons lived with their two daughters and son-in-law harmoniously all of their lives. With the advent of the Great Depression, the family lost the Blackwell home along with the Manilla Apartments. They would eventually relocate to Ponca City where Dott, at the age of forty, applied for her first, and only, job with the Continental Oil Company. (Dott lied about her age by subtracting thirteen years when applying for the job and she got away with it.)

After moving to Ponca, the family would often take a weekly Sunday afternoon drive back to Blackwell to view their former home. Traveling in their ancient Nash automobile, they would cover their legs with the car's red plaid lap robe in the winter and in the spring and summer months, the two hanging glass wall vases at the back seat would be filled with freshly cut flowers. Sylvester Jack Walton and Virgie Greene Walton were my grandparents and their only son, Ray Earl Walton, was my father. — JBW

203/215 W. PADON

Miss Louise's Family Homes

Alfred Bryan Porter was born in Hardin County, Tennessee, and his wife, Lucille Mitchel Porter was from the state of Kentucky. They were married on March 8, 1922. In 1921, Alfred had come to Blackwell to work for the Charlie Fyffe Funeral Home. In 1943, Alfred Porter opened the Porter Funeral Home at 215 South Main.

In 1954, the Porters purchased the house located at 215 West Padon. This fine home was built in 1918 by L. C. Moore, who had made his fortune in the Three Sands oil fields. The beautiful house with its white stucco facade and bright green tile roof is in the Arts and Crafts style of architecture, and many of the window mullions repeat that style in their design. The Moore-Porter house has a very open first floor plan with its spacious entrance foyer, its large living and dining rooms and its library. In fact, during the Porter years in the home, the first floor

203 WEST PADON.

215 WEST PADON.

was often used as a funeral chapel seating up to 100 people. In 1977, the Porters sold the property at 215 West Padon which they had owned for nearly twenty-five years.

Next door to the Moore-Porter house is another Porter house. Located at 203 West Padon, this turn-of-the-century structure was built before 1900 by the Stevenson family who moved into Blackwell from their rural farm. This frame Victorian style house sits on a large corner lot, and the outstanding element of its exterior is the turret located at one corner of the house. Just below the turret's roof line is a wide frieze of decorative garlands and flowers that gives this fine old house an elegant air.

At the first floor level of the turret, the walls are in a series of facets, but as you ascend the front hall stairs, the turret walls become circular and its decorative windows, with their colored glass borders, are curved to match the circular wall. Once inside the not-too-large foyer, you are greeted by this interesting staircase that wraps around the turret walls and up to the second floor of the house. Another unique feature of the stairs is that they still have their original natural stained finish.

There are two very large rooms off the foyer that also connect together. One is the living room and the other is the parlor. Both rooms have their own fireplaces with the parlor mantel being Victorian and original with the house. The living room mantel is decorative glazed ceramic tile, circa 1920s. Other rooms on the first floor are the formal dining room, kitchen and a downstairs bedroom. There are two bedrooms at the second floor level of the house.

The Porters had two daughters, Louise and Mary Jane. From 1942 until 1945, Louise Porter worked in the State Department's foreign mail office in Washington, D. C. In 1951, on New Years Eve, Louise Porter left New York City to serve a tour of duty with the United States Department of War in Tokyo, Japan. She remained in Japan until 1954, when she continued her journey around the world (quote, "With the help of my father," end quote.) Upon returning from her around the world travels, Louise returned to the family home at 203 West Padon, where Miss Louise Porter resides today. —JBW

203 WEST PADON CARRIAGE HOUSE.

194 ~ HISTORIC HOMES OF PONCA CITY AND KAY COUNTY

In 1893, Joel H. Dyer and A. G. West came to Oklahoma from Kansas to establish a general dry goods store in the township of Blackwell. They purchased lots and, six months after the founding of the town, established the West-Dyer Store. Located on North Main Street, the small store carried a general line of goods. In 1896, Joel Dyer's brother, C. L. (Lee) Dyer, joined the firm and in the early 1900s, Joel Dyer bought out his original partner, A. G. West, but did not change the original store name. In 1913, a new West-Dyer's store building was constructed on East Blackwell. In 1924, my uncle, Edward Kopisch, purchased a five-piece bedroom suite from West-Dyer's. This fine set of Berkey & Gay furniture was a wedding present for his bride, Manilla Walton Kopisch. Today that wedding present bedroom suite is in our guest bedroom in Tulsa, Oklahoma.

The two Dyer brothers, Joel and Lee, were originally from Tennessee. Lee would marry Emma Frank, also a Tennessee native. From that union two sons were born, F. Vassar and Dowis Dyer. (Dowis was named for Greene Dowis. See "The G.E. Dowis

1607 S. MAIN

The West-Dyer Story

House," page 184.) Vassar and his wife, Clotene Jane Shidler Dyer, had one son, Frank, who married Joy Walker from Konawa, Oklahoma.

In 1924, Lee Dyer's son, F. Vassar, entered the family business, and in 1951, Vassar's son, Frank, followed him. In 1982, Joel Dyer, a son of Frank, would become the fourth generation of Dyers in the family business.

For several years the Vassar Dyer family lived at 227 West Vinnedge. In 1942, they purchased the Ralph Leachman home at 1607 South Main. The house was built in

1937 at a cost of $7,500. The architect was R. J. Hamilton of Wichita, Kansas. Ralph Leachman was the owner of several of Blackwell's movie theaters including the luxurious Rivoli Theater. The Leachmans had two daughters whom I remember seeing while visiting relatives in Blackwell. We were shopping at the local Kress Store and saw the two sisters wearing matching white rabbit fur coats. I was only eight years old, but I thought they were "knockouts."

The exterior of the Leachman-Dyer house is in the Southern Colonial style. One enters the house into a center foyer with a partially exposed winding staircase rising to the second floor. This narrow and steep

WEST-DYER IS FOUND IN CITY IN EARLY DAYS

Joel Dyer And A. G. West Organized What Is Now Oldest Store In City.

In 1893, the same year the little town of Blackwell was founded, two men came down into Oklahoma from Kansas to establish a general dry goods store.

These two men bought lots in Blackwell, and in March of the following year, after the opening of the Cherokee Outlet and about six months after the founding of Blackwell, they established their store.

The two men were Joel H. Dyer and A. G. West. The tiny store was West-Dyer's, now Blackwell's oldest and one of its largest and most modern mercantile firms.

That first store was a 20 by 40 building on North Main street, handling a general line of dry goods, the beginning of a sound business institution.

Two years later, in 1896, C. L. Dyer, Joel's brother, joined the firm and together the three partners enlarged and improved their business.

A new two story building was constructed in 1900, a 25 by 100 structure with a floor space of 2,500 square feet. In 1906 another addition doubled the store's size with a 50 by 100 building and 5,000 square feet of floor space.

Built In 1913

The present home of West-Dyer's was built in 1913. Its first floor was 50 by 120 feet, its mezzanine 20 by 50 feet and its second floor 50 by 80 feet, providing 10,000 square feet of floor space.

The new building was one of the most modern in Oklahoma. It was built of concrete and steel fireproof construction. A system of ventilation was provided to give fresh air at all times. Prism glass supplied an abundance of daylight and electricians provided the store with plenty of electric light.

The three operated the business until 1910 when West sold his interests. The firm, however, has retained the name of West-Dyer in honor of West, one of the pioneers of Blackwell both in business and civic affairs.

Vassar Dyer, son of C. H. Dyer, entered the firm in 1924 and under the guidance of the three Dyers the store has continued to grow.

Joel Dyer is president and manager of the office and gift department; C. H. Dyer is vice president and manager of the dry good department; Vassar Dyer is secretary and manager of appliances, floor covering and furniture departments and the advertising.

THE
CONSOLIDATED GAS
UTILITIES CORPORATION

CONGRATULATES

West-Dyer's

On The

FORMAL OPENING

Of Its New Furniture and Appliance Departments

Visit the Grand Opening! Be sure to see the Electrolux and other displays of Gas Appliances—they are just what you need for your modern home.

staircase would never meet today's building codes, (It is almost impossible to get a king size bed mattress to the second floor) but its decorative iron rail and balusters are certainly a thing of beauty. To the left of the foyer is the formal living room and across the foyer is a downstairs bedroom with its own bath. This room could also serve as a library or study. A rather large back hall behind the staircase opens into the living room, kitchen, and a breakfast-room-size dining room. Upstairs there are three bedrooms and two baths.

In 1992, Vassar Dyer's grandson, Joel Dyer, and his wife, Debbie, moved into the family home at 1607 South Main, where they reside today. Although the Leachman-Dyer home seems to be located in Blackwell's "Tornado Alley" (once a heavy timber was blown into the upstairs master bedroom while its occupants were sleeping), this beautifully scaled and proportioned structure has become one of Blackwell, Oklahoma's fine historic homes.

The West-Dyer Store closed its ladies and men's apparel departments and became a furniture and appliance store in 1948, but it remained in business until 1999, when, after over 100 years, it closed its doors forever. —JBW

114 URBANA

The Turvey Farm

George Turvey's English ancestors operated garden nurseries and flower shops in North Hampton, England. George immigrated to the United States and first settled in Pittsburgh, Pennsylvania, then moved to Illinois before coming to Kansas. George and his wife, Mary, had five sons, George Jr., Samuel, Jim, Harold, and Harry, and one daughter, May. George Turvey, Sr. made the 1893 Land Run and staked his claim on land that was located south of the new township of Blackwell. The 160-acre Turvey farm included a large barn and eventually a meat packing operation. In 1902, George and Mary built their Victorian style farmhouse on their farm.

The original two-story farmhouse had lap wood siding at the first floor and shingle siding at the second floor and roof gables. The front porch was an excellent example of Classical details blended with the Victorian style of design. Its wood columns sitting on Classical style bases, the simple balusters at the railings and the spandrels above the porch openings tell us that the Turvey house was built with a detailed set of drawings. In the 1904 photograph of the house, note the small gable above the front porch and how it duplicates the larger roof gable also located on the front of the house.

George Turvey, Sr.'s son, Samuel Harvey, married Lydia, the daughter of a widow who left Germany after her husband died. Lydia's and her sister's mother would eventually marry a Carl Missel and settle in Blackwell. Sam and Lydia had four children, Sam Jr., Ray, Dorothy, and Anilee. The Sam Turvey family moved to Douglas, Arizona, where they operated a meat shop and an asparagus farm. They would later return to Blackwell and enter into the family meat packing business. The Turvey Meat Packing Company was well recognized in the industry for over seventy years.

The Turvey farmhouse at 114 Urbana, though well maintained, hardly resembles its 1904 photo. This is primarily true because of the lack of original trim and the removal of the original front porch. The Blackwell City Swimming Pool is located on land that was once a part of the Turvey farm. This land was given by the Turveys to the City of Blackwell to be used to build the swimming pool.

Samuel Harvey Turvey is remembered by two of his great granddaughters, J. T. Goodall and Barbara Turvey Brauchi, as a very kind and generous person who was always protective and considerate of children. As a child, the story was told how Sam had saved his pennies until he had a nickel. With his nickel in hand, he walked into Blackwell to purchase a sack of candy. Sam did not open his bag of treats until arriving home to share his bounty with his siblings.

I do not think I ever had that much willpower. —JBW

HISTORIC HOMES OF PONCA CITY AND KAY COUNTY ~ 197

The Lowery Mansion

Dr. Allen Lowery was born on July 18, 1860, on his family's farm in Kentucky. Until he was five years old, Allen spent much of his time hiding from the Yankee soldiers who would raid his father's farm. As a young man, Allen was a country school teacher and later operated a small-town drug store. He put himself through medical school in Louisville, Kentucky, and shortly after Oklahoma was opened for settlement, he and his family came to Blackwell, where he formed a partnership with his brother-in-law, Dr. William H. Padon.

Through the years, Dr. Lowery had many unique and interesting experiences. One was thanks to a bank robber known as "Diamond Dick," who was shot by a sheriff's posse and brought to Dr. Lowery's office to have the bullet removed. On another occasion, when he was traveling to a distant ranch to deliver a baby, his horse and buggy got mired in quicksand when fording the Salt Fork River near Tonkawa. Only with the help of a farmer and his team of horses could the doctor's horse and buggy be retrieved.

The Lowery mansion was built in 1900 by the Seattle, Washington, contractor who had just completed the original Blackwell High School building. The mansion was located on the northwest corner of West Bridge and South Padon Street. Unfortunately, after a devastating fire, the structure was taken down by the local Roman Catholic Church.

Dr. Allen Lowery's two favorite hobbies were getting up at the crack of dawn to watch the visiting circus unload and attending the Negro Minstrel tent shows that occasionally visited Blackwell in its early years.

After his death in 1932, his family found a long list of the names of patients who owed him fees. Beside the name of each debtor, Dr. Lowery had written, "Paid in full by acts of kindness." —JBW

198 ~ HISTORIC HOMES OF PONCA CITY AND KAY COUNTY

With the advent of the French Revolution in 1790, the patriarch of the DeCamp family and his wife lost their heads to the guillotine. One of the reasons for their untimely deaths was that the name, DeCamp, in French, means "Aide to the King."

After their parents' executions, one son changed his name and remained in France. Another son relocated to the Netherlands, and the five remaining sons relocated to America. One of these settled in the state of New York, two in Ohio, and two in California. One of the DeCamp descendants, Charles, was born in Meggs County, Ohio.

At the age of twenty-one, Charles DeCamp filed and proved up on a homestead and lumber claim near Liberal, Kansas. Later he moved to Chetopa, Kansas, where, with another brother, Will, he opened a new and used furniture store. It was in Chetopa that Charles met Rachel Ellen Rich. Charles and Rachel were married on December 26, 1895; a snowstorm had postponed their planned Christmas wedding by one day.

In the fall of 1898, Charles and Will

424 S. A STREET
The Frenchman's House

THE ORIGINAL DECAMP HOUSE AFTER A SIDE WING WAS ADDED IN 1906.

LEFT: TODAY'S FRENCHMAN'S HOUSE.
BELOW: THE ORIGINAL HOUSE IN 1899.

built a houseboat and, with their families, floated down the various rivers until they reached the future site of Tulsa, Oklahoma. The large houseboat could easily accommodate both families with each living at the opposite ends of the enclosed structure. Upon their arrival in what would become "Tulsey Town," they sold the boat, and Charles and his family went to Anthony, Kansas, in search of a location for another furniture store. On May 8, 1899, Charles and Rachel and their son, Oral, arrived in Arkansas City, Kansas. From there they traveled by train to the new townsite of Kildare. There they boarded a stagecoach and traveled to Blackwell, where Charles first worked for A. O. Blackwell, constructing store buildings for Blackwell's new town.

Charles DeCamp opened his new and used furniture store on the northwest corner of Main and McKinley Streets in Blackwell. It was an immediate success, and he soon sent for his brother, Will, to join him in the business. The brothers would eventually relocate their store to the northeast corner of Main and Oklahoma Streets. With this move, it became the largest furniture store in northern Oklahoma.

The Charles DeCamp house is located at 424 South A Street in Blackwell. Built in 1899, it started as a modest three-room frame structure but in 1906, a wing was added to one side. In 1914, another wing was added to the first addition giving the house an "H" shaped plan. In 1923, the legs of the plan were enclosed and a second floor was added, making the DeCamp house as it appears today.

The DeCamp brothers advertised their popular furniture store with the slogan "You furnish the girl and we will furnish the home." Charles and Will DeCamp closed their furniture store, once the "largest in northern Oklahoma," in 1917, prior to the start of World War I. —JBW

221/315/323 S. FIRST STREET

Blackwell's Triplets

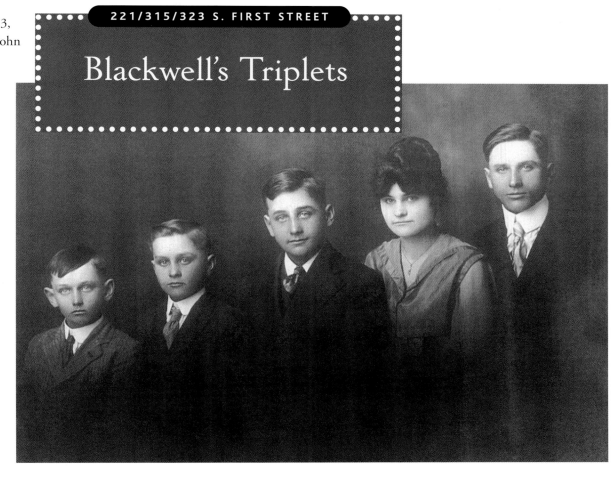

On September 16, 1893, the Welsh brothers, John and James, made the Run in a horse-drawn cart filled with bedrolls and a small supply of food and water. Another brother, Robert, also made the Land Run, atop a white racing horse. John Welsh staked his claim nine miles northeast of Blackwell while Robert staked on an adjoining claim. Brother James was unable to find a claim so he returned to his family home in Peabody, Kansas. The two Welsh brothers who remained stood their claim against all contesters, each building one-room "claim shacks" and cultivating and planting their lands as required by the homestead laws in Oklahoma Territory.

On July 28, 1897, Robert Edwin Welsh married Rosa Sarah Rogers in Peabody, Kansas. Their three-day honeymoon trip was spent traveling to Robert's 160-acre claim in Oklahoma Territory. The covered wagon was drawn by four horses leading a milk cow and was loaded with all of the couple's worldly belongings, including a crate of chickens, a gift from the bride's parents. On the last night of the trip there was a heavy rainstorm, but the travelers decided to forge

208 WEST PADON; ABOVE, THE ROBERT AND ROSA WELSH CHILDREN, EVERETT, KENNETH, HAROLD, MABEL, AND ROBERT.

ROBERT AND ROSA WELSH, CA. 1910; BELOW, THE HOUSE AT 208 WEST PADON IN DECEMBER, 1917.

on to the homestead since they were so close. At one point the team of horses refused to move another step so the couple pitched camp under the wagon. The next morning Robert and Rosa discovered that they were on the bank of a steep cliff and, had the horses not stopped, they would have tumbled to their fate and probably been killed.

John and Robert Welsh lived as neighbors and raised their families together on their land claims for twenty years. John and Carrie Welsh had three children, Ruth, Vera Constant, and Blanche Margaret, and Robert and Rosa Welsh had four sons, Robert, Harold, Kenneth, and Everett, and one daughter, Mabel Lenore. Their farms had orchards of peach, plum, apple, and apricot trees, and the sisters-in-law spent long hours canning the harvested fruit and vegetables. There was also plenty of milk and cream from which golden butter was churned.

In 1917, oil was discovered on the Welsh brothers' farms. They had leased the oil rights to oilman, Lew Wentz, and soon more wells were drilled on the farms for there were no spacing requirements for oil rigs at that time. It has been said that Lew Wentz often commented that his road from rags to riches had started in the Dilworth field with the leases on the Welsh brothers' farms.

Both families would soon relocate into Blackwell to provide better schooling for their children. Robert and Rosa's first home in Blackwell is located at 208 West Padon. In 1924, John and Robert built three identical "triplet" homes in Blackwell. John's triplet home is at 315 South First Street, Robert's is at 223 South First Street, and the third triplet house, which was built as the parsonage for the First Methodist Church, is located at 221 South First Street. House plans were from the Sears and Roebuck catalogue.

TOP TO BOTTOM: THE HOUSES AT 315, 323, AND 221 S. FIRST STREET. THE 221 S. FIRST STREET HOUSE WAS THE METHODIST CHURCH PARSONAGE. HOUSE PLANS CAME FROM THE SEARS AND ROEBUCK CATALOGUE AND WERE THE "AUBURN" DESIGN.

These fine identically designed houses are in the Craftsman style. Through the years, each has changed in appearance with color trim accents, roofing materials, and varieties of landscaping. But, upon closer inspection of Blackwell's triplet houses, it is evident that they all came from the same page of the home-builder's catalog of house designs.

A bit of trivia perrtaining to the story is that John Welsh's wife, Carrie Freeman Welsh, was a first cousin to the well-known actress Katherine Hepburn. Once when Miss Hepburn was visiting Carrie in Blackwell, she was stopped for driving way above the speed limit in downtown Blackwell. Hepburn pulled over to the curb and entered a local attorney's office to ask for legal counsel. While talking to the attorney, she draped her new fur coat over a hot radiator in the office and the coat caught fire. So her trip to Blackwell cost Katherine Hepburn a traffic violation ticket, an attorney's fee, and the cost of replacing a new fur coat. —JBW

The Goodson Ranch

Ola Goodson grew up in Carrolton, Missouri. His father was the town's Baptist minister and his mother was a small German lady who gave all of her children short names as they were easier to call when naming the long list: Ira, Guy, Mat, Ola, Ode, Abby, and Lucy.

Ola Goodson was a true cowboy. He first saw his future wife, with her five Christian names, Dora Alice Julia Dolly Lane Barry, on the road while she was driving a cow to pasture. (This was an everyday task for Dora.) Ola tipped his hat and said, "Dora Barry, you are the girl I am going to marry." Her reply was, "You may be one of the three men that I shall marry." (A gypsy fortune teller had told Dora she would be married three times.) In 1897, Dora Alice Barry married Ola Goodson.

In 1903, Dora Barry Goodson became the legal owner of the land claim she had "proved up." The Goodsons' other land claims were those purchased by Ola from a Dr. Manchester and another purchased from John Clark. It was on the Clark land claim that Ola and Dora Goodson built the "Big House" on what they referred to as the "Homestead." Located three miles south and two miles east of Blackwell, the large frame structure with its third floor turret was built by E. A. Taton. (A distant relative of mine.)

In later years, Dora recalleed the Goodson farm and ranching activities. "We farmed wheat, corn, alfalfa, oats, barley, maize, sweet clover, soy beans, and Austrian winter peas. We were among the first farmers in Kay County to employ fertilizer for crops and to use soil conservation practices for waterways and terraces. We also raised sheep, pigs, chickens, turkeys, ducks, and white-faced cattle. After the death of my husband, I continued the operation of the farm and ranch, managing over 3,000 acres of land."

The Goodsons had two daughters, Polly Goodson Cullison and Jennie Goodson Cannon. The Goodsons moved into Blackwell so the the girls could attend school. After the move, Ola tried to teach Dora to drive the family car. He forgot to tell her where the brake pedal was located so after starting the car, Dora drove into the closed garage door and on into the garage. Ola was furious with his wife. After the confrontation was over, Dora informed Ola she would never drive again, and she never did.

Ola Goodson died in 1933, and Dora Alice Julia Dolly Lane Berry Goodson died in 1969, at the age of ninety-five. Dora never lost her sense of humor. When her family doctor, Dr. L. H. Becker, asked her how she felt during a hospital stay in her last year of life, Dora replied, "I still feel with my hands." —JBW

TONKAWA

Six months after the opening of the Cherokee Strip, W. W. Gregory and Eli V. Blake applied to the federal government for permission to use their land claims as a townsite. One hundred and twenty acres of the Gregory land and eighty acres of the Blake land were included in the original townsite. When permission was granted, a company was formed to sponsor a city lot drawing, which took place in Arkansas City, Kansas.

The first telephone line in Tonkawa was installed in 1896, and a bridge across the Chikaskia River was completed in the same year. In 1899, the Santa Fe Railroad extended its lines south to Tonkawa and the first wheat crops were shipped from the town. —JBW

609 E. GRAND
The House That Petroleum Built

On February 7, 1924, the *Tonkawa News* headlined an article, "The House that Petroleum Built, not a House but just a Comfortable Home." The story read, "So Sam McKee, pioneer Kay County farmer, characterizes the new $35,000 structure he is building in Tonkawa. McKee, who once scratched a living for himself and family of eleven on virgin prairie, might easily have built a $350,000 home since a petroleum Aladdin rubbed a magic lamp above his once poor homestead a few years ago. McKee has money enough to satisfy one of far more complex tastes than he. However, moderation in all things seems to be Sam McKee's motto."

Samuel Hunter McKee was born on February 23, 1862, in Warsaw, Ohio. At the age of twenty-three, he moved to Kansas, where he married Mary Jane Hayhurst in 1887. Sam and Mary Jane had four children, Mary, Walter, Lucy, and Earl. In 1893, Sam made the Cherokee Strip Run and staked his claim on land that he soon discovered had already been settled by a "Sooner" so he purchased another claim from its owner for $206 and moved his family onto his new 160-acre farm. Six months afterwards Mary died, and in 1899 he married Lutitia Robbins. From that union six more children were born.

Sam McKee toiled hard to eke out a living for his large family for twenty-three years. In 1922, his luck changed with the discovery of oil on his farm. With sixty-eight producing oil wells on his land and with the help of a friend named Lew Wentz, Sam McKee soon became a millionaire. One of his oil wells, the #45, became the most lucrative well in Oklahoma at that time.

The exterior of the house is dark red brick with deep overhangs that seem to be supported by decorative brackets at each corner. The roof is red clay tile in the barrel shape pattern. The large entrance foyer's grand staircase is rather simple in design but with a touch of elegance. To the left of the foyer is the thirty-foot-long living room with its decorative tile mantelpiece. Off the living room is the large glassed sun porch, which has its own tile fireplace matching the ceramic tile floor. At the end of the foyer a small back hall leads to a first floor bedroom and bath and on into the kitchen and breakfast room.

To the right of the entrance foyer is the formal dining room. Like many of the other furnishings in the home, the beautiful mahogany twelve-piece dining room suite is original with the house. The Steinway grand piano that once graced the living room was given to the Tonkawa High School and is still in use today. The original light fixtures and wall sconces in the living and dining rooms and the foyer have a frosted bronze finish. Soft brown all-wool carpeting throughout the house was installed in 1935 but appears to have been installed only yesterday.

Sam McKee spent the remainder of his life trying to lead a simple life. He enjoyed spending time with his family and participating in his favorite sports, hunting and fishing, He died at the age of seventy-two in 1933. —JBW

401 N. ELEVENTH STREET
Tonkawa's Mail-Order House

On November 22, 1909, A. D. McFadden and his wife, Anna Russell McFadden, purchased sixteen lots from the University Preparatory School for $1,755. The McFaddens would build their farm house on the property from what was referred to as a "mail order" house.

The precut material package was purchased from the Aladdin Company, located in Illinois, at a cost of $850. The mail order kit included a living room, dining room, kitchen, and pantry and a first floor bedroom. The second floor contained two bedrooms and a bath. The dining room included a built-in china cabinet with leaded glass doors, and the entire house was lit with gas fixtures that were used until the 1940s. The exterior included a front porch and screened back porch.

The story is told that A.D.'s brother, John, did the plastering in the house and painted some of the rooms, including the living and dining rooms. Because John worked for the railroad, he painted them the color of the railroad's Pullman cars of the era. This color scheme was dark green on the bottom part of the walls and dark red above with a gold band separating the two colors. (I wonder where John got the paint.)

Upon the death of A. D. McFadden in 1929, his daughter, Retta, and her husband, Charley Bidwell, moved into the house with A. D.'s widow, Anna. In the late 1930s, Charley purchased a cow to provide milk for his family. The cow's milk was so good that the neighbors soon wanted to buy the Bidwell milk. Shortly Charley had purchased a fine herd of Jersey milk cows to keep up with the demand. Retta would bottle and cap the milk for Charley to deliver and sell for ten cents a quart.

In September of 1948, the Bidwells gave a warranty deed to the Tonkawa Board of Education for twelve of the original McFadden building lots. This land would be used as the building site for a new elementary school.

After the death of Charley Bidwell in 1955, his granddaughter, Willa Mae Barnhill Fuhr, and her husband, Alan Fuhr, moved into the McFadden family home with grandmother Retta. Through the years, Alan and Willa Mae's five children would attend the first through sixth grades in the elementary school that was built on land purchased in 1909 to build Tonkawa's mail-order house, which has housed four generations of the McFadden family. —JBW

302 S. FOURTH STREET
The Wiley William Gregory House

At noon on Saturday, September 16, 1893, more than 100,000 homesteaders made the land run into the Cherokee Outlet. The Outlet was an area over 9,000 square miles in size and located in what today is northwest Oklahoma. The area included 40,000 parcels of land open to adventurous settlers who wished to stake claims on them.

Two pioneers who made the Run were Eli V. Blake and Wiley William Gregory. The two staked their claims adjacent to each other. Federal law permitted claimants to organize townsites on their homesteads, so Blake and Gregory decided that a portion of their land was to be such a townsite. The next town from the Blake-Gregory townsite was Blackwell, located eight miles to the north, and with the Salt Fork and Chikaskia rivers nearby, the surrounding agricultural potential was excellent for farming.

Both Blake and Gregory contributed sizable portions of their land for the townsite, which they named Tonkawa after the Tonkawa Indians who lived on a reservation three miles east of the town. By 1895, the town's first two saloons were opened, and a lumberyard and real estate office were in existence. The real estate office offered nearby farms as well as town lots for sale. Another establishment on Main Street in 1895 was the Tonkawa Hotel, where lodging was one dollar and meals were twenty-five cents. Joe Hendrick built the first barber shop and, besides his tonsorial talents, Hendrick owned the first public (and probably the only) bathtub in Tonkawa.

The Gregory home is located at 302 South Fourth Street. This modest Victorian style house was alive with gingerbread ornamentation when first built. These decorative accents included the front and side porch's turned-wood columns capped with ornate wood brackets and cut-out spandrels. The front gable of the Gregory house was covered with wood "fish scale" shingles painted with contrasting bands of color and capped with a Victorian style decorative ridge beam. The fish-scale shingle treatment was also used on the small mansard roof at the front porch. Like many of the houses of its period, the Gregory house's exterior was painted in several color hues, making for a bright (and sometimes rather gaudy) exterior. Unfortunately, this multi-color scheme went out of style and most of the houses of that era are now painted white. —JBW

208 ~ HISTORIC HOMES OF PONCA CITY AND KAY COUNTY

501/709 E. GRAND

The First Banker's House

The founding of Tonkawa's first bank occurred in the late 1890s when the area was experiencing rapid growth and good crops. In the summer of 1898, W. H. Poffenberger, a banker from Iowa, came to Oklahoma Territory to explore the possibility of opening a bank. In Ponca City, he learned of the abundant wheat harvest in the area and decided to visit nearby Tonkawa. Upon his arrival, the community leaders of Tonkawa convinced Poffenberger that their town offered all of the prerequisites for a successful bank.

Upon his return to Iowa, Poffenberger informed his senior partner, Dr. Samuel T. Goodman, of his discovery. Goodman agreed to visit Tonkawa but, because of previous business experience, he preferred to locate the bank in an area where corn, not wheat, was the major agricultural commodity. Forewarned of Goodman's prejudice against wheat, the Tonkawa business leaders took the banker on a tour of area farms that cultivated corn. Dr. Sam Goodman was impressed with what he saw, and upon his return to Iowa he dispatched Poffenberger back to Tonkawa with $26,000 to start a bank.

In October of 1898, the Bank of Tonkawa opened for business, operating from a local hotel room. In December of

1898, Goodman arrived in Tonkawa to formally organize the bank, and in early 1899 he relocated his new bank to a Grand Avenue building.

The Samuel T. Goodman home is located at 709 East Grand and is in the Victorian style of architecture. The two-story house has many interesting features, including the wrap-around porch with its curved roof line. The large second-story bay window and the roof gable on the front of the house, covered with cedar "fish scale" shingles, are other interesting exterior features that make the house cry out "Victorian, Victorian."

Dr. and Mrs. Goodman had three children, two daughters, Mamie and Jennie, and one son, Clark. During its lifetime, the Goodman home has also served as the parsonage for Tonkawa's First Methodist Church.

Jennie Goodman Walling and her husband, Vic Walling, built their family home near Jennie's parents' home. Located at 501 East Grand, it is a Victorian two-story structure not unlike the Samuel Goodman house. —JBW

TOP: VIC AND JENNIE WALLING HOUSE AT 501 EAST GRAND. BOTTOM: THE SAMUEL T. GOODMAN HOUSE AT 709 EAST GRAND.

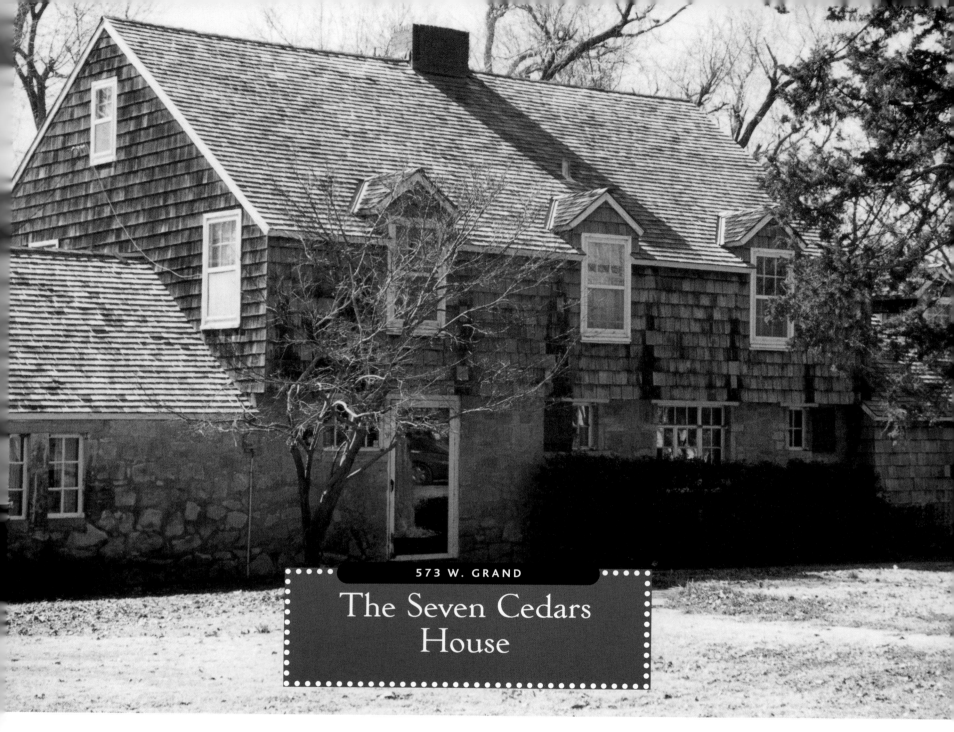

573 W. GRAND
The Seven Cedars House

Dr. Dewey Mathews came to Tonkawa in 1926 and purchased the medical practice of Dr. McKenney. His new office waiting room consisted of two rocking chairs, an oak roll-top desk, a library table, and a rug. Dr. Mathews carried a copper sterilizer in the bottom of his medical bag, which he took on house calls. The sterilizer held his delivery instruments and his baby scales were included in his medicine and pill bag.

During Dr. Mathews' early practice,

house calls cost three dollars, office calls ranged from one to three dollars, and a trip to Three Sands was seven dollars. In later years Mathews would become the college doctor for what is now known as Northern Oklahoma College.

When Dr. Mathews and his wife, Pauline Carter Mathews, built their house in 1936, the seven native cedar trees in the front yard were full grown. Pauline did not want these mature trees cut down, so with the help of her architect, William N. Caton of Winfield, Kansas, the house was designed so that the seven cedars could remain. So what did the Mathews name their new home? Seven Cedars, of course.

The house is designed in the New England farm house style, and it is wonderful. The exterior has native stone at the first floor and shingle siding at the second level. The long single-story wing at the east end of the house is a living room that terminates at a tall fireplace chimney. The massive wood front door has a carved monogram, "D L M," for Dewey Lee Mathews, and at the bottom rail of the door are carved a series of elves and animals. All of this unique carving was executed by Pauline's father.

Beyond a small entrance foyer is the staircase opposite the front door. Enclosed behind a three-quarter-high pine-paneled wall capped with a series of spindles, this space seems warm and friendly. To the left one steps down into the long, long living room with its vaulted and beamed ceiling of dark wood. At the opposite end of the room is the unusual fireplace wall. Centered in the wall, the fireplace with its wide surrounds of cut limestone panels reaches upward, not quite touching the ceiling. On either side of the fireplace are matching open book shelves while at the top is a continuous shelf running the width of the fireplace wall.

Behind the living room wing is a long screened porch overlooking the back yard. Among the furniture on the porch is a long table that can seat fourteen diners. (I counted and that number is correct.) Off the living room and at the rear of the house is a small room that has served several purposes: first as a children's play room, next as a cozy dining room, and today as a convenient study. The wood floors in the living room, foyer, and study are wide planked pine with recessed pegs, and the kitchen and its eating area floors have red quarry tile floors. The second level of the home has three bedrooms. In the 1940s, the third-floor attic was remodeled into a large space for Dewey, Jr. and Carter William Mathews. Dewey and Pauline also had two daughters, Sally and Elizabeth.

In later years, their children, grandchildren, and great-grandchildren of Dewey and Pauline Mathews would gather for numerous family reunions at "Camp Carefree," as Seven Cedars was called by subsequent generations. Today, Sally Mathews McQuade resides in her family home.

Dewey and Pauline Mathews moved into their newly completed home for Christmas, 1936—what a wonderful Christmas memory to have had.

As a side note, after graduating from Ponca City High School in 1947, I attended Northern Oklahoma Junior college for two years. During my stay in Tonkawa, I would often walk or drive around the town admiring the many beautiful old homes. My tour would always end in front of the Mathews home, for then and even today, this fine example of a comfortable and lovely New England farm home is my favorite house in Kay County. —JBW

The nine-room Colonial Revival-style house at 102 South Twelfth Street was built in 1922 for a pioneer doctor, Dr. J. A. Jones. The house features generously proportioned rooms with ten-foot ceilings and oak interior woodwork, doors, and floors. The French doors in the living and dining rooms have beveled glass panes with matching crystal doorknobs. The oak staircase leads to the second floor with its four bedrooms and a sleeping porch. A bay window at the end of the upstairs hall holds an oak window seat.

Dr. Jones commissioned an engineer to design the unique ceiling light fixtures in several of the first floor rooms. This same woman engineer also designed the light fixtures for the Tonkawa Masonic Temple.

In 1900, John Jones came to Tonkawa from La Belle, Missouri, with his parents, two brothers, and two sisters. He had attended the School of Osteopathy and Medicine in Kirksville, Missouri, and then taught school to earn his tuition and expenses to attend medical school. Upon graduation and upon passing his medical exam with high honors, Dr. Jones opened his medical practice in Tonkawa. Through the years, Jones had many offers to leave Tonkawa and become associated with medical groups in larger communities but he chose to stay in Tonkawa, serving his neighbors and friends. He would continue to practice there until three months before his death in 1933.

Dr. Jones also owned the Palace Pharmacy in the 100 block of East Grand Avenue. His daughter Gladys still remembers the the installation of the new soda fountain at the Palace, the cigar counter with the open cigar boxes that lured prospective customers to choose their favorite, and even a wallpaper sales and display in the back of the drug store. Gladys married Clarence Burr. After the deaths of her parents, Gladys and Clarence and their three sons lived in the Jones family home. Through the years, Gladys taught music lessons in the home to many pupils in the community.

In the back yard of the Jones-Burr home is an underground storm cellar. The cellar's interior is lined with brick and has a domed ceiling. At one time, Gladys grew her African violet collection in that cellar. Both Gladys and her mother were known as avid gardeners and flower lovers. The lilac bushes and wisteria they planted still bloom each spring. An enormous papershell pecan tree, planted by Dr. Jones, continues to bear an abundant crop of pecans each year. —KA

101 S. TWELFTH STREET

Jones-Burr House

201 N. SECOND STREET

The Plumb Houses

Albertus (Bert) Plumb described his memories of the Land Run of 1893:

A few days prior to the opening of the Cherokee Outlet, we prepared ourselves with blankets and provisions, and went to the booth to register for the opening. Thousands were lined up for the registering. I stood in line for two days and nights. When night came we spread our blankets where we stood and remained there for the night. If we left our places at any time, the man next to us in line would hold our place until we returned. It was reported that during the registration a farmer living nearby sold enough drinking water to pay the mortgage on his farm.

September 16, 1893, at high noon, the gun was fired that signaled our departure in every mode of conveyance then known. Off with a mad rush we started and pell mell over the broad, freshly burned prairies, we scattered in desperate efforts to beat the other fellow to a claim.

Bert Plumb did stake a claim and soon had plowed a furrow around it. He and his adjacent neighbor erected a sod house spanning the line of their claims. One room of the two-room structure was for Bert on his claim and the other was across the line for his neighbor.

During the dry years after the Run, Bert Plumb traveled to the Arkansas River bottom lands and husked corn for three cents per bushel. From that money he purchased a grubstake and returned to his claim.

Bert Plumb built his first house at 201 North Second. It is a large two-story structure with a wrap-around porch. Today the first Albertus Plumb house has been restored. The second Plumb house is at 508 East Grand. Its airplane bungalow-style exterior is in keeping with many similar homes built in its era. The massive brick porch bases support well-proportioned wood columns that contribute to a pleasing and well-proportioned exterior.

In later years Plumb recalled, "After the dry years, which tried our mettle, we were blessed with abundant rainfall and good crops. After that we prospered and improved our claims and the country in every way."
—JBW

508 E. GRAND

THE SECOND PLUMB HOUSE AT 508 EAST GRAND; TOP: THE FIRST PLUMB HOUSE AT 201 NORTH SECOND STREET.

101 S. THIRD
The Major's House

Major D. H. Clark was a veteran of the Civil War, an Indian fighter, and a quartermaster and supply officer during World War I. Clark would trade a piece of residential property in Tonkawa for a farm that Lee Shawver homesteaded on, known as the Shawver lease. After the trade, the Shawver lease would become part of the Tonkawa oil field, in its time the greatest oil pool yet discovered.

Major Clark was left an orphan when he was but a lad living in a log cabin in the hills of Kentucky. Though his early life was a struggle against poverty, he managed to attend school and equip himself for a military career. In April of 1861, he enlisted in the Fourteenth Kentucky Volunteer Cavalry as a private. At the end of the Civil War, he resumed his studies and was appointed to West Point in 1867. In 1873, Clark graduated from the Academy with a second lieutenant's commission. He would see active service against the Indians, fighting in New Mexico, Arizona, Montana, and the Dakotas, eventually retiring as a major.

Soon after his retirement, Major Clark arrived in Tonkawa, and in 1904 he instituted the first military organization at the University Preparatory School in Tonkawa. In 1916, Clark was called back into service with the entry of the United States into World War I.

At the termination of his work at the Preparatory School, Clark traded some of his Tonkawa property for the farm that would bring him his great riches.

The Clark house is a typical two-story Colonial Revival structure. The front entrance and covered porch are all in graceful harmony with each other, except for the lack of the original wood porch columns that must have been more in scale with the original front entrance. The original wood shutters have been replaced with plastic shutters that are a bit too narrow for the scale of the windows. Except for these few minor replacements, the Major Clark house appears very similar to the original structure.

In 1923, Major D. H. Clark attended the fiftieth reunion of his West Point graduating class, and of the few remaining old West Pointers, Clark was said to be "the sturdiest of them all." —JBW

1401 E. "N" AVENUE

The Doenges Story

Reverend Rudolph C. Doenges was determined to find a home for his wife and six children when he purchased the "Wayman Place" in January of 1918. Reverend Doenges had become very ill and was forced to give up his pastorate of the First Methodist Church in Blackwell, Oklahoma. In searching for a family home his major requirement was a location with adequate schools, and Tonkawa, located ten miles south of Blackwell, fulfilled that requirement. Located at 1401 East N Avenue, the "Wayman Place" consisted of six acres of land, well fenced, with a chicken house, barn, tool shed, a good outdoor privy, a fine well, a six-room house, and a well-maintained orchard.

For all of this, Doenges paid the modest price of $1,700. He paid $700 down on the property with a note due of $1,000 at a later date. As a result of the yellow fever he had suffered during military service in Cuba, Doenges was able to buy life insurance with a "binder" allowing for a cash settlement on the policy. After a bitterly contested effort, Doenges was able to obtain a $1,000 settlement and thus received a clean title on the property he had purchased for his family. Reverend Rudolph Doenges died on March 8, 1918, in his new family home.

The Doengeses' eldest son, Soland Doenges, wrote of his memories in growing up in Tonkawa in Marilee Helton's wonderful *Pieces of the Past,* published by the Tonkawa Historical Society.

One of our nearby neighbors operated the local dairy with a herd of thirty milk cows. He asked our mother if one of the boys would be able to help out at the dairy. So I went to work for him starting early in the day with milking at 5:30 A. M., straining and running the hand-turned separator and bottling and delivering the morning deliveries. Then a quick run home for a clean up and on to school. After school, I would change my clothes, then do the evening milking and milk deliveries and back home for study and supper.

As summer approached, other jobs opened up and family friends on a farm west of Blackwell, "persuaded" us to provide a good home to an old mare called "Lady." Using a light one-horse wagon, my brothers, Oswald and William, were able to deliver groceries for the Yount Grocery Store in Tonkawa. They

409 NORTH SIXTH STREET

THE DOENGES HOME AT 1401 EAST "N" AVENUE.

delivered groceries six days a week for $9 a week. I was paid $6 a week for my work at Yount Grocery so the three of us took home a total of $15 a week, a magnificent sum!

The chief custodian at the University Preparatory School hired my brother, Oswald, to help with the janitorial work, and the school's chief engineer of the steam plant hired me as a part-time assistant. My job was to come in after school each evening, rake out the ashes and clinkers from the boilers, haul out the ashes, and then haul in coal for the next day. This work was done with heavy wheelbarrows.

The next morning, my dear mother would awaken me at 4:00 A. M., prepare my breakfast and, with my kerosene lantern in hand, I walked to the power plant while she watched from the window. I would always signal to her upon my safe arrival. I returned home at 7:00 A. M., and mother would have a galvanized bathtub of hot water ready in a closet adjacent to our kitchen. After bathing and another breakfast, I would hurry on to school.

On one occasion, during his janitorial work, Oswald learned that a contract was to be let for the repainting of the dome on Central hall. With our mother's help, we submitted a bid "to scrape loose paint from the dome and apply two coats of 'oil based' paint." We were given the job by the president of the college and with help from friends, we collected paint brushes and ten gallons of "lead base" paint. The project started at noon on a Friday and was completed on Saturday.

The problem began on Monday morning when Dr. Caldwell, the college president, returned to the campus to discover that the dome on Old Central had been painted a bright green. Dr. Caldwell announced to us that he would not pay for our work and the job must be done over using white lead paint. We were devastated and, after telling mother of our plight, she immediately went to the president's office, closed the door and, upon leaving the meeting, she had a check in hand for our painting contract.

In later years, Mrs. Lulu Soland Doenges became the librarian for the college and also taught classes in German, for she was of German descent and spoke the languages fluently. In later years she relocated to a charming bungalow style house at 409 North Sixth Street.

A footnote to Lulu Doenges: During World War II, the prisoner of war camp north of Tonkawa housed a number of German soldiers. Mrs. Doenges would travel to the camp on Sunday afternoons to visit with the prisoners, often bringing them homemade jellies and cookies. Was Lulu Doenges a German sympathizer? No, she was just a kind and caring lady offering friendship and hope to these boys who had been caught up in the ravages of war. — JBW

400 EAST GRAND

The McCafferty Story

Mr. and Mrs. C. E. McCafferty arrived in Tonkawa on January 6, 1905, having purchased a small inventory of furniture and caskets from Bowker & Bowker, which was located at 119 East Grand. On January 10, 1905, four days after their arrival, they opened their doors to the public, and two years later, they purchased the Charles Bull Furniture Store at 107 East Grand. From then until 1926, they operated a thriving furniture and undertaking business.

McCafferty often recalled the hectic but prosperous days of the oil boom, when he bought furniture by the carload. On occasion, he had it delivered directly to customers without unloading it at the store, so great was the demand for household furnishings. They delivered loads of furniture to

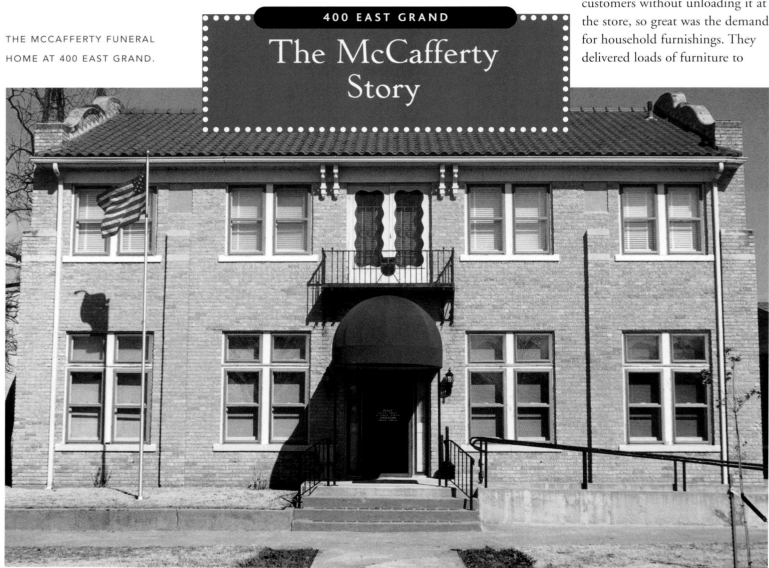

THE McCAFFERTY FUNERAL HOME AT 400 EAST GRAND.

218 ~ HISTORIC HOMES OF PONCA CITY AND KAY COUNTY

houses not yet completed and into which families moved before the roof was finished. McCafferty sold carloads of fine wicker chairs, which were taken to oil well sites for the drillers to use. Beds, springs, and mattresses were sold by the carload, and pianos and Edison phonographs went as fast as they could be stocked.

In the early days, practically all funeral work was done in homes and churches. Caskets were all black (white for children) and came untrimmed from the manufacturer. The funeral director lined and decorated the inside and added the handles and any other decorative hardware.

McCafferty's big black hearse was drawn by matched black or gray horses in the beginning. In 1917, he purchased his first motor funeral car, a Reo. In 1926, Mr. and Mrs. McCafferty sold the furniture store in downtown Tonkawa and constructed their beautiful funeral home facility and, next door, their family residence. Located at 400 East Grand, the funeral home was built at a cost of $50,000. The exterior of the building is buff brick with a red tile roof. The

architecture is in the Spanish style with accents of cut stone trim and a small balcony above the front entrance. The McCafferty family home to the east is in the "airplane bungalow" style.

In 1955, *The Tonkawa News* featured an article commemorating the fiftieth anniversary of the McCafferty Funeral Home. The article concluded with the following,

A funeral home is a business that is operated for a profit. But like the work of doctors and ministers, it is a public service, a service that for years has taken C. E. McCafferty into many Tonkawa area homes. He has witnessed grief, tragedy and the quiet death of old people. He has always been strength and support when people needed him. — JBW

THE BULL-MCCAFFERTY FURNITURE STORE. TOP: THE MCCAFFERTY FAMILY HOME, LOCATED NEXT DOOR TO THE FUNERAL HOME.

One of Tonkawa's early industries was the Tonkawa Milling Company, the "Home of White Wonder Flour." Located on Grand Avenue east of the railroad tracks, the business was started by Rudolph Finkey and E. E. Ensley. The first electricity was brought to Tonkawa by Ensley because his customers were buying Wichita's bleached flour. To meet the competition, Ensley ordered generating equipment for electricity which was used in the bleaching process in the manufacture of flour. The dynamo for this power plant was often operated until ten o'clock in the evening to provide power for Tonkawa's first theater, an open air dome established by Fred Olmstead in 1910.

An early-day advertisement in the local newspaper read, "The Tonkawa Mill and Elevator Company makes their flour from the best home-grown wheat. Sold in 24 pound sacks, our hard wheat flour for bread is $1.10 for 'Pure #7 White' brand and $1.15 for our 'Tonkawa Chief' brand. Soft wheat flour for pastry and biscuits is marketed under the brand names of 'White Wonder,' and the firm's premium brand, at $1.25 per bag, and 'Quality' brand, priced at $1.15."

The first grain elevator was built next to the railroad tracks soon after the railroad came to Tonkawa in 1899. Constructed by "Lord" R. T. Brook, it was soon purchased by A. J. Esch.

In 1842, at the age of twenty-two, Bernard Esch arrived in Delphos, Ohio, with a group of forty-two persons from Osnabruck, Germany. The group's mission was to establish a German Catholic community in Ohio. In 1881, Bernard, his wife, Catherine, and their six sons moved to Kansas, having purchased over 2,000 acres of farm and ranch land between Maple City and Dexter, Kansas.

Shortly after the opening of the Strip into Oklahoma, Theodore Peter Esch (the third son) and Alexander Joseph Esch (the fourth son) leased Indian land two miles east of Tonkawa. They later purchased the land and operated the "Esch Brother's Farm & Livestock" business. At the time the brothers arrived in Oklahoma, Alec had thirty-five cents in his pocket, and during their first year, the Esch boys had to sell the corn in order to buy salt to season the corn, which was the primary food they ate daily.

In 1900, Alec purchased a homestead

one mile east of Tonkawa. In 1895, while Alec and Tate were still "batching," Alec was working in the garden when he paused to watch a caravan pass by. The procession included a covered wagon, a horse and buggy, farm implements, a cow or two, and some horseback riders. It was the George McGuckin family with about half of their fourteen children, moving to an Indian lease just south of the Esch farm. Little did Alec realize that his future wife, Mabel McGuckin, was in that caravan. Alec and Mabel were married in 1903, and in that same year, they moved into their new farm home on Christmas day

Alec and Mabel had five children. As their family increased, they added additions to their home. Through the years, generation after generation of the Esch family have lived in the family farmhouse as they continue to do today. Sitting on the northeast corner of old Highway 60 and Highway 177, the house sports large black wood letters spelling out the name "ESCH." You can't miss it. —JBW

201 S. FIRST STREET

The C.C. Bell House

In deciding to make the Land Run in 1893, Charles Curry Bell thought that he might be fortunate to get a good piece of land, and if not, he would have had an interesting experience.

In 1880, C. C. Bell married Mary Rebecca Montgomery, and from this union were born five children, Annie E., Josephine, Mary R., C. C., Jr., and John Montgomery.

Charles Bell did make the Run in 1893 and staked his claim near the present town of Lamont, Oklahoma. He recalled the large crowds awaiting the opening of the Run. "Sandwiches and cold drink vendors went up and down the waiting lines during the morning and many filled their canteens with water or lemonade. One man near Bell asked each vendor many questions about the quality of their lemonade. Frequently, annoyed by his questions, they would say, 'Try it and see for yourself.' After taking a generous drink he would always reply, 'It ain't worth a damn.' In this way he got all the free lemonade he wanted."

Bell soon disposed of his claim and remained in the cattle business in Kansas. Later he purchased what was known as the Little V Ranch located on the Salt Fork River, south of Tonkawa.

The C. C. Bell home is located at 201 South First Street. With its gambrel roof, the architecture is definitely Dutch Colonial in style. The fireplace in the Bell home has an interesting tile surround, and the front bay living room window matches a similar bay window in the dining room. The interesting gambrel roof is a series of graceful curves with its front gable displaying a very decorative shingle pattern.

In 1920, the cutting and threshing of wheat with the same machine took place for the first time in this part of the country on the Bell ranch. This wonderful labor and time-saving machine was the "Deering Combine Thresher-Harvester" made by International Harvester Company. The machine was pulled by a tractor, with a filling wagon going along with it. The only stops made were to change wagons when the trailing wagon was filled. There was one man on the tractor, one on the machine, and one on the grain wagon, with two men and a team of mules to haul the wheat away and scoop it in the bin. This machine did an excellent job of threshing, leaving a trail of straw behind. Putting straw back on the ground was considered to be of great value to succeeding crops. Some thought you should plow it under, while others contended that it should be burned, but whether in the form of straw or ashes, it imparted fertility to the soil.

Annie E. Bell was my English professor at Northern Oklahoma College. I considered her quite elderly at the time even though she had not reached the mandatory retirement age. Her thin white hair was tied with a small bun, and she seemed to have little interest in the college life on the campus. One time, after a sports victory, the students declared an unofficial walk-out. The teachers were required to convene their classes and take roll call. As some of us were walking across the campus, Miss Bell opened her classroom window in Old Central and rallied us to continue with our walk-out.

That incident completely changed my opinion of Professor Annie E. Bell. —JBW